With goodwishe

A Richardson

Oxford   June 1995.

PARENTING, SCHOOLING AND CHILDREN'S BEHAVIOUR

Parenting, Schooling and Children's Behaviour

Edited by
ANN BUCHANAN
BARBARA L. HUDSON
Centre for Research into Parenting and Children
University of Oxford

Ashgate

Aldershot • Brookfield USA • Singapore • Sydney

Published by
Ashgate Publishing Ltd
Gower House
Croft Road
Aldershot
Hants GU11 3HR
England

Ashgate Publishing Company
Old Post Road
Brookfield
Vermont 05036
USA

British Library Cataloguing in Publication Data
Parenting, schooling and children's behaviour :
    interdisciplinary approaches
    1. Children - Social conditions
    I. Buchanan, Ann II. Hudson, Barbara L.
    362.7
Library of Congress Catalog Card Number: 98-73508

ISBN 1 84014 556 0

Printed and bound by Athenaeum Press, Ltd.,
Gateshead, Tyne & Wear.

Contents

List of Figures

List of Tables

Foreword

This book originated from the inaugural seminars arranged by *The Centre for Research into Parenting and Children* in Michaelmas Term 1997 at the Department of Applied Social Studies and Social Research, Oxford University.

Earlier in 1997, academics from the Oxford University Departments of Public Health, Educational Studies, Psychiatry, and Applied Social Studies who were researching into issues around parenting, schooling and children's behaviour problems, came together and set up an informal network of researchers.

The stated aims of the Centre were:

- to develop a better understanding of the well-being of parents and children; what causes problems (health, educational, psychological and social) and how they may be ameliorated;
- to build interdisciplinary research links;
- to act as a discussion forum for researchers from different disciplines and for practitioners (health, education, psychological and social) who work with children and families;
- to disseminate research findings.

The first members of the Centre were:

Dr Ann Buchanan: University Lecturer in Applied Social Studies;
Dr Kathy Sylva: Reader in Educational Studies;
Dr Sarah Stewart-Brown: Director of the Health Services Research Unit, Department of Public Health;
Dr Frances Gardner: University Lecturer in Clinical Psychology, Department of Psychiatry;
Mrs Teresa Smith: Director of the Department of Applied Social Studies and Social Research;
Dr Jane Barlow: MRC Research Fellow at the Health Services Research Unit;
Dr JoAnn Ten Brinke: Postdoctoral Research Fellow at the Department of Applied Social Studies and Social Research;

Professor Carolyn Webster-Stratton, University of Washington, Seattle, joined the group during her sabbatical; and
Eva Lloyd from Barnardo's contributed a national child care agency perspective to the seminars.

The initial seminars attracted a wide-ranging audience both from within Oxford and from further afield. The informal discussions before and after the seminars were especially valued. Those who came to the seminars asked that the papers be written up so that the ideas and the findings from research could be made more widely available. The following chapters are based on the original presentations. Some material has been updated in the light of new findings.

Ann Buchanan
Oxford, May 1998

Contributors

Dr Ann Buchanan, PhD, MA, CQSW

Ann Buchanan is University Lecturer in Applied Social Studies and Dean of St Hilda's College, Oxford. Before entering academic life in 1990, she spent ten years working as a child psychiatric social worker in an inner urban area. Her current research interest is long-term outcomes for children. Her research is based on secondary analysis of longitudinal studies but is informed by studies of users' perspectives, particularly children's. Recent research grants have come from Mental Health Foundation, NHS Executive (Anglia and Oxon), Joseph Rowntree Foundation and Barnardo's. Her book *Intergenerational Child Maltreatment* (Wiley, 1996) has become a standard text in child protection.

Dr Jane Barlow, DPhil, MSc, BA

Jane Barlow currently holds an MRC NHS Training Fellowship at the Health Services Research Unit, Institute of Health Sciences, Oxford University. She graduated from Warwick University with a degree in Sociology and Social Administration before coming to Oxford University where she undertook an MSc in Sociology. She then undertook research for her DPhil on the psychosocial consequences of screening for raised cholesterol levels. Her main research interests are in child welfare interventions, and she is presently conducting a randomised-controlled trial to investigate the effectiveness of a home-school linked parenting education programme.

Paul Colman, MA, MSc

Paul Colman is currently a research officer and statistics demonstrator at the University of Oxford, Department of Educational Studies. After completing a Psychology degree at the University of Cambridge, he moved to the London

Institute of Education and took an MSc in Child Development. During this time, he investigated the assessment of cognitions of children with behavioural problems with Dr Stephen Scott at the Institute of Psychiatry. He is interested in the development of social competence from attachment and theory of mind perspectives.

Dr Frances Gardner, MA, MPhil, DPhil

Frances Gardner is University Lecturer in Clinical Psychology at the University Department of Psychiatry, Park Hospital, Oxford. Before that, she was Lecturer at the Institute of Psychiatry and Senior Clinical Psychologist at the Maudsley Hospital working with families in Camberwell. She was also Lecturer in Education at Warwick University. Her current research interests include a Wellcome-funded longitudinal observational study of parenting style and the early development of children's behaviour problems. Other grants include co-investigator on the MRC Hip Trial, investigating the psychosocial effects on parents of babies with hip instability. She is a member of the Steering Committee of the DoH ECMO Trial advising about the measurement of psychological outcomes in children with neonatal respiratory illness. She is co-editor of the 'Measurement Issues' series in *Child Psychology and Psychiatry Review*.

Barbara L. Hudson, MA, CQSW

Barbara L. Hudson is University Lecturer in Applied Social Studies at the University Department of Applied Social Studies and Social Research. She was previously at the London School of Economics and before that, a psychiatric social worker. A former editor of the *British Journal of Social Work* she has also co-edited a series of psychiatry texts. Her main interests are cognitive-behavioural approaches in social work and the development of evidence-based social work.

Eva Lloyd, BA, BSc, Dip Ling

Eva Lloyd holds a position as Principal Officer Research and Development in the Policy, Planning and Research Unit at Barnardo's. Before that, she spent six years in a similar post in the Policy Division at Save the Children UK. Having started her working career in the UK teaching Dutch at London University's Bedford College and obtaining a Psychology degree during that time, she joined the Thomas Coram Research Unit at London University's Institute of Education in 1985. There she was a member of multi-disciplinary research teams conducting major Department of Health funded studies into early day care and preschool services. Her current research interests include family support, early childhood services, parenting education and prisoners' children. She is the author of a number of publications in these areas and also co-edited *Motherhood: meanings, practices and ideologies* (Sage, 1992). She holds honorary research fellowships at the Centre for Family Research at Cambridge University and the Centre for Child Care Research at the Queen's University in Belfast.

Mrs Teresa Smith, MA, DipSocAdmin

Teresa Smith is Director of the Department of Applied Social Studies and Social Research. She has worked at the Department since 1974 as University Lecturer in Applied Social Studies. Before that, she worked in one of the Educational Priority Area Projects in South Yorkshire. Her research interests include 'mapping' disadvantage and services, preschool and day-care policy, and community work. Recent research grants have come from the Department of Health and The Children's Society and the Joseph Rowntree Foundation.

Dr Sarah Stewart-Brown, FRCP, FFPHM, PhD, MA, BM, BCh

Sarah Stewart-Brown is Director of the Health Services Research Unit in the Department of Public Health. After graduating from Oxford in 1974, she worked in the National Health Service first as a paediatrician and subsequently as a public health doctor in London, Bristol and Worcester. She has held academic appointments at the Department of Child Health and the Department of Epidemiology and Community Health, at the University of Bristol and at the Department of Social Medicine at the University of Birmingham. Her current research interests centre around the importance of emotional well-being for the health of both adults and children. Her current research projects include systematic reviews of the effectiveness of child health and school health services and a community controlled trial of a home-school linked parent education programme. She holds grants from the Medical Research Council, the NHS Health Technology Assessment Programme and the NHS Executive (Anglia and Oxford).

Dr Kathy Sylva, PhD

Kathy Sylva is Reader in Educational Studies at the University of Oxford Department of Educational Studies. After earning a PhD at Harvard University, she moved to Oxford where she taught psychology while serving on the Oxford Preschool Research Group. Her book *Childwatching at Playgroup and Nursery School* broke new ground by questioning an unbridled 'free play' ideology. With Teresa Smith and Elizabeth Moore, she evaluated the High/Scope preschool programme with its emphasis on 'plan, do, review' in each session. She moved to London to begin research on assessment and curriculum in primary schools. In *Early Intervention in Children with Reading Difficulties*, she and Jane Hurry showed that Reading Recovery is a successful intervention and cost-effective as well. She has returned to Oxford where she leads the DFEE research on effective provision of preschool education. A dominant theme throughout her work is the impact of education not only on 'subject knowledge' but on children's problem-solving, social skills and commitment to learning.

Dr Ted K. Taylor, PhD

Dr Taylor received his PhD from York University in Toronto, Canada in 1994. He worked in children's mental health services in Canada for several years as a psychologist implementing and evluating the Parents and Children Series programme. At present he is collaborating on a prevention study in Kindergarten to Grade 3 in multi-ethnic communities, funded by the National Institute on Drug Abuse.

Dr JoAnn Ten Brinke, Dr PH, MPH, BA

JoAnn Ten Brinke is currently a postdoctoral fellow at the Department of Applied Social Studies and Social Research, Oxford, on a project funded by the Joseph Rowntree Foundation on the influence of early parenting on adult outcomes. She received her Bachelor of Arts in Anthropology from Pomona College in 1985, and was a research assistant for three years at Harvard School of Public Health. She received her Doctorate in Public Health from the University of California at Berkeley in 1995, with a focus in Environmental Health Science and minors in Biostatistics and Energy and Resources. Her dissertation research on volatile organic compounds in indoor air was based at Lawrence Berkeley National Laboratory. She is a co-author on papers published in *Environment International* and *Atmospheric Environment*.

Professor Carolyn Webster-Stratton

Carolyn Webster-Stratton is Professor and Director of the Parenting Clinic at the University of Washington. She is a licensed clinical psychologist and nurse practitioner and has published numerous scientific articles on conduct disordered children and parent training. She has had extensive clinical and research experience in helping families with conduct disordered children. She has developed and evaluated video-tape-based training programmes for parents regarding effective parent management skills as well as communication, problem-solving and anger management. Her books *Troubled Families: problem children* and *The Incredible Years* have been used to train therapists, teachers and parents. In addition, she has developed a social skills and problem-solving curriculum (Dinosaur Curriculum) for training younger children, ages 4–8 years. Currently she is conducting a study evaluating a partnership, which combines teacher training with parent and child training for young children who are highly aggressive and noncompliant.

In recent years, her interventions, originally designed for helping children who were diagnosed with conduct problems, have been used in efforts to reduce the occurrence of aggressive behaviour problems and to promote children's academic and social skills. In 1997 she received the National Mental Health award for excellence in prevention (in the United States).

The authors of the individual chapters and the two editors would also like to acknowledge the help of Helen Wills, who was tireless in her efforts in giving secretarial and administrative support to the project.

PART I
INTRODUCTION

1 The Background

ANN BUCHANAN

Summary

- This chapter sets the context. Despite considerable progress over the last hundred years in raising standards of health and education, the paradox remains that the number of children with emotional and behaviour disorders appears to be rising. These disorders seriously limit the life chances of many thousands of young people. If the quality of life for those who in the past may not have done so well is to be improved, steps need to be taken to prevent the disabling effects of these disorders.
- Central to the disorders is how a child is parented. How parents parent, and how children thrive, however, takes place within a wider social context. Children interact with parent(s) and the wider family. Parents and children interact with schools and their local neighbourhood. Schools and communities interact with current economic conditions, local/national policies, attitudes, norms and societal expectations.
- Children's emotional and behavioural disorders have consequences and costs for parents, individuals, schools, communities, and whole populations. It makes sense, therefore, that interventions to promote children's emotional well-being should take place in all these domains; that the researchers from different disciplines come together to share their knowledge and expertise, and that interventions for these children are based on 'what works'.

As we approach the twenty-first century, we may reflect on the momentous educational, health and social achievements of the last hundred years that have done so much to improve the well-being of children. As we reflect on our successes, however, we may also want to consider from where the next great leap forward will come. Smith and Rutter (1995, p. 763) note the paradox of our times:

> It might be expected that as living conditions have improved over the course of this century, they [psychosocial disorders in young people] would have become progressively less frequent. The evidence from our study firmly contradicts that commonly held assumption. Physical health has improved in step with better living conditions, as shown by the steadily falling infantile mortality and a steadily increasing life expectancy. However, against expectation, psychosocial disorders have shown no such fall in frequency .... The evidence suggests that many have become substantially more prevalent.

Smith and Rutter support their claims by examining five disorders: youth crime and conduct disorder; trends in substance misuse; depressive disorders; eating disorders and suicide and suicidal behaviour among adolescents. In varying degrees, these disorders seriously interfere with the life chances of thousands of young people. The strong message from this work is that if the quality of life is to be improved of those who in the past may not have done so well, ways need to be found of preventing the disabling effects of emotional and behavioural disorders in children.

The human, societal and financial costs of such disorders are great. These are the children who form the bulk of those who are 'socially excluded' – the present concern of the government's Social Exclusion Unit. If progress is to be made in integrating these children, there needs to be a partnership and a sharing of knowledge and resources between the key stakeholders: parents, schools, health, community, social, voluntary and psychological services. This book is part of this process.

The 'Ecological' Framework of Parenting, Schooling and Child Development

Although parents have always been held responsible for their children's behaviour, it is increasingly evident that parenting cannot be seen apart from its wider social context. Parents around the world have similar tasks in promoting their child's development and well-being throughout childhood as well as preparing them for adult life.

How parents parent, and how children thrive, however, takes place within an interacting ecological framework (Bronfenbrenner, 1979). Factors within *the child* interact with factors within *the parent(s)* and *the family* including the 'shared environment' of brothers and sisters. These in turn interact with factors present *outside the family,* at school and in their local neighbourhood. A good school can compensate for problems in other areas of a child's life whereas children attending a poor school are more likely to truant, to have weak educational attainments and to leave school early (Gray et al., 1980). School and community factors interact with factors in *the wider environment* such as the current economic conditions, local/national policies, attitudes, norms and societal expectations.

Along the life course and at each of the different levels there will be factors for both parents and children that increase risk for psychosocial disorders and factors that are protective. Risk and protective factors are not absolute or static, nor are they all good or all bad. On the whole, parents and children are more likely to cope with a single stressful experience that occurs in isolation than with multiple stresses. The timing of experiences is important: children may be developmentally more vulnerable, and parents may be emotionally less strong, at particular moments in time. Compensatory experiences such as success in school or work may increase parents' and children's 'resilience' to cope with other psychosocial stresses (Rutter, 1995).

Within the broader 'ecology' of child development, parent/child relationships are central. How parents and children react to each other's personality; how they react to the many interacting stresses and strains of their increasingly complex world; how successful they are in finding compensatory experiences for the many adversities that come their way; all these will be predictive of children's emotional well-being.

Parenting in a Fast Changing World

Certainties about parenting can be rendered less certain at times of great social change. Although the family has always been evolving, in the last 30 years the rate of family change has been particularly rapid. David Utting (1995) notes that in the UK:

- marriage rates have reached their lowest point since records began more than 150 years ago;
- cohabitation has increased in a quarter of a century from being the experience of six per cent to 60 per cent of brides before their wedding day;
- nearly one in three births (31 per cent) occurs outside marriage compared to one in 16 (six per cent) 30 years ago;
- there are fewer large families and fertility rates have declined from 2.9 in 1964 to 1.8 children per woman;
- the annual divorce rate has had a sixfold increase since 1961. If current trends continue, four out of ten new marriages will end in divorce;
- one in five families with dependent children (21 per cent) is headed by a lone parent compared with one in 12 (eight per cent) in 1971. The proportion of families headed by single mothers who have never married has grown from one per cent to seven per cent;
- one in 12 dependent children (eight per cent) are living in stepfamilies. By the age of 16 about six per cent of children will have lived in married-

couple stepfamilies and seven per cent in cohabitating-couple stepfamilies; and
- employment patterns over 15 years have become increasingly polarised between 'dual earner' families and homes where nobody has a paid job (Buchanan and Ten Brinke, 1997, p. 2).

These changes have brought new stresses for both parents and children. There is considerable evidence (Amato and Keith, 1991; Cherlin, Furstenberg, Chase-Lansdale et al., 1991) that divorce and family breakdown is associated with psychological difficulties for children. One of the problems in blaming family breakdown is that with family disruption come a host of other problems. In the short term, there may be a period of emotional distress. This may be related to the family break-up, or to disturbances and fraught family relationships that came before the disruption, or may be related to the difficulties that come as a result of the break-up.

Elliott and Richards (1991) found that many of the emotional and behavioural difficulties seen in children after divorce in fact predated the divorce. Sweeting and West (1995) in the west of Scotland study found that poorer health and lower self-esteem in children were associated with high levels of conflict between parents.

Divorce can also push parents below the poverty line. Weiss (1984) found that five years after the divorce, children and families were on average living on half the level of income of intact families. There is considerable evidence that lone parents (the separated and divorced and the never-married) are economically disadvantaged when compared to couple parents (Bradshaw and Millar, 1991). With economic disadvantage come a range of other disadvantages such as poor parental and child health, poorer educational achievement in children and a more stressed parenting style (Amato and Keith, 1991).

As Rutter noted in 1974:

> Good parenting requires certain permitting circumstances. There must be the necessary life opportunities and facilities. Where these are lacking even the best parents may find it difficult to exercise these skills.

Although overall, most families in the UK are better off, there has been an increasing divide between the rich and the poor. For example, in 1965, 32 per cent of couple families with children fell into the bottom 10 per cent of all incomes, whereas by 1991 this figure was 42 per cent. Children's early experience of disadvantage is a comparative experience. They compare themselves to others at their school. Buchanan and Ten Brinke (1997) found that disadvantage was associated with a greater likelihood of behaviour problems in adolescence and the risk extended to age 33, manifesting itself as a tendency to depression.

Parents traditionally play an important role in preparing their young to make the transitions into adult life. Parents, however, may be unaware of the coping strategies needed in a modern and very different society to the one in which they grew up. In addition, parents themselves are under pressure from increasing expectations. Owning your own home may not be possible on one salary. For many families, two salaries are a requirement to meet the mortgage repayments. Ferri and Smith (1996) have shown that although most parents are coping well, long working hours and job insecurity is having adverse effects on family life. These findings underline the real difficulties that modern parents face in reconciling their work and family responsibility – including evidence of the failure of the free market to deliver affordable alternative child care for working parents (Ferri and Smith, 1996).

Although the improving living conditions have, on one hand, meant a reduction in some stresses for children and young people, for example, experiencing the death of parent, brother or sister; on the other hand, as expectations rise and as more children and young people enter further education, there are the stresses of examinations, exam failures and the potential rejection at the tertiary stage of education. In addition, young people are faced with a plethora of choice. Whether to take, or not to take, the widely available substances that may be part of their peer culture; whether to engage in sexual relationships; whether or not to leave home; whether or not to cohabit.

Why is an Increase in Psychosocial Disorders in Young People a Matter of Concern?

The first concern, as evidenced by the rising number of exclusions, is that children with emotional and behavioural disorders may take their problems into school. School, as shown by the educational achievements of the last century, offers the 'best chance' of redressing early life disadvantages. The dilemma is that those children who stand to benefit most by education are amongst those most likely to miss out. The present government is currently producing a report for the Prime Minister on how to reduce the scale of truancy and how to find better solutions for those who have to be excluded from school (Social Exclusion Unit, Cabinet Office, 1998).

The second concern is that children with such disorders may develop mental health problems in adult life. Originally, it was felt that emotional and behavioural disorders were essentially apart and different from adult psychological disorders. More recently, the growing interest in the causes of depressive disorders in children and young people has shown that there are important links between childhood disorders and disorders in adulthood (Harrington, 1992; Harrington, Fudge, Rutter, Pickles and Hill, 1990). As Kovacs and Devlin (1998, pp. 47–63) note:

> The weight of evidence that youngsters with emotional disorders are likely to have similar difficulties in young adulthood will presumably put to rest any lingering notions that depressive or anxiety disorders in young people are a temporary phase.

Similarly, many studies demonstrate the strong links between early disruptive behaviour and later antisocial behaviour.

> Eighty-four per cent of children found to be 'uncontrolled' at age 11 met criteria for stable and pervasive antisocial disorder when reassessed at 13. Antisocial behaviour at 13 was predicted by 'externalising' behaviour at age 3 and behaviour problems at age 5, long before a diagnosis of conduct disorder could be made. Further these early behaviours were stronger predictors than IQ, mothers' attitudes, language level or any other variable tested (Robins, 1991, p. 202).

Although most antisocial children recover without developing an antisocial personality in adult life, there is an impressive body of research that demonstrates there is some degree of continuity between disruptive behaviour and conduct disorders in childhood and adult behaviour problems including crime (Smith, 1995).

The opening paragraph of a wide-ranging policy and practice review by the Health Advisory Service of the National Health Service (1995) summarises the many key issues:

> The mental health of children foreshadows the mental health of future generations of adults, … the implications of poor attention to children's and young people's mental health are not only their and their families' continued suffering, but also a continuing spiral of child abuse, juvenile crime, family breakdown and adult mental illness, all of which can lead to more child and adolescent mental health problems.

The Human and Economic Costs of Poor Mental Health

The Green Paper, *Our Healthier Nation* (1998) concludes that 'mental health is a key component of a healthy active life'. Poor mental health is a risk factor for many physical health problems. The Health Survey for England notes that 20 per cent of women and 14 per cent of men may have had a mental illness. It is estimated that mental disorders accounted for 17 per cent of total expenditure on health and social services in 1992/3 and between 15 per cent and 26 per cent of days off work for incapacity (Department of Health, 1998).

The Green Paper also notes that there are marked inequalities in who suffers most from mental health problems. There are particular concerns about the risk of suicide amongst men who are unskilled workers and women born in Sri Lanka, India and the East African Commonwealth. Depressive illness, which may have its origins in childhood, is one of the most common predictors of suicide. Although in recent years, suicide levels in the UK have generally been falling, of special concern are levels of suicide amongst young men and certain ethnic groups.

So What Can be Done to Promote the Emotional Well-being of Children?

International health programmes often use the metaphor of 'the river of risk'. We can equally well apply this metaphor to children with emotional and behavioural disorders:

> Downstream agencies are trying to rescue 'drowning' children ... Upstream, people are trying to ascertain whether children swimming in the river are 'at risk' for 'drowning' and should be rescued ... still further upstream children are jumping or falling into the river because of some combination of family and community dysfunction. We are surprised to see that very little is being done either to teach children to swim or, more importantly, to keep them from falling into the river.(Chamberlin, 1994, pp. 36–7)

The metaphor describes different levels of prevention/intervention. Stopping children falling into the water or teaching them to swim is about *primary prevention*. In this context, this means adopting measures that lower the risk of emotional and behavioural disorders for the child population as a whole. Public health policies have an important role to play here.

As Skuse (1998, p. 135) notes:

Primary prevention strategies that are aimed widely, perhaps at the broader community from which the family comes could turn out to be significantly more efficient and effective public health approaches to some under-socialised behaviour disorders than a reliance on individualised forms of treatment aimed at the family itself.

Noting children who have some combination of family and community dysfunction and who have 'fallen into the water' is about primary prevention of high-risk groups. This level targets populations who may be at greater risk of developing emotional and behavioural disorders because of the circumstances in which they live, or the groups to which they belong. The key task is to identify these areas or groups so that services may be readily available to them. It is recognized that most people who live in these priority areas, or who belong to particular high-risk groups will not have mental health problems. For example, children who have been in care are a particularly high risk group for further psychological problems (Cheung and Buchanan, 1997), but most children who have been in care do not have mental health problems (Buchanan and Ten Brinke, 1997).

'Rescuing' children who are drowning is *about secondary prevention*. The purpose is to 'rescue' or treat those who already have emotional and behavioural disorders. The focus here is mainly on 'individual' approaches. The key players are specialist educational, psychological, psychiatric and social services and the large national charities such as Barnardo's who run 'treatment' centres for a range of conditions.

Each level of prevention/intervention interacts with the next level. Although population approaches may lower the risk of developing emotional and behavioural disorders in all children, some communities will be more at risk than others. There will always be a need for individual treatment approaches. If, however, primary and secondary level approaches are successful, many fewer children will need individual treatment. Since the numbers of children with emotional and behavioural disorders are rising and since resources are limited, it becomes increasingly important that more work is undertaken 'upstream'. For both humanitarian and economic reasons, preventing a child developing a disabling behavioural disorder is preferable, and the evidence suggests may be more successful, than treating the child once the disorder is established.

'Our Healthier Nation'

These ideas link into the Green Paper (Department of Health, 1998). Key themes in the Paper are the association between poverty and disadvantage and poor health, and the need to lessen inequalities, if the nation's health and emotional well-being is to be improved. In order to do this, the Paper suggests that there are responsibilities at different levels. The National Health Service as a whole, and especially the branches dealing with Public Health, formulates strategies and policies that promote good health in people (*Population approaches)*; local authorities that deal within areas and communities formulate local policies to promote good health in the community and identify risks that are associated with particular communities *(Community approaches)*; while local professionals such as school nurses, family doctors and specialist mental health workers treat individuals who have health problems (*Individual approaches).*

Another major theme in the Green Paper is the role of individual and parental responsibility:

> Individual responsibility is not only just about (ourselves) ... It is also about the example that we set to those around us. The example and boundaries that parents set are central to the health of their children. It is in stable and caring families that children learn self-confidence to become secure and independent individuals. (Department of Health, 1998)

In outlining strategies for improving the nation's well-being, the Green Paper places a strong emphasis on the role of schools:

> **The Healthy Schools Initiative** will raise awareness of children as well as teachers, families and local communities to the important opportunities that exist for improving health, particularly the physical and mental health of children and young people. The initiative will include the development of parenting skills and the importance of recognising responsibility to ourselves and to others ... (Department of Health, 1998)

Among other things, it is intended that the Healthy Schools Initiative will create an environment that promotes the *emotional* well-being of children.

Promoting the emotional well-being of children

- *The research evidence indicates*: poor mental health in children is associated with greater health problems, poorer education/employment outcomes and greater social problems both during childhood and in human life.
- There are inter-generational continuities.
- There are human, economic and social costs.
- Despite improving health and education, the number of children with psychosocial disorders is rising.

Levels of intervention

	Public Health	**Education**
Population Aim: *to promote* emotional well-being in all children	Focus on factors which promote emotional well-being in children e.g. enhancing parenting skills *Delivered*: Child Health Services, voluntary sector, parents' groups	Focus on factors which promote emotional well-being in schools, preschool education, reduction of bullying, truancy and exclusions and emotional literacy *Delivered*: through schools to all children

	Primary Health/ Community Health	**Education**	**Social service and voluntary bodies**
Community Aim: to *facilitate* services that promote emotional well-being in communities at risk	Programmes for areas of high need e.g. health visiting, new parents' groups	Effective preschool education for children at risk of behaviour problems. Parents' groups in schools	Open access in areas of high need to parent support and other services

	Education	**Social services**	**Voluntary bodies**
Group Aim: to *provide* services for groups who may be at high risk	'Special needs' education services	Range of provisions e.g. after-care services for children who have been looked after; after schools clubs	Range of excellent projects for groups of children who are at risk e.g. homeless children

	Psychiatric/ psychological services	**Education**	**Social services**	**Voluntary organisations**
Individual Aim: *treatment/ rehabilitation* of children	Assessment and treatment of children with emotional and behavioural disorders	Remedial services for children with educational difficulties. Education psychologists etc. EBD schools etc.	The whole range of services for children who are being looked after or supported in the community	Range of services for children with EBD who may not get help elsewhere e.g. runaway children, substance abusers

Figure 1.1   Improving the emotional well-being of children: Interventions and responsibilities at different levels

The Need for Effective, Economical, Accessible and Widely Available Services

Central to all the new initiatives, is the growing realisation that if we want to improve services for children with emotional and behavioural problems we have to find effective and cost-efficient remedies.

A recent discussion paper from the Maudsley Hospital on child and adolescent mental health services (Goodman, 1997) reminds us that far from improving children's lives, some interventions may actually do harm. There is the salutary tale of the Cambridge-Somerville study. In this study, boys at high risk of becoming delinquent were randomly allocated to no-intervention or a planned package of social and psychological support. Thirty years later the intervention was found to make a highly significant difference on measures of criminality, alcoholism, psychosis and early death. Those who took part in the social support programme did *far worse* than those who had not taken part in a treatment programme (McCord, 1992). Goodman (1997, p. 1) emphasises the need to use effective treatments:

> Many of the treatments currently delivered … are of dubious or minimal value. … There is considerable scope for obtaining services that are more effective and better value for money by diverting available resources from treatments of dubious value into treatments that have been shown to work…

It is not that we do not know 'what works'. In the Maudsley paper (Goodman, 1997) there is a useful discussion on the issues. In a hypothetical catchment area with a total population of 250,000, Goodman summarises the estimated prevalence of particular disorders, and the treatments that are known to be effective in remediating the particular disorder. For example, some 1–5 per cent of 5–15 year olds will suffer from severe hyperkinesis or Attention Deficit Hyperactive Disorder. Three treatments that have been demonstrated as effective are: medication, diet and behavioural therapy. In cases of severe depression in childhood, the prevalence is one per cent amongst 11–15 year olds and four per cent amongst 16-17 years olds. The effective treatments are cognitive behavioural therapy, interpersonal therapy and medication (in a minority).

The major theme from this Maudsley paper is that child psychiatric services should only focus on children and young people with core mental health problems such as anorexia nervosa, schizophrenia, severe depression, obsessive-compulsive disorder and severe hyperactivity. Other children with emotional and behavioural disorders should be treated by primary health care services and other agencies. Their justification for this is that:

> Though troubled children and teenagers are common, many of them have social or educational problems rather than health problems. These require social and educational solutions, not health interventions.(Goodman, 1997, pp. 4–5)

The justification is also that with less severe emotional and behavioural problems, labelling children as having a 'mental' health problem may be more damaging than the condition itself. In addition, the efficacy of psychiatric treatment for this group is less certain. There is, however, considerable evidence that education and social programmes can be very effective. As Webster-Stratton notes in chapter 8, there is now a range of proven therapies and services that can reduce the number of children with behaviour problems, reduce delinquency, improve mental health and help parents improve their child-rearing.

The central problem, however, is that these effective therapies are not widely used. Researchers such as the contributors to this book have had to learn the hard lesson. It is not enough to demonstrate the good news that an intervention 'works'. The good news needs to be disseminated into practice.

About This Book

There are four parts to this book. The first sets the context; the second describes the characteristics of children with emotional and behavioural disorders; the third looks at possible interventions that 'work' and the final part considers how to implement evidenced-based interventions in practice.

Three different perspectives are explored in Part II. Sarah Stewart-Brown considers children's behaviour problems from a public health perspective. She argues that since such problems are the most common of all forms of disability in childhood, children's behaviour problems are a public health concern. The challenge for public health is to improve the overall psychological well-being of all children. She feels that well-validated population-based programmes that enhance parenting skills offer the best chance of achieving this.

In the second chapter, Ann Buchanan and JoAnn Ten Brinke acknowledge the importance of a public health perspective, but argue that it is also helpful to know which groups of children may be more at risk of psychological difficulties and what factors may protect them from such problems. They report on two studies. The first study considers factors that may be associated with 'recovery' from emotional and behavioural disorders. The second study considers whether the rise in the number of children with emotional and behaviour disorders is related to the rise in the number of children who have experienced family disruption.

Frances Gardner in chapter 4 moves away from the big picture and describes her observational research on parent-child interactions. She demonstrates how particular parenting styles contribute to the development of conduct disorders. She describes some of her work in developing early positive interactions between the parent and the child.

The focus of Part III is more directly on interventions, in particular interventions that have proven efficacy.

Kathy Sylva and Paul Colman take the education perspective. The key theme here is the role of preschool intervention to prevent behaviour problems and school failure – 'inclusion' rather than 'exclusion' from the educational system.

In chapter 6, Jane Barlow describes the findings from her systematic review of parent-training programmes for children aged between 3–10 with externalising disorders.

The perspective moves again in chapter 7. Here Teresa Smith takes a community perspective. First, she describes her research into family centres and some of the dilemmas in measuring effectiveness. In the second part of her chapter she describes how the needs of disadvantaged areas can be 'mapped'.

In Part IV there are two further important chapters. The first is by Carolyn Webster-Stratton from the US. Professor Webster-Stratton has over 20 years' experience of running parenting programmes and has led some of the most important randomised controlled trials in this field. Although she describes this work, her central message is how to persuade administrators and practitioners to adopt and implement programmes such as her own that are proven to be effective. Digging into her cookie jar, she uses the biscuit metaphor to describe the process in three areas.

Eva Lloyd's chapter takes this theme further. As a Principal Officer for Research and Development she has the task of introducing evidence-based social welfare in a large national child care agency. The final chapter draws together some of the findings.

Each well-intentioned intervention will not be successful, but through well-designed evaluations, the effectiveness of future efforts can be increased and the hiatus that separates the intention and realisation of aims can be diminished. (Kaufman and Zigler, 1992, pp. 287–8)

References

Amato, P.R. and Keith, B. (1991), 'Parental Divorce and the well-being of children: a meta-analysis', *Psychological Bulletin*, 110, pp. 26–46.

Bradshaw, J. and Millar, J. (1991), 'Lone parent families in the UK', *Department of Social Security Research Reports 6*, London, HMSO.

Bronfenbrenner, U. (1979), *The Ecology of Human Development: Experiments by Nature and Design*, Cambridge, Mass., Harvard University Press.

Buchanan, A and Ten Brinke, J-A. (1997), *What happened when they were grown up? Outcomes from parenting experiences*, York, Joseph Rowntree Foundation.

Chamberlin, R.W. (1994), 'Primary Prevention: the missing piece in child development legislation' in R.J. Simeonsson (ed.), *Risk, Resilience and Prevention*, Baltimore, Md, Brookes Publishing.

Cherlin, A.J., Furstenberg, F.F., Chase-Lansdale, P.L., Kiernan, K.E., Robins, P.K., Morrison, D. and Teitler, J. O. (1991), 'Longitudinal studies of effects of divorce on children in Great Britain and the United States', *Science*, 252, pp. 1386–9.

Cheung, S.Y. and Buchanan, A. (1997), 'Malaise scores in adulthood of children and young people who have been in care', *Journal of Child Psychology and Psychiatry*, 38, pp. 575–80.

Department of Health (1998), *Our Healthier Nation*, (Green Paper), London, HMSO.

Elliott, B.J. and Richards, M. (1991). 'Children and divorce: educational performance and behaviour before and after parental separation', *International Journal of Law and the Family*, 5, pp. 258–76

Ferri, E. and Smith, K. (1996). *Parenting in the 1990s*, London, Family Policy Studies/Joseph Rowntree Foundation.

Goodman, R. (1997), *Child and Adolescent Mental Health Services: Reasoned advice to Commissioners and Providers*, Maudsley Discussion Paper No., 4, London, Institute of Psychiatry.

Gray, G., Smith, A. and Rutter, M. (1980), 'School attendance and the first year of employment', in L. Hersov and I. Berg (eds), *Out of School: Modern perspectives in truancy and school refusal*, pp. 343–370, Chichester, John Wiley and Sons Ltd.

Harrington, R.C. (1992), 'Annotation: the Natural History and Treatment of Child and Adolescent Affective Disorders', *Journal of Child Psychology and Psychiatry*, 33, pp. 1278–1302.

Harrington, R.C., Fudge, H., Rutter, M., Pickles, A. and Hill, J. (1990), 'Adult outcomes of childhood and adolescent depression: I Psychiatric Status, *Archives of General Psychiatry*, 47, pp. 467–473.

Health Advisory Service (1995), *Bridges over Troubled Waters*, London, HMSO.

Kaufman, K., and Zigler, E. (1992), 'The prevention of child maltreatment: programming, research and policy' in J. Willis, E. Holden and M. Rosenberg (eds), *Prevention of Child Maltreatment, Developmental and Ecological Perspectives*, New York, John Wiley and Sons, Ltd.

Kovacs, M. and Devlin, B. (1998), 'Internalizing Disorders in Childhood', *Journal of Child Psychology and Psychiatry*, 39, 1, pp. 47–63.

McCord, J. (ed.) (1992), *Advances in Criminological Theory Vol. III: Facts, frameworks and forecast*, New Brunswick, NJ, Transaction.

Robins, L.N. (1991), 'Conduct Disorder', *Journal of Child Psychology and Psychiatry*, 32, pp. 193–212.

Rutter, M. (1974), 'Dimensions of parenthood: some myths and some suggestions' in *The Family in Society*, Department of Health and Social Security, London, HMSO.

Rutter, M. (1995), 'Causal concepts and their testing' in M. Rutter and D. Smith, (eds), *Psychosocial Disorders in Young People*, Chichester, John Wiley and Sons Ltd.

Skuse, D. (1998), Editorial, *Journal of Child Psychology and Psychiatry*, 39, 2, pp. 135–136.

Smith, D. (1995), 'Youth Crime and Conduct Disorders: Trends, Patterns and Causal Explanations' in M. Rutter and D. Smith, (eds), *Psychosocial Disorders in Young People*, Chichester, John Wiley and Sons Ltd.

Smith, D. and Rutter, M. (1995), 'Time Trends in Psychosocial disorders of Youth' in M. Rutter and D. Smith, (eds), *Psychosocial Disorders in Young People*, Chichester, John Wiley and Sons Ltd.

Social Exclusion Unit (1998), Consultation letter, 23 February 1998, Cabinet Office, London.

Sweeting, H. and West, P. (1995), 'Family life and health in adolescence: a role for culture in the health inequalities debate?', *Social Science and Medicine*, 40, pp. 163–75.

Utting, D. (1995), *Family and Parenthood. Supporting Families, preventing breakdown*, York, Joseph Rowntree Foundation.

Weiss, R.S. (1984), 'The impact of marital dissolution on income and consumption in single-parent households', *Journal of Marriage and the Family*, 46, pp. 115–27.

PART II
SETTING THE SCENE

2   Public Health Implications of Childhood Behaviour Problems and Parenting Programmes

SARAH STEWART-BROWN

Summary

- *This chapter presents the epidemiological research on childhood behaviour disorder and argues that this disorder is not a clinical entity but the tail end of a spectrum of behaviour. Other examples of disorders with these epidemiological characteristics include hypertension (high blood pressure), high cholesterol and alcohol misuse. There is strong theoretical and research evidence to suggest that these disorders are more effectively prevented using a 'population' rather than a high-risk or secondary prevention approach.*
- *Parent training programmes have been used by the statutory services (social, health and education) in both high-risk and secondary preventive approaches for some years. The research evidence showing that programmes are effective in these settings is strong. At present, the voluntary sector is the main provider of parent training using a population approach. Preliminary and qualitative and observational studies suggest that these are also effective in a population setting, but no trials have been carried out.*
- *Childhood behaviour disorder is now the most common cause of disability in childhood and there is good evidence to suggest that it is an important risk factor for many common disorders of adolescence and adulthood, including mental illness, family violence, and unhealthy lifestyles. The most promising solution to this twentieth century epidemic is parent support and training for all parents. More research is needed to define which types of programmes should be provided and how.*

The Public Health Implications of Behaviour Problems

Behaviour problems in childhood are an important public health concern for a number of reasons. They have now become the most important cause of disability in childhood (Bone and Meltzer, 1989). They are a risk factor for mental illness in adulthood (Newton, 1988) and mental illness is one of the most important causes of disability in adulthood (Murray and Lopez, 1996). They are predictive of social outcomes such as marital breakdown, criminality and violence (Newton, 1988), which are important causes of mental illness, both in their own right and secondarily, through their influence on spouses and victims. They are a risk factor for drug and alcohol misuse, which are themselves risk factors for a range of physical health problems. Longitudinal studies are beginning to show a direct relationship between behaviour problems and a range of physical health problems in adulthood (Power et al., 1991).

Functional categories of disability: children 5–9 yrs OPCS 1985–88

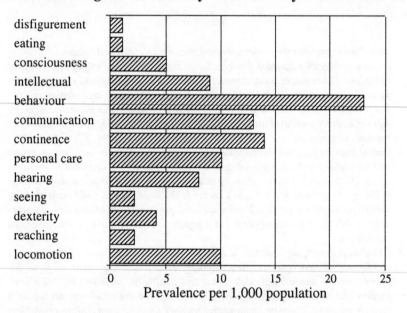

Figure 2.1   Prevalence of disability in childhood: Great Britain
Source: Based on data in Bone and Meltzer, 1989.

Parenting Programmes

Parenting programmes appear to offer a promising solution to childhood behaviour problems. A range of these programmes is available, developed by different professionals, based on different theoretical models (Smith, 1996).

Psychiatrists and psychologists have developed programmes based on social learning theory and behaviour modification principles for parents whose children attend their clinics because of behaviour problems. Counsellors and psychotherapists have developed programmes based on psychotherapeutic principles to help parents understand how their own conscious and unconscious feelings affect their parenting. Educationalists have developed programmes to improve literacy skills, children's classroom behaviour and educational achievement (Alexander, 1997). These programmes may be offered by people from a variety of professional backgrounds. In the UK at the moment the voluntary sector is the biggest provider of parenting programmes. What these programmes have in common is that they provide parents with the opportunity to develop their understanding of children's emotional development and their ability to provide emotionally supportive home environments. All programmes aim to improve parents' communication skills so that they can listen to their children more effectively and respectfully. To be effective programmes need to offer non-judgmental support to parents. Programmes run for parents in groups appear to be more effective than those run on an individual basis (Barlow, 1997).

Parenting programmes are offered both to parents whose children have established behaviour problems and to parents who simply want to learn more about parenting (open access). The former are usually provided by health or social services; the latter usually by education services or the voluntary sector. In between these two approaches both groups offer parenting programmes on a preventive basis to parents whose children are at high risk of developing problems; for example, those living in deprived communities and teenage parents. It has also been proposed that children should undergo a screening test, for example at school entry, to ensure that all those who are developing behaviour problems are identified early and that their parents are offered a programme. These different approaches represent the range of public health interventions, from tertiary prevention or treatment (for children with established behaviour problems), through to secondary prevention of emerging problems by screening, and primary prevention either on a population approach (open access and universal provision) or a high risk approach (access restricted to certain social groups).

The effectiveness of these parenting programmes has been investigated in different types of controlled trials (see chapters 6 and 8). The most rigorously evaluated programmes are those based on behaviour modification. Most studies have evaluated the effectiveness of programmes for parents whose children have established behaviour problems, but some have demonstrated that these programmes can also be effective in preventing the development of these problems (Webster-Stratton, in press, a and b; Sandler, 1992). The latter trials have been undertaken only with parents in high risk groups. Open access parenting programmes have not yet been studied in controlled trials. Evaluative studies on these programmes are based on measures at the beginning and end of programmes, which demonstrate improvement. They have also collected the views of participating parents on the value of the programme.

Further Public Health Implications of Parenting Programmes

Antenatal parenting programmes have been shown in two controlled studies (Parr, 1996; Eliot et al., 1988) to have a direct positive impact on the emotional well-being of parents, offering protection against post natal depression. A controlled study of a preschool parenting programme also showed a beneficial effect on maternal self esteem (Mullin et al., 1994).

Epidemiological and qualitative studies are beginning to identify links between parenting styles and the adoption of unhealthy lifestyles. Teenagers from families where communication is poor and there is little emotional support are at greater risk of substance misuse than their peers (Nutbeam, 1989; Barnes, 1984). These unhealthy lifestyles are now responsible for a very large proportion of premature death and disease. Programmes that improve communication and increase emotional support in the home may well prove protective against substance misuse.

A promising analysis of the causes of social inequalities in health (Wilkinson, 1996) defines social stress rather than the inequitable distribution of income as the critical cause of this major public health problem. The same study defines social cohesion and social support as protective against inequalities in health. By improving parents' ability to make and sustain relationships with other adults as well as their children parenting programmes could have an important part to play in the development of social cohesion.

Through their impact on the emotional environment in which children are raised parenting programmes therefore have the potential to impact on a wide range of major public health problems.

Behaviour Problems: Definitions and Terminology

The terminology used to describe childhood behaviour problems differs in different professional groups. The child psychiatrists have defined a number of different clinical entities: internalising disorder in which the child appears fearful, anxious, clinging and tearful and externalising disorder in which the child is destructive, aggressive, disobedient, hyperactive or attention seeking. These have also been labelled neurotic and antisocial behaviour respectively. Externalising disorder is further subdivided into attention deficit disorder, characterised by hyperactivity and poor concentration and a group of disorders, characterised by hostility and disregard for the rights of others. In the latter, the label and definition differ according to the age of the child (Oppositional Defiant Disorder under eight years, conduct disorder in youths and antisocial personality disorder over 18 years). There is considerable overlap between these different entities with children frequently showing signs of more than one. The identification of explicit criteria in the classification of behaviour problems has been a very difficult task; no one classification has proved completely defensible and the criteria have changed over time. This may be part of the reason why teachers and social workers use a single label – emotional and behaviour disorder – for children who exhibit these problems in schools. Previously such children were called maladjusted.

An important feature of all the definitions, however, is that they are a description of behaviours which may be exhibited by normal children under certain circumstances. It is therefore only the frequency and constellation of the symptoms that makes them a problem of concern to psychiatrists, teachers and social workers.

Epidemiological Studies of Behaviour Problems

Epidemiological studies or community surveys are carried out to estimate the prevalence of a condition or problem and to identify the characteristics of people most likely to have the problem. Studies of abnormal behaviour in children of the sort that might indicate psychiatric disorder have been carried out since the 1950s (Verhulst and Koot, 1992). In a few studies very large numbers of children have been assessed clinically (Anderson et al., 1987; McGee et al., 1990) to identify those who have a psychiatric disorder. Most studies have used questionnaires or rating scales (child behaviour inventories), in which parents, teachers or the children themselves record the presence or absence of a range of behaviours to screen for children most likely to have psychiatric disorder. Responses to these inventories are then scored, and children with high scores representing more abnormal behaviours are invited to attend for a clinical assessment. These studies have provided a range of estimates of prevalence of psychiatrically defined behaviour problems ranging from seven per cent to 26 per cent. Some of this variation may indicate real differences between the different communities but some is also likely to be due to differences in the definition of behaviour problems used in different studies.

These studies are of course all predicated on the assumption that there is a clinical entity or a series of clinical entities, which can be defined by abnormal behaviour. The difficulties which psychiatrists have faced in trying to define a system of classification and estimate the prevalence of behaviour problems suggests that this assumption may not be valid and that it may be preferable to regard behaviour problems as a spectrum in which the 'deviant behaviours' are a symptom of emotional distress. In this model the frequency and severity of distress dictates the frequency and severity of the behaviour problem. When the distress is prolonged and severe the deviant behaviour becomes 'normal' for that child.

This model is supported by the child behaviour inventory data gathered in epidemiological surveys. The early child behaviour inventories (Rutter et al., 1970; Eyberg and Ross, 1978; Achenbach et al., 1991) contained only negative statements, such as 'talks too much', 'cheeky', 'fights frequently with other children', 'not liked by peers', 'steals'. Some items, such as 'picks nose in public' or 'behaves like a child of the opposite sex', might no longer be seen to be deviant behaviours. New inventories (Goodman, 1994; Hind and Haggard, 1998) also include a range of positive items: 'helpful and obedient' and 'well liked by peers'. Clearly the content of these inventories determines the number of children who will be identified as likely to have a psychiatric disorder.

The results from surveys using child behaviour inventories are usually analysed categorically, that is children are described as having abnormal behaviour or not having it, according to whether their scores fall above or below a cut off point. They can however also be analysed as shown in Figures 2.2 and 2.3. These show frequency distributions of scores on two different child behaviour inventories and they vary in shape. The Rutter scale shown in Figure 2.2 for 16 year olds demonstrates a positive skew, that is, there are a small number of children with very high scores and most children have low scores. The frequency distribution of the more recent Behaviour Assessment Inventory (Figure 2.3) is more normally distributed, that is it approximates more closely to the bell shaped curve characteristic of a normal distribution.

The shape of the distribution of scores on these inventories can be

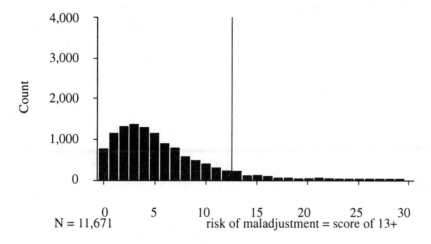

Figure 2.2   Distribution of scores on the Rutter 'A' Child and Behaviour Checklist: 16 year olds

Source: National Child Development Study, 1974.

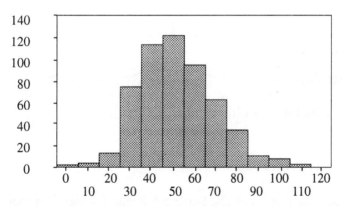

Higher scores represent more behaviour problems

Representative sample of 545 children living in Nottinghamshire, Derbyshire, Leicestershire, Renfrewshire and Avon.

Figure 2.3   Distribution of scores on Behaviour Assessment Inventory (BAI): 2–9 year olds

Source: S. Hind and M. Haggard, MRC Institute of Hearing Research.

manipulated by statistical transformation or by subtle differences in the way
the questions are phrased or the answers scored. However scores on all
inventories in all the populations where they have been used, have one thing
in common; they are continuous with no suggestion of a bimodal distribution.
It is very different from the distribution of, for example, blood sugar levels in
a condition like diabetes. A plot of the blood sugar levels in a representative
sample of the population shows two distinct peaks with very little overlap as
in Figure 2.4. The first peak represents the sugar levels of normal people and
the second the sugar levels of people with diabetes. The frequency distribution
of blood sugar levels suggests that diabetes is a well-defined clinical entity,
whereas that for childhood behaviour problems suggests that it is not.

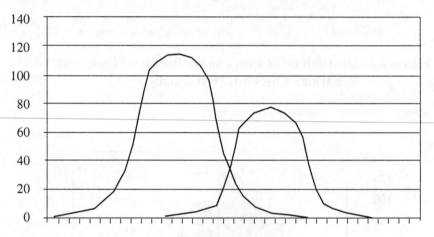

Figure 2.4   Example of a bimodal distribution

Implications for Prevention

The frequency distribution of childhood behaviour disorder is of more than
just theoretical importance. Rose (1989) writing of the mental health of adult
populations, for which the frequency distribution is similar, has identified
several implications of this type of distribution. The questions which health
professionals should be asking with a health problem distributed in this way
is not 'does he/she have the problem?' but 'how much of the problem does
he/she have?'. The health problems represented by the tail end of a distribution
like this (high blood pressure, raised blood cholesterol levels, alcohol misuse)
are not an entity. They are part of and belong to the body of the distribution

curve; they also move with the body of the curve. For all these problems when the prevalence varies over time or in different populations it can be shown that the proportion of people who have a severe level of the problem varies in proportion to the population mean (Rose, 1985). The more alcohol the average individual drinks the more people there will be who misuse alcohol.

Health problems with this sort of distribution are most effectively tackled by population approaches to prevention rather than by secondary prevention or high-risk approaches. Population approaches aim to shift the entire distribution so that everyone has a bit less of the problem. This contrasts with the high risk approach in which the aim is to find communities with a high level of the problem and offer programmes which reduce the risk, or secondary prevention in which the aim is to find individuals with a high level of the problem and to reduce their individual level. Alcohol taxation or reducing dietary salt intake are examples of the population approach. Screening and medication for people with high blood pressure or counselling for people who are misusing alcohol are examples of secondary prevention and high-risk approaches. Both from a theoretical base and from a research base the population approach can be shown to be more effective (Rose, 1985).

Studies in which the scores of children on the child behaviour inventories have been analysed categorically (see above) can provide a useful and different perspective from those analysed continuously. In this type of analysis for example it is possible to demonstrate that at any specified level of severity, behaviour problems are more common in social classes IV and V than they are in social classes I and II (Figure 2.4). The difference between classes is most marked for conduct disorder. This sort of distribution often suggests that a high-risk approach to prevention might be worth trying because it appears reasonable to concentrate resources on those at greatest risk. However, although behaviour problems are more common in social classes IV and V, paradoxically most of the children with this problem are in social class IIIM (Figure 2.5.) This 'population paradox' occurs because the number of children in social classes IV and V is small relative to the number in the other social classes. In situations such as this a high-risk approach to prevention is rarely efficient. Perhaps the most important thing to note from Figure 2.5 is that all three types of childhood behaviour disorder are common in all social classes.

Epidemiological studies therefore support the provision of universal parenting programmes rather than provision for high risk groups, or secondary prevention. These three approaches are not mutually exclusive and may be provided together. At present however the great majority of UK parenting programmes, provided or funded by statutory organisations, are confined to

Social class

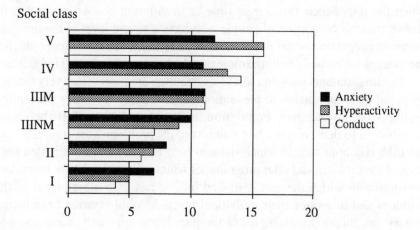

**Figure 2.5   Per cent of children age 10 years with childhood behaviour
problems in each social class as defined by Rutter Scale
(Woodruffe, 1993)**

Social class

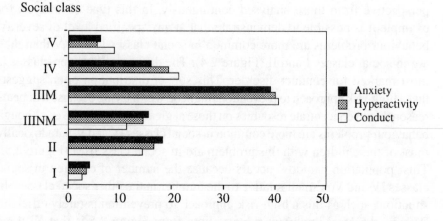

Prevalence of CBD from Child Health and Education Study: social class distribution of
children 1–14 yrs from DS 8 1981 (Woodruffe, 1993)

**Figure 2.6   Social class distribution (per cent) of children with
childhood behaviour disorder at 10 years of age**

parents of children who already have behaviour problems or to those at high risk. Funding for research programmes has also been confined to this group. Apart from the relative inefficiency of this approach problems will also arise because of stigmatisation. If parenting programmes are seen to be provided only for parents who are failing or likely to fail, none will want to attend. Population approaches can be more difficult to implement than high-risk approaches. One of the main problems with their implementation is that it is necessary to persuade people in the middle of the distribution, which usually includes the policy makers, that they might need to change.

The Next Steps

Universal parenting programmes have the potential to impact on the commonest cause of disability in childhood, and through their impact on health-related lifestyles, mental health and social inequalities, on the commonest causes of disability and premature death in adulthood. There is therefore an urgent need to set up research programmes which define the extent of this potential, and establish the most effective of the range of different approaches.

In the meanwhile the feasibility of universal provision needs consideration. Only a small number of health, education or social services are currently providing parenting programmes in the UK. Celia Smith (1996) has estimated that voluntary sector programmes are reaching upwards of four per cent of parents. Although the voluntary sector could not provide programmes for all parents tomorrow, given secure funding and consistent government or statutory sector support they could probably reach this target over the course of a decade. Another voluntary organisation, the Pre-school Playgroups Association, achieved a similar feat with only a small amount of government funding or support in the 1970s and 1980s. Writing from the point of view of parenting programmes in support of education, Alexander (1997) has estimated that parenting education and family support could be provided at the cost of between £300 per child (a costing based on one full-time support worker per secondary school) and £1,800 per child (based on one worker per primary school). These figures represent respectively 0.5–3 per cent of the education budget. Given that parenting programmes appear to be of central importance to all three of the statutory services dealing with children, jointly funded universal programmes provided by both the statutory sector and the voluntary sector are clearly feasible in the long to medium term.

References

Achenbach, T.M . and Edelbroch, C.S. (1991), *Manual for the child behaviour checklist: 4–18 profile*, Burlington VT, University of Vermont Dept of Psychiatry.

Alexander, T. (1997), *Family Learning*, London, Demos Arguments Series.

Anderson, J.C., Williams, S., McGee, R. and Silva, P.A. (1987), 'DSMIII disorders in preadolescent children', *Archives of General Psychiatry*, 44, pp. 69–76.

Barlow, J. (1997), *Systematic Review of the effectiveness of the parent training programmes in improving behaviour problems in children aged 3–10 years*, University of Oxford, Health Services Research Unit Report Series.

Barnes, G.M. (1984), 'Adolescent alcohol abuse and other problem behaviours: their relationships and common parental influences', *Journal of Youth and Adolescence*, 13, pp. 329–84.

Bone, M. and Meltzer, H. (1989), *The prevalence of disability among children, OPCS surveys of Disability in Great Britain Report 3*, London, HMSO.

Eliot, S.A., Sanjack, M. and Leverton, T.L. (1988), 'Parent Groups in Pregnancy: A preventive intervention for post natal depression' in Gottlieb, B.J. (ed.), *Marshalling Social Support: Formats Processes and Effects*, California, Sage Publications Ltd.

Eyberg, S.M. and Ross, A.W. (1978), 'Assessment of child behaviour problems: the valuation of a new inventory', *Journal of Child Psychology*, 16, pp. 113–6.

Goodman, R.A. (1994), modified version of the Rutter parent questionnaire including items on children's strengths: a research note, *Journal of Child Psychology and Psychiatry*, 35, pp. 1483–94.

Graham, P. (1991), *Child Psychiatry: a Developmental approach*, 2nd edn, Oxford, Oxford University Press.

Hind, S. and Haggard, M. (1998), personal communication MRC Hearing Unit Nottingham.

McGee, R., Feehan, M., Williams, S., Partridge, F., Silva, P.A. and Kelly, J. (1990), 'DSM-III disorders in a large sample of adolescents', *Journal of the American Academy of Child and Adolescent Psychiatry*, 29, pp. 611–9.

Mullin, E., Quigley, K.and Glanville, B.A. (1994), 'Controlled evaluation of the impact of a parent training programmes on child behaviour and mothers general well-being', *Counselling Psychology Quarterly*, 7, pp. 167–79.

Murray, C.L. and Lopez, A.D. (1996), *The global burden of disease*, Harvard School of Public Health, on behalf of WHO and World Bank.

Newton, J. (1988), *Preventing Mental Illness*, London, Routledge & Kegan Paul Ltd.

Nutbeam, D., Aar, L. and Catford, J. (1989), 'Understanding children's health behaviour: the implications for health promotion for young people', *Social Science Medicine*, 29, pp. 317–25.

Parr, M. (1996), 'Support for couples in the transition to parenthood', PhD thesis University of London.

Power, C., Manor, O., and Fox, J. (1991), *Health and Class: the Early Years*, London, Chapman and Hall.

Rose, G, (1985), 'Sick Individuals, Sick Population', *International Journal of Epidemiology*, 14, pp. 32–8.

Rose, G. (1989), 'The mental health of populations' in Williams, P., Wilkinson, G. and Rawnsley, K. (eds), *The scope of epidemiological psychiatry: essays in honour of Michael Shepherd*, London, Routledge.

Rutter, M., Tizard, J. and Whitmore, K. (1970), *Education Health and Behaviour*, London, Longman.

Sandler, I.N. (1992) in West, S.G., Bacca, L., Pillow, D.R. et al., 'Linking empirically based theory and evaluation: the family bereavement programmes', *Journal of Community Psychology*, 20 (4), pp. 491–521.

Smith, C. (1996), *Developing Parenting Programmes*, London, National Children's Bureau.

Verhulst, F.C. and Koot, H.M. (1992), *Child Psychiatric Epidemiology: Concepts, Methods and Findings, Developmental Clinical Psychology and Psychiatry 23*, California, Sage Publications Ltd.

Webster-Stratton, C. (in press a), *Preventing conduct disorder in the Head Start: Strengthening Parenting Competencies in Children*, Journal of Consulting and Clinical Psychology.

Webster-Stratton , C. (in press b), 'Parent training with low income clients: promoting parental engagement through a collaborative approach' in Lutzer, J.R. (ed.), *Child Abuse: A Handbook of Theory Research and Treatment*, New York, Plenum Press.

Wilkinson, R.G. (1996), *Unhealthy Societies: the afflictions of inequality*, London, Routledge.

Woodruffe, C., Glickman, M., Barker, M. and Power, C. (1993), *Children, Teenagers and Health: the key data*, Buckingham, Open University Press.

3 Children Who May be at Risk of Emotional and Behavioural Problems

ANN BUCHANAN AND JOANN TEN BRINKE

Summary

- *This chapter gives an overview of factors associated with emotional and behavioural disorders in children. In order to focus interventions effectively, be they public health, educational, psychological or social, it is helpful to know what factors place children at risk and what factors may protect children from such disorders. The chapter draws on two studies by the authors. Both these studies were based on longitudinal data from 17,000 children who took part in the National Child Development Study (NCDS).*
- *The first study identifies risk and protective factors for emotional and behavioural problems at 7, 11, and 16.*
- *The second study looks in more depth at the associations between parental background and psychological problems in adolescence and in adult life. It asked, what difference did it make to later psychological well-being whether a child was brought up in a birth, step, widowed or lone parent family? It also asked to what extent did an early experience of extreme social disadvantage and/or experience of public 'care' influence later mental health?*

Whether our approach to children with emotional and behavioural disorders stems from a public health, educational, psychological or social perspective, we need basic information about the psychological problems that children are experiencing. We need to know not only the characteristics of the disorders, their extent and consequences, but also what factors place children at risk for such a disorder; what factors may protect them. In addition, we need to know what factors are associated with 'recovery' once a child has such a disorder. If interventions to improve the emotional well-being of young people are to be focused effectively, all services need this information.

The two studies reported here are part of this process. Both studies use longitudinal data from the National Child Development Study (NCDS). The

34

first study explores risk and protective factors that are associated with behavioural problems at different ages and factors that are associated with 'recovery' from behaviour problems. The second looks in more detail at the associations between parental background – whether a child has been brought up by their natural parents, or step-parents or a widowed or lone parent, and whether they had experienced extreme disadvantage or been in care – and psychological problems in adolescence and in adult life.

Background

Children's Behaviour Problems and the Ecological Approach

As discussed in chapter 1, parenting, schooling and children's development take place within an interacting 'ecological' framework (Bronfenbrenner, 1979). Risk and protective factors for behavioural problems in childhood are also nested in these ecosystems (person; family; school/community; nation). Risk factors in the person, for example, such as a biological disposition to depression, may be compensated for by protective factors, such as a high IQ which may also bring better problem-solving skills. Personal risk and protective factors interact with those of the family, the community and the national situation. The likelihood of a person who is born with a tendency to depressive illness developing a full-blown clinical depression will be increased if that person's mother also has the same tendency and that mother lives in an economically disadvantaged community at a time of national economic recession. Protective factors in the person, such as resilience in the face of adversity; within the family, such as financial well-being; and in the community, such as excellent schools and community support, may compensate for or act as 'buffers' against a biological predisposition to depression and consequently lead to very different outcomes.

'Internalising' Versus 'Externalising' Behaviour Problems

Traditionally studies on childhood behaviour problems, as discussed elsewhere in this book, are broken down into two clinical subgroups: disruptive or antisocial disorders, and neurotic or anxiety disorders. Broadly speaking, the first group refers to 'externalising' disorders and the second to 'internalising' disorders:

> Thus 'internalising disorders' refers to conditions whose central feature is disordered mood or emotion. In contrast 'externalising disorders' are ones whose central feature is behaviour. As general category labels, the terms 'emotional' disorders versus 'behavioural' disorders are synonymous with 'internalising' versus 'externalising' conditions.(Kovacs and Devlin, 1998, p. 44)

Within these two broad groups there are a number of subgroups. Internalising disorders comprise both depressive and anxiety disorders. Both these disorders encompass a variety of diagnoses. The American Psychiatric Association DSM IIIR lists more than 10 types of anxiety disorders alone (American Psychiatric Association, 1987). Similarly, 'externalising' disorders, as discussed by Frances Gardner in chapter 4, also have a number of sub-categories, for example: Attention Deficit Hyperactive Disorder (ADHD), Oppositional Defiant Disorder (ODD) and Conduct Disorder (CD). During late adolescence, antisocial disorders are more common in boys whereas emotional disorders are more common in girls. All internalising disorders occur at a lower rate in childhood than in adolescence or adulthood (Kovacs and Devlin, 1998).

There is a continuing debate about co-morbidity. Broadly speaking the main debate is about co-morbidity within the two broad categories. Throughout childhood and adolescence, internalising disorders are more likely to be co-morbid with one another (for example anxiety and depression), than with externalising disorders (Cohen, Cohen, Kasen et al., 1993). Internalising disorders, however, co-occur with externalising disorders at rates typically higher than by chance (Caron and Rutter, 1991). It may be that antisocial behaviour leads to problematic social interactions that in turn lead to rejection. Such rejection may increase the risk of depression in adult life (Kovacs and Devlin, 1998).

The literature on 'externalising' disorders paints a rather gloomy picture of continuity between behaviour problems in childhood, and later antisocial behaviour:

> For example, the antisocial child may be troublesome and disruptive at school, the antisocial teenager may steal cars and burgle houses, and the antisocial adult male may beat up his wife and neglect his children. These changing manifestations reflect changes both within the individual (e.g. maturation) and in his environment.(Farrington, 1992, p. 258)

Adverse family and environmental factors such as punitive parenting styles, social adversities and parental disagreements are strongly correlated with externalising disorders especially where these develop into antisocial behaviour. Biological factors probably play a lesser role, although some twin studies are finding genetic links (McGuffin and Thapar, 1997). The adult outcome of children with an anxiety disorder in childhood is less clear cut. Kovacs and Devlin (1998, p. 51) conclude:

> Findings from epidemiological, community-based, clinically referred and special samples converge generally supporting the predictive validity of internalising disorders in the young years ... from childhood into adolescence and from adolescence into young adulthood.

However, Rodgers (1990), in a prospective longitudinal study of more than 1,000 women, has shown that such childhood disorder is only associated with adult psychopathology when there are precipitating environmental stresses in adult life. It is possible that 'within person' temperamental traits render some children more sensitive to negative stimuli (Clark et al., 1994). This suggests that although these children may have a biological propensity to an internalising disorder, for this to become a problem the presence of adverse environmental factors may be required.

Smith (1995) notes that although there is an impressive amount of evidence, particularly relating to antisocial disorders, that demonstrates the continuity between childhood and adult life, there is also considerable evidence of discontinuity. Campbell (1995) in discussing behaviour problems in preschool children suggests that around half will have difficulties that extend into adolescence. This, of course, also means that around half will not.

Three important points are raised. First, looking back, many or even most adults with psychological disorders will have had some problems in childhood, but looking forward only half of the children who have behavioural problems in early childhood will grow up to have psychological disorders in adult life. We need to know more about factors that are associated with 'recovery'.

Second, much of the research focuses on risk and pathology. There is much less emphasis on factors that may protect children from adverse outcomes. If we are to develop effective interventions, we need to know more about protective factors.

Third, most of the literature centres around personal and family characteristics associated with these disorders. As Bronfenbrenner (1979) has demonstrated, risk and protective factors interact within the wider ecological framework. Since teacher responses and events in the wider community may shape subsequent behaviour it is critical to look beyond personal and family characteristics to understand the ecology within which the child develops and interacts in order to develop effective interventions.

The National Child Development Study (NCDS)

NCDS is an excellent vehicle for exploring child to adult trajectories. NCDS is a study of some 17,000 children who were born in one week in March, 1958 in England, Scotland and Wales. The aim of the study was to collect a range of social, educational and health data on factors that may influence human development over the entire life span. To date follow-ups have been carried out in 1965 (age seven years), in 1969 (age 11 years), in 1974 (age 16 years), in 1981 (age 23 years) and in 1991 (age 33 years). Information has been collected from parents, teachers and the school health service and in the later sweeps from the NCDS cohort members themselves. Over the years some of the original members have been lost to the study. At age 33, information was obtained from 11,363 members. Despite the losses, generally, the overall representative nature of the study has been maintained (Shepherd, 1993). Amongst ethnic minorities, however, losses have been particularly high and unfortunately the data cannot be used reliably to explore issues relating to these groups.

Study One: 'Recovery' from Emotional and Behaviour Problems

The aim of this study was to use longitudinal data from NCDS first to identify risk and protective factors that were associated with behavioural problems at different ages and secondly to identify factors that were associated with 'recovery' from behaviour problems. The findings of the study will be reported in full elsewhere (Buchanan and Ten Brinke, forthcoming).

How the Study was Undertaken

The National Child Development Study offers an unrivalled opportunity to test hypotheses on person, family, school and social/environmental factors that may be associated with emotional and behavioural disorders.

The first stage of this study was a wide-ranging review of the literature. From this and from the first author's clinical experience, potential risk and protective factors were identified. These covered person, family and school/community variables operating at birth, age seven, 11 and 16. The potential risk and protective factors were then linked to available data in NCDS.

The next stage was to establish the behavioural measures. In NCDS, behavioural measures were taken of every child at age seven, 11 and 16 years.

In 1974 at age 16 the full Rutter 'A' (parental report) Health and Behaviour Checklist was used (31 questions). At both age seven and 11 years a shortened parent-report version was used. Twenty-three items from the Rutter 'A' Health and Behaviour Checklist were available at all three ages seven, 11, 16; complete behavioural data were available for 8,657 children. A shortened Rutter 'A' at each age was developed based on the set of 23 questions available. Tests concluded that there was a very high correlation between the short and long version of the Rutter 'A' at age 16 ($r = 0.95$; $p < 0.0001$).

Factor analysis confirmed that two sets of behaviours in the shortened Rutter 'A' grouped together. Seven behaviours were identified as belonging to a 'disruptive' or an externalising group, while another seven behaviours were identified as belonging to an 'unhappy' or internalising group. Taking the 20 per cent with the highest scores of the shortened Rutter 'A', these were then divided into a 'disruptive' group and an 'unhappy' group.

There was a good correlation between the subgroup 'Unhappy' age 16 from the short Rutter 'A' and the subgroup 'Neurotic' on the full Rutter 'A' ($r = 0.80$; $p < 0.001$). Similarly there was a reasonable correlation between the subgroup 'Disruptive' age 16 from the short Rutter 'A' and the subgroup 'Conduct disorder' on the full Rutter 'A' ($r = 0.61$; $p < 0.001$).

For the risk and protective clusters identified earlier, the Odds Ratio (and 95 per cent Confidence Interval) was used to assess the likelihood of falling into the 'disruptive' or 'unhappy' groups. In the following Table 3.1 those factors with a significant association (risk = 'r', or protective = 'p', $p < 0.05$) with the 20 per cent top scorers of either the 'disruptive' or the 'unhappy' group at one or more of the three ages (seven, 11, 16) are listed.

These variables were then used to assess their role in 'recovery' from behaviour problems at seven. Those children who fell into the top 20 per cent of high scorers at seven were deemed to have 'recovered' if they fell below the top 20 per cent cut-off at 11 and 16.

Necessary Cautions

Caution needs to be exercised in reading these tables. These tables only identify some factors that may be important. They are not, and cannot be, conclusive. In different samples and at different times there may be other factors that are more important. We need to remember that NCDS data relates to children born forty years ago when social conditions, health care and family lives were very different. Important factors may be missing, either because an appropriate NCDS variable was not available, or because the factors were identified as not significant in the earlier analyses and therefore dropped. It may be that some factors, such as low birth weight, become more significant in combination with other factors such as poor social circumstances.

Person Factors Associated with Internalising and Externalising Disorders

The following tables show the associations between having a particular factor and the likelihood of one or both types of disorders. For example, the factor low birth weight is compared to those children without low birth weights. These analyses are simple two-by-two correlations. They do not tell what may have caused the link. Soiling, for instance, is listed under person factors, but for most children who soil the cause is probably related to an interaction between physical factors (a tendency to constipation being the most common), family and school factors (Buchanan, 1993). Similarly behaviour problems may come as a result of the soiling problem or vice versa.

Table 3.1   Person factors: associations between factors and the likelihood of being in the top 20 per cent of children with behaviour disorders

Factor	Unhappy			Disruptive		
	7	*11*	*16*	*7*	*11*	*16*
Female	ns	r	r	p	p	p
Low birth weight < 5lb	ns	ns	ns	r	ns	ns
Mother smoked prior to pregnancy	ns	r	r	r	r	r
High reasoning skills (as measured at 11)	p	p	p	p	p	p
Clumsy (Doctor's diagnosis)	ns	r	r	ns	r	r
Asthma at 7 (Doctor's diagnosis)	r	r	ns	r	ns	ns
Poor hearing at 7 (Doctor's assessment)	ns	ns	ns	ns	r	ns
Treatment for emotion/behaviour	r	r	ns	r	r	ns
Soiling at 7	r	r	ns	r	r	r

R = risk (p < 0.05); p = protective (p < 0.05); ns = not significant

Some clear messages emerge from this initial analysis. First, as reflected in the literature, girls at all ages are much less likely to have a disruptive disorder than boys (Kovacs and Devlin, 1998). Secondly, children who have high reasoning skills at age 11 are protected against all types of behaviour disorders at all ages. Plomin (1994) has suggested that there is an interplay between 'nature', for example a child's temperament, and 'nurture'. Children with high IQs are better able to find the 'niche' in day-to-day living which matches their personalities. For example, children who may have an inherent 'unhappy' or depressive tendency may be able to use their problem solving skills to find a way to reduce the stresses upon them. Similarly, potentially disruptive children may find positive ways of controlling their impulsivity.

The data also identifies a number of other person factors that place particular children at risk. It is possible that children who are clumsy develop emotional and/or disruptive problems when they become the butt of bullying in the less supportive environment of secondary schooling. Similarly, it is known that children who have soiling problems are likely to have relationship difficulties with their peers and parents (Buchanan, 1993). Asthma places children at risk in early and middle childhood. Mrazek and Schuman (1998) noted that children who had early onset (between three and six years of age), had significantly more emotional and behavioural problems at age six than children who did not have asthma or who developed asthma later. The finding that children who receive treatment continue to have emotional and behavioural problems, probably says less about the efficacy of the treatment than the likelihood that only children with severe problems were referred to such services.

More surprising were the high risks for children whose mothers smoked during pregnancy. Children whose mothers smoked during their pregnancy were at risk of both an 'internalising' and 'externalising' behaviour disorder at almost all ages. Butler and Golding (1986) also found this association in the 1970 cohort study. This variable may interact with other factors, for example, pregnant mothers who are depressed may be more likely to smoke. Whatever the explanation, a useful indicator of children who are likely to have later problems, is those whose mothers smoked in pregnancy.

Family Factors Associated with Internalising and Externalising Disorders

In the following table most of the data relates to the specific time period. For example, 'Birth family' indicates that the child was living in that type of family at age seven, or at age 11 or at age 16. Where there are gaps under the specific age column, the information was not available. For example, under the factor of 'three or more moves', information on family mobility was not available at age 11. 'Severe Disadvantage' is not included under age seven, as this category was calculated when the cohort member was age 11. Severe disadvantage was defined as the presence of four out of the following five factors: four or more children in one family, more than 1.5 individuals per room, privately rented or local authority accommodation, lack of sole use of bathroom etc., receipt of free school meals).

In some cases a factor was so important, such as 'Family difficulties at age 7 – domestic tension', that the presence of the factor at this age is then carried over into assessing whether it has any influence at a later age. Where this happens it is clearly stated.

The first impression is that there are fewer identified risk and protective factors associated with 'unhappy' children. This could be a failure of the methodology in identifying such factors or it could be, as Kovacs and Devlin (1998) have suggested, that internalising disorders are more 'within the person'. If this is true, the factors that have been identified are useful.

The second impression, is that family adversities, as well documented in the literature, are strongly associated with 'disruptive' type behaviour.

In the first section on structural family variables, manual social class is associated with 'disruptive behaviour' at all ages. Children being brought up by birth parents at age 16 have a measure of protection against emotional and behaviour disorders at age 16 while those brought up in step families are associated with risks for disruptive behaviour at all ages. As we will see in the second study described here, these findings are not as clear-cut as they may seem.

The most striking finding is the risk associated with a care experience, especially when compared to children brought up in severe disadvantage. This has been reported elsewhere (Cheung and Buchanan, 1997) and will be discussed further, later in the chapter.

Surprisingly, at age 16 having a working mother is protective against disruptive behaviour. It is hard to explain this finding unless this is associated with increased financial well-being. Less surprising are the risks associated with high family mobility. Moving house carries risk for children who have to change school and who may lose contact with their friends.

In Table 3.2, a third group of findings relates to a range of family adversities and various levels of social service and probation involvement. Poor parental mental health as well documented in the literature and as summarised by Campbell (1994) and Kovacs and Devlin (1998) is a risk factor for both internalising and externalising disorders but the main risks relate to the early years and to adolescence. Conflict or domestic tension in the family at age seven has a particularly strong long-term association with psychological difficulties. Many writers report on the links between parental conflict and psychological difficulties in children (Hess, 1995; Cockett and Tripp, 1994; Sweeting and West, 1995). Similarly there is much support in the literature for the conclusion that children brought up in families who are themselves

Table 3.2   Family factors: associations between factors and the likelihood of being in the top 20 per cent of children with behaviour disorders

	Unhappy			Disruptive		
Factor	7	*11*	*16*	7	*11*	*16*
Structural factors						
Manual social class at birth	ns	ns	ns	r	r	r
Birth parents	ns	ns	p	ns	ns	p
Step parents	ns	ns	ns	r	r	r
Lone (single, separated, widowed)	ns	ns	r	ns	ns	ns
Severe disadvantage at 11		ns	ns		ns	r
Care (experience of having been in care)	r	ns	r	r	r	r
Owner occupied house	ns	p	ns	p	p	p
3 or more moves since birth	r		r	r		r
Mother works	ns	r	ns	r	r	p
Family adversities						
Parental mental health problems	r	ns	r	r	ns	r
Family financial difficulties	r	r		r	r	
Family difficulties at age 7 (alcoholism)	ns	ns	ns	r	ns	r
Family difficulties at 7 (domestic tension)	r	r	r	r	r	r
Social services involvement	ns	ns	r	r	ns	r
Family involvement in courts or with Probation Service because of offending	r	ns	ns	r	r	r
Family involvement with NSPCC or courts because of childcare	ns		ns	r		ns
Family involvement						
Outings with father at 7	p			p		
Father's role in management at 7	p			p		
Father reads to child at 7	ns	ns	ns	p	p	p
Mother's interest in child's education	ns	ns	ns	p	p	p
Father's interest in child's education	ns	p	ns	p	p	p

R = risk (p<0.05); p= protective (p<0.05); ns = not significant

involved with 'the law' will be more likely to have antisocial disorders (Farrington, 1995) as will children who have been maltreated or neglected (Loeber and Stouthamer-Loeber, 1986).

The final group of analyses on family factors explored what might be interpreted as 'family involvement' indicators. More recently there has been considerable interest in the protective function of 'involvement': parents who do things together with their children (for example, Sweeting and West, 1995) or are 'involved' with their education. A key finding here is the protective role of 'involved' fathers: fathers who were involved in the management of their children; fathers who read to their children age seven; fathers who were interested in their children's education.

School Factors Associated with Internalising and Externalising Disorders

Table 3.3   School factors: associations between factors and the likelihood of being in the top 20 per cent of children with behaviour disorders

	Unhappy			Disruptive		
Factor	*7*	*11*	*16*	*7*	*11*	*16*
Preschool						
LA nursery or nursery class	ns	ns	ns	r	r	r
Private nursery class	ns	p	ns	ns	ns	p
Other organised preschool provision	ns	ns	r	ns	ns	ns
Teaching methods and child's skills						
Systematic teaching of phonetics at 7	p	p	ns	p	ns	p
Streamed class	ns	r	ns	ns	ns	r
Reading teacher's rating	p		ns	p		p
High reading skills at 11		p			p	
Attendance						
Attendance 90% or more	r		p	ns		p
Admitted truancy		r			r	
More than three schools since 11th birthday		r			r	

R = risk (p < 0.05); p = protective (p < 0.05); ns = not significant

The associations between different types of preschool experience and emotional and behavioural disorders supports the findings of Sylva (chapter 5) that not all types of preschool provision are equally effective. Here, however, the risks associated with Local Authority nurseries or nursery classes may be an artefact of the period. In the 1960s when these children were growing up, children who gained a place in a local authority nursery were likely to be those whose parents had considerable difficulties.

The suggestion that early teaching of phonetics when learning to read was protective against 'unhappy' and 'disruptive' type behaviours, was interesting. A possible interpretation is that this method of teaching reading helped the more anxious child and the more impulsive child to achieve better reading skills. How the class was organised – streamed or not streamed — also impinged on the likelihood of an emotional or behaviour disorder. Streamed classes were a risk factor for being unhappy, and placed 16 year olds at risk – presumably those in the lower streams – of having a behaviour disorder.

Good attendance is likely to protect children against behaviour problems, although a risk factor for unhappy problems in childhood, while truancy at age 16 is likely to be a risk factor. Changing schools is also a risk factor for both types of behaviour.

A final group of analyses which are not shown here explored young people's attitudes to school at age 16. There was a very strong association between disruptive behaviour and negative attitudes to school and school work (such as, school is a waste of time; homework is a bore; I find it difficult to keep my mind on my work; I do not like school). The association between such attitudes and internalising disorders was also important. Adolescent attitudes about schooling may be a result of how they have cognitively processed their earlier experiences. There is a growing realisation that we cannot make assumptions about how young people are processing their experiences, but we need to know this if we want to help them (Caprara and Rutter, 1995).

Recovery from Behaviour Problems after Seven

Unfortunately, because the number of children who recovered from behaviour problems was low, separation into internalising and externalising disorders resulted in small groups, roughly five per cent of the children with behavioural data. A child was deemed to have 'recovered' from a behaviour problem if the child's behavioural score fell into the top 20 per cent at seven but whose score was not in the top 20 per cent at either 11 or 16. Here again these are simple bi-variate analyses.

For 'unhappy' children, three factors were significantly associated with unlikelihood of recovery: poor hearing as assessed by the doctor at seven, a care experience and domestic tension at age seven between the parents. For children with disruptive behaviour, there were other factors, social services involvement and a 'streamed' class (presumably this meant being in a stream with other children who had behavioural problems). Surprisingly, the father reading to the child emerged as associated with 'recovery'. This could be

Table 3.4   Factors associated with 'recovery' after seven (significant factors only)

Likely or unlikely to 'recover'

		Unhappy	Disruptive
Person	Poor hearing (doctor's assessment at 7)	unlikely	ns
Family	Care (any experience)	unlikely	unlikely
	Family difficulties at 7 (domestic tension)	unlikely	ns
	Social services involvement	ns	unlikely
	Father reads to child at 7	ns	likely
School	Streamed class	ns	unlikely

interpreted in different ways. It could mean that the child had a father who was involved and interested or it might mean that the child's reading was better because someone developed the child's interest in reading. Although there was no information in NCDS on mother's reading to the child, mother's interest in the child's education did not have the same association.

Study Two: Parental Background and Psychological Problems in Adolescence and Adult Life

The purpose of the second study was to look in more detail at the associations between a child's parental background and the likelihood of experiencing psychological difficulties in adolescence and in adulthood. This study is reported in full elsewhere (Buchanan and Ten Brinke, 1997).

There is a substantive literature on the association between family breakdown and psychological difficulties (Chase-Lansdale, Cherlin and Kieman, 1995; Cherlin, Kiernan and Chase-Lansdale, 1995). In the first study reported here we saw that boys who had been brought up in a step-family were at significant risk of disruptive behaviour at all ages. With family breakdown, however, especially during a transitional period, may also come a range of other difficulties such as a lower standard of living and a greater likelihood of living in poverty. In a few extreme cases family breakdown may also be associated with a child's entry into care.

The research questions in this second study were: did the risk of psychological problems relate to the type of family in which a child had been brought up, or did the psychological difficulties relate to the disadvantage and problems that might have come as a result of family breakdown? A related question was, to what extent did any risk established extend into adult life?

How the Study was Undertaken

The following parental groups were established using data from NCDS. For the full methodology see Buchanan and Ten Brinke (1997). Parental backgrounds relating to the structure of the family were separated out from those relating to the social context. The different groups were:

Birth	Children living with two birth parents until age 16;
Restructured	Children living with step-families at age 16;
Widowed	Children living with a lone parent where the other parent had died;
Lone parent (other)	Children living with a lone parent for other reasons;
Disadvantaged/birth	Children living with birth parents but who had also experience severe social disadvantages (such as living in overcrowded accommodation, or in housing lacking basic amenities or receiving free school meals);
Disadvantaged/ restructured	Children living with step-parents at 16 but who had also experienced severe disadvantage;
Care/birth	Children who at age 16 who were living with birth parents and who had also had an experience of being looked after by local authorities; and
Care/restructured	Children living in step-families at age 16 who also had an experience of being looked after by local authorities.

Of the 8,441 NCDS members for whom there was psychological data available at age 16 and at age 33, 97 per cent fell into these parental categories. The frequencies were equally divided between women and men. Additional analyses were undertaken to evaluate the effect of those lost to the study to see if those either missing or excluded biased the results in any way. These analyses supported the overall results reported.

Children who at age 16 had a Rutter 'A' score of 13+ were deemed to have a psychological problem at age 16, and those who had a Malaise score of 8+ were deemed to have a psychological problem at age 33.

Psychological Risks

Figure 3.1 shows that at age 16 those at greatest risk of psychological problems were those living in disadvantage and those who had been in care. At age 33 a similar picture emerged but there were some important gender differences. Firstly, except for the care groups, women were more likely to be at risk for depression. Secondly, early experience of disadvantage, had a much greater effect on women than men. For men the long term links with a care experience was more pronounced.

After controlling for social class, presence of partners, employment and qualifications, and self-reported heavy smoking and drinking, *the structure* of the family, that is, being brought up in a step-family without extreme disadvantage or a care experience did not significantly influence the risk of psychological problems. The only exception was that men who had been brought up by lone parents for reasons other than the death of a parent were at risk of psychological problems at age 33.

The *context* of the family, however, when others factors were controlled, remained a significant influence leading to a tendency toward depression at age 33. Men who had been in care were significantly at risk of depression and similarly women who had been brought up in disadvantage were at risk.

What are the Implications of these Findings?

The findings of this second study suggest that it is not so much the fact of family disruption that has psychological consequences for children, but what may be associated with it. The study did not measure poverty per se, but extreme disadvantage; it did not measure parenting problems but situations where children went into local authority care. The implication of these findings is that most children, regardless of their parental background, survive without too many psychological scars. The most serious risks appear to relate to the extremes of disadvantage and the extremes of parenting breakdown.

What Works to Prevent/Alleviate Psychological Problems?

From the two studies reported here, a fairly simple message emerges. A knowledge of risk and protective factors and factors associated with 'recovery' from psychological problems offers the possibility for not only creating an environment where children are less likely to suffer such difficulties, but also for tailoring individual interventions for young people who may already have significant difficulties. This is a hopeful message.

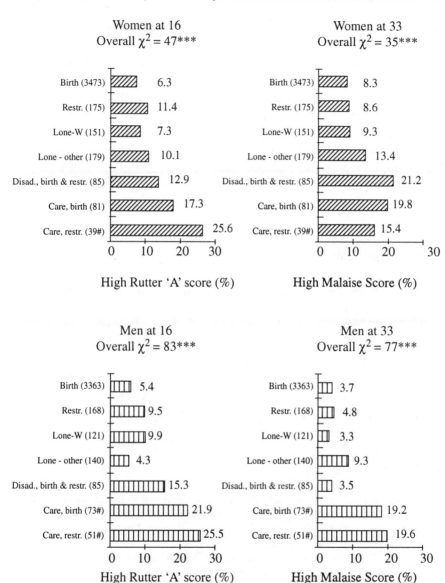

Figure 3.1 **Percentages of men and women in each parental group with maladjustment at 16 (as measured by a Rutter 'A' score of 13+) or a tendency to depression at age 33 (as measured by a Malaise score 8+)**

Conclusions

As already mentioned, no firm conclusions can be drawn from this study about the reasons for the associations seen. The interpretations that have been suggested can only be hypothetical. The factors identified, however, may be of interest as markers to identify those children who are likely to have problems and those children who are likely to be protected from such difficulties. These are not conclusive lists. There may be other factors that are more important. The literature suggests (for example, Rutter, 1995) that children with multiple adversities or multiple risk factors are likely to be more at risk than those with single adversities or risk factors. Further work on this is forthcoming.

Acknowledgements

The work on children who may be at risk of emotional and behavioural problems undertaken by Ann Buchanan and JoAnn Ten Brinke was funded by the NHS Executive Anglia and Oxford; the views expressed in this publication are those of the authors and not necessarily those of the NHS Executive Anglia and Oxford. Similarly the work on parental background and psychological problems in adolescence and in adulthood was funded by the Joseph Rowntree Foundation. Again, the views expressed here are those of the authors and not necessarily those of the Foundation.

References

American Psychiatric Association (1987), *Diagnostic and statistical manual of mental disorders, 3rd edition revised (DSM-III-R)*, Washington DC, American Psychiatric Association.
Bronfenbrenner, U. (1979), *The ecology of human development. Experiments by nature and design*, Cambridge, Mass., Harvard University Press.
Buchanan, A. (1993), *Children who Soil*, Chichester, John Wiley and Sons Ltd.
Buchanan, A. and Ten Brinke, J.A. (forthcoming), *'Recovery' from Behaviour Problems*, NHS, Oxford and Anglia.
Buchanan, A. and Ten Brinke, J.A. (1997), *What Happened when they were grown up?*, York, Joseph Rowntree Foundation/York Publishing Services.
Butler, N. and Golding, M. (1986), *From Birth to Five; A Study of the Health and Behaviour of British Five year olds*, Oxford, Pergamon Press.
Campbell, S.B. (1995), 'Behaviour problems in PreSchool children: A Review of Recent

Research', *Journal of Child Psychology and Psychiatry*, 36, 1, pp. 113–49.

Caprara, G. and Rutter, M. (1995), 'Individual Development during Adolescence' in Rutter, M. and Smith D.J. (eds), *Psychosocial Disorders in Young People, Time Trends and their Causes*, Chichester, John Wiley and Sons Ltd.

Caron, C. and Rutter, M. (1991), 'Co-morbidity in Child Psychopathology: Concepts, Issues and Research Strategies', *Journal of Child Psychology and Psychiatry*, 32, 7, pp. 1063–80.

Chase-Lansdale, P.L., Cherlin, A.J. and Kiernan, K.E. (1995), 'The long-term effects of parental divorce on the mental health of young adults: a developmental perspective', *Child Development*, 66, pp. 1614–34.

Cherlin, A.J., Kiernan, K.E. and Chase-Lansdale, P.L. (1995), 'Parental Divorce in Childhood and Demographic Outcomes in Young Adulthood', *Demography*, 32, pp. 299–318.

Cheung, S.Y. and Buchanan, A. (1997), 'Malaise Scores in adulthood of children and young people who have been in care', *Journal of Child Psychology and Psychiatry*, 38, 5, pp. 575–80.

Clark, L.A., Watson, D. and Mineka, S. (1994), 'Temperament personality; and the mood and anxiety disorders', *Journal of Abnormal Psychology*, 103, pp. 103–16.

Cockett, M. and Tripp, J. (1994), *The Exeter Family Study. Family Breakdown and its impact on children*, Exeter University Press.

Cohen, P., Cohen, J., Kasen, S., Velez., C.N., Hartmark, C., Johnson L, Rojas, M., Book, J. and Streuning, E. L. (1993), 'An epidemiological study of disorders in late childhood and adolescence – Age and gender specific prevalence', *Journal of Child Psychology and Psychiatry*, 34, pp. 851–67.

Farrington, D.P. (1992), 'Explaining the beginning, progress and ending of antisocial behavior from birth to adulthood' in McCord, J. (ed.), *Advances in criminological theory, Vol. Ill: Facts, frameworks and forecast*, New Brunswick, NJ, Transaction.

Hess, L.E. (1995), 'Changing Family Patterns in Western Europe' in Rutter, M. and Smith D.J. (eds), *Psychosocial Disorders in Young People, Time Trends and their Causes*, Chichester, John Wiley and Sons Ltd.

Kovacs, M. and Devlin, B. (1998), 'Internalizing Disorders in childhood', *Journal of Child Psychology and Psychiatry,* 39,1, pp. 47–63.

Loeber, R. and Stouthamer-Loeber, M. (1986), 'Family factors as correlates and predictors of juvenile conduct problems and delinquency' in Tonry, M. and Morris, N. (eds), *Crime and Justice: an annual review of research*, Vol. VII 7, 29, 149, Chicago: University of Chicago Press.

McGuffin, P. and Thapar, A. (1997), 'Genetic basis for bad behaviour', *Lancet*, Vol. 350, August 9, p. 411.

Mrazek, D. and Schuman, W.B. (1998), 'Early Asthma Onset: risk of Emotional and Behavioural Difficulties', *Journal of Child Psychology and Psychiatry*, 39, 3, pp. 247–54.

Plomin, R. (1994), *Genetics and Experience: The Interplay between Nature and Nurture*, Newbury Park, Ca., Sage.

Rodgers, B. (1990), 'Behavior and personality in childhood as predictors of adult psychiatric disorder', *Journal of Child Psychology and Psychiatry*, 31, pp. 393–414.

Rutter, M. (1995), 'Causal concepts and their testing' in Rutter, M. and Smith D.J. (eds), *Psychosocial Disorders in Young People, Time Trends and their Causes*, Chichester, John Wiley and Sons Ltd.

Shepherd, P. (1993), Appendix 1 in Ferri, E. (ed.), *Life at 33*, London, National Children's Bureau.

Smith, D.J. (1995), 'Patterns and Trends in Youth Crime' in Rutter, M. (ed.), *Psychosocial Disorders in young people. Challenges for Prevention*, Cambridge, Cambridge University Press.

Sweeting, H. and West, P. (1995), 'Family Life and health in adolescence: a role for culture in the Health inequalities debate?', *Social Science and Medicine*, 40, pp. 163–75.

4 Observational Studies of Parent-Child Interaction and Behaviour Problems: Their Implications for Parenting Interventions

FRANCES GARDNER

Summary

- *This chapter begins with a definition of children's behaviour problems, and a discussion of their implications and developmental course. The most effective interventions are likely to be based on the findings of well-designed studies of the influence of modifiable risk factors on the development of behaviour problems.*
- *It will briefly examine measures and research designs used to try and demonstrate the causal influence of parenting style on the development of behaviour problems. It will briefly review the evidence for Patterson's 'Coercive Family Process' model of parent-child interaction.*
- *It will argue that there is good evidence that we need to examine positive interactions, not just discipline skills and conflictual encounters, in order to gain a fuller picture of the parenting influences on children's behaviour problems.*
- *Findings from recent studies of parents' involvement in joint play, and their positive strategies for resolving and preventing conflict are discussed. Evidence is accumulating from longitudinal observational studies that these positive interactions play an important role in the development of behaviour problems over time. Implications for intervention are drawn throughout.*

Definition of Children's Behaviour Problems

Acting-out or externalising behaviour problems are known by a number of labels in the literature on younger children, including conduct problems, antisocial, hard-to-manage or noncompliant behaviour. These terms all refer to an empirically-derived cluster of problems, known as oppositional defiant disorder in DSM-IV (American Psychiatric Association, 1994), and defined as a 'recurrent pattern of negativistic, defiant, hostile behviour'including tempers, noncompliance, spiteful, angry and resentful behaviour. These behaviours need to occur more frequently than in other children of the same age, and to cause impairment in the child's social or school functioning. The term 'Conduct Disorder' in DSM-IV refers to more serious antisocial behaviour usually developing later in childhood and often includes oppositional behaviours plus harmful aggression, destructiveness, theft, and rule breaking. The term 'behaviour problems' is used here to refer to the cluster of oppositional behaviours defined above.

Why are Behaviour Problems Important?

Behaviour problems in children are common, persistent, difficult to treat (Kazdin, 1993), costly to society and have a very poor prognosis (Loeber, 1990; Robins, 1991). Longitudinal studies show that antisocial behaviour originates in the preschool years, resulting from a combination of difficult early temperamental characteristics (Bates, Bayles, Bennett, Ridge and Brown, 1991; White, Moffitt, Earls, Robins and Silva, 1990) and dysfunctional family interaction (Campbell, 1995; Dishion, French and Patterson, 1995; Loeber and Hay, 1994; Patterson, Reid and Dishion, 1992; Reid, 1993). These behaviour patterns show a well-documented developmental progression starting with hard-to-manage toddlers, who tend to be difficult mainly in the home. About 50 per cent of these children go on to have more serious oppositional and conduct disorders in middle childhood (Campbell, 1995; Richman, Stevenson and Graham, 1982), followed by delinquency in early adolescence. The consequences of this behaviour for individuals, families, schools and society are considerable. Antisocial children are more likely to be rejected by peers, to fail at school and to truant. Their disruptive behaviour in class makes life very difficult for teachers and other pupils, and often leads to school exclusion. The outlook for adult life is also poor. Robins' (1991) longitudinal studies, which followed children over several decades, found strong continuities between child and adult disorder. Children with conduct disorders had very high rates of antisocial personality disorder, other mental illness and criminality. Those who escaped these major problems nevertheless had an increased risk of social difficulties such as divorce, unemployment and drug abuse.

The fact that behaviour problems start young, are stable and have a clear progression to more serious outcomes makes a strong argument for carrying out early intervention to help prevent later disorder. Behaviour problems appear to be more difficult to treat later in childhood when difficulties become entwined with the child's peer relations, school failure and petty crime, and the child and his family feel stigmatised, isolated and hopeless (Webster-Stratton, 1998).

How do Parenting Styles Contribute to the Development of Behaviour Problems?

The most thoroughly researched causal factor in the development of behaviour problems is family interaction. Evidence converges from several different kinds of research design; all supporting the contention that parenting style makes a strong contribution to the development and maintenance of behaviour problems. I will first outline important features of research measurement and design that have made possible these conclusions, and then describe some of the studies in more detail.

Systematic Observational Techniques

The development of systematic observational techniques for assessing parent and child behaviour in their natural context has been essential to the development of this field. These techniques are the only way to assess in fine detail what takes place, moment-by-moment, during an interaction. Understanding interaction on this level has proved very useful for predicting child outcomes and for devising effective interventions (Forehand and McMahon, 1981; Gardner, 1997; Gardner, Sonuga-Barke and Sayal, 1998; Patterson and Forgatch, 1995; Patterson, 1982). Some of the first detailed observational measures of parent-child interaction in the home were developed by Patterson and colleagues (Patterson, 1982; Reid, 1978), who paid careful attention to testing the reliability and validity of their measures. Earlier studies of parenting and behaviour problems used interview measures of parenting style (Baumrind, 1967; Sears, Maccoby and Levin, 1957), but the validity of these instruments was not well tested against observational and other techniques (Maccoby and Martin, 1983), and neither did these studies contribute directly to the development of interventions. More recently, there have been attempts to validate newer, more focused interview measures of parenting against direct observational findings. Some studies have found reasonable convergence (Webster-Stratton and Spitzer, 1991; Webster-Stratton, 1998) and other studies slight (Deater-Deckard, Dodge, Bates and Pettit, 1996) or poor convergence (Patterson et al., 1992, p. 68) between observational and interview measures. There have not been enough studies to allow us to say which aspects of parenting, if any, can be adequately measured using self-report, and which techniques are most useful. The evidence to date suggests that direct observations are the most useful way of measuring parent-child interaction.

Research Designs for Examining the Causal Role of Parenting

Correlational designs Many studies have used correlational designs to demonstrate associations between parenting style and problem behaviour. These studies are very important in describing systematically how parenting varies across families, and how it relates to child behaviour problems (Campbell, 1995; Dumas, LaFreniere and Serketich, 1995; Gardner, 1989; 1994; Patterson, 1982). However, correlational designs are conventionally viewed as insufficient for demonstrating that parenting influences problem behaviour, since any associations found may be interpreted in a number of ways (Loeber and Farrington, 1994). For instance, correlations may be interpreted as showing that parenting influences child behaviour, but equally the causal direction could be the other way round, or the association could be due to other factors, e.g. the influence of a hostile neighbourhood, or genetic factors, which may affect both parenting and child behaviour. Rutter (1994a) takes a more constructive view, pointing to strengths of correlational designs, which are not always recognised. He argues that it is absolutely essential to establish correlations between variables before deciding which questions to test in costly longitudinal studies. Rutter suggests circumstances in which correlational designs can be an important part of a series of tests of a causal hypothesis, for example, where the opportunity for a 'natural experiment' occurs, and in the testing of competing hypotheses. The latter might involve testing which of two possible risk mechanisms is most plausible. For example, there is a well-known association between broken homes and conduct disorder, and Rutter (1978; 1994b) was able to test which of two hypothesised mechanisms, parental separation or discord, was most closely associated with conduct disorder.

Longitudinal designs These have the advantage of being able to show how a risk factor predicts an outcome that is measured later in time, but do not completely get round the problem of interpreting the direction of causality (see Loeber and Farrington, 1994; Rutter, 1994a, for a fuller discussion of their strengths and limitations). A number of longitudinal studies have shown that parenting influences later behaviour problems, whilst controlling for the powerful predictive effects of earlier levels of behaviour problems (e.g. Gardner et al., 1998; Zahn-Waxler et al., 1990; Shaw, Keenan and Vondra, 1994a).

Intervention and experimental designs These are powerful designs for establishing causes, but suffer from the drawback that the effects of contrived interventions may tell us more about the possible impact of parenting in the context of a therapeutic intervention, than about its naturally occurring effects. Bryant (1985) and Loeber and Farrington (1994) suggest that a solution may be to combine experimental intervention with naturalistic longitudinal studies, in order to bring together the advantages of both. Many studies of behaviour problems have employed one of these designs, providing evidence for the causal role of parenting style, but few studies have combined these two approaches. There have been numerous controlled trials of parent-training interventions which attempt to change parents' style of dealing with difficult behaviour, and show predicted improvements in child behaviour (Cunningham, Bremner and Boyle, 1995; Patterson, 1982; Tremblay, Pagani-Kurtz, Masse, Vitaro and Pihl, 1995; Webster-Stratton, Kolpacoff and Hollinsworth, 1989; Webster-Stratton, 1994; 1998). Some studies show that changes in parent behaviour are crucial predictors of child outcome (e.g. Patterson and Forgatch, 1995) providing further evidence for the causal role of parenting variables. There have also been some examples of more tightly-controlled experimental interventions which manipulate only one or two specified aspects of parent behaviour, thus allowing more precise identification of the effects of particular parenting variables on child behaviour. For example, Patterson et al.(1992), Forgatch (1991) and Reid, O'Leary and Wolff (1994) have shown that teaching more consistent discipline strategies led to decreases in antisocial behaviour.

Behaviour genetic studies using twin and adoption designs These are important because they have the power both to show how weak or strong is the genetic influence on behaviour problems, and to tell us more about the extent and nature of environmental influences, such as parenting (Plomin, 1994), and whether these influences are shared between sibs or unique to that child. For example, an adoption study by Deater-Deckard and Plomin (1998), and a large twin study by Eaves et al. (1997) found a moderate influence of both genetic and shared environmental factors on conduct problems. However, these and other studies have mainly used self-report measures of behaviour (e.g. Simonoff et al., 1995) and have found that the relative contribution of these factors varied, sometimes a great deal, depending on the informant and the type of measure used. There have been fewer studies of genetic influences on observed behaviour, which is noteworthy, since one twin study found no genetic effects on observed aggression (Plomin, Foch and Rowe, 1981). This stands in contrast to many questionnaire studies, which find large genetic effects on aggression. Other studies suggest the importance of environmental influences that are not shared by the twins or sibs, but are unique to individuals (Plomin, 1994). These findings raise interesting questions about the extent to which parents direct their behaviour selectively to different children in the family. This could result from factors such as child temperamental differences (nongenetic) or variations in parental mental state or attitudes affecting one child and not the other at an important developmental stage. These factors would interact with parenting styles to produce individual child outcomes. Behaviour genetic design also offers the exciting possibility of using observational methods to examine genetic and environmental sources of influence on parenting and child behaviour, and on the associations between parent and child behaviour.

Social Factors and Parenting

As well as parenting, wider social factors have an influence on behaviour problems. Rutter's (1978) epidemiological studies found a set of 'family adversity' factors, including maternal depression, marital discord, overcrowding, low social class and paternal antisocial behaviour, that were strongly related to conduct disorder in middle childhood. These findings have been replicated in later studies, including Shaw, Vondra, Hommerding, Keenan and Dunn's (1994b) study of toddlers from low-income families. Both Shaw et al. (1994b) and Richman et al. (1982) found that adversity factors that most closely reflected family relationships (discord and depression) were the strongest predictors of behaviour problems, suggesting that family dysfunction has a greater influence on child behaviour than material poverty. It is assumed that adversity factors act to make parenting more difficult, and that parenting is the common pathway through which these adversities impinge on young children's behaviour. There is evidence that good parenting, along with other factors such as the child's gender and temperament, may help to buffer the effects of adverse social circumstances on behaviour problems (Pettit, Bates and Dodge, 1997; Rutter, 1978; Sanson, Oberklaid, Pedlow and Prior, 1991; Shaw et al., 1994b).

Implications for Intervention

From numerous studies which have employed the kinds of research design described above, we can draw the very broad conclusion that parenting has a powerful influence on child behaviour problems, although it is by no means the only influence. It follows that interventions based on teaching parenting skills are likely to be successful, and indeed randomised controlled trials show that this is the case. If good parenting helps to buffer the effects of social circumstances on behaviour problems, then we would expect that parenting interventions would help ameliorate some social adversities, e.g. parental depression, discord and social isolation, though in more severe cases it may be necessary and effective to intervene directly with these risk factors as well as teach parenting skills (Webster-Stratton, 1994).

The next sections examine studies that attempt to identify the key parenting mechanisms influencing child problem behaviour.

Parenting Style and Behaviour Problems: Patterson's Work

The earliest work in this field came from Patterson (1982; Patterson et al., 1992), who began his pioneering work on parenting interventions in the late 1960s, developing these effective therapies in tandem with basic observational research on family interactions, within a social learning theory framework. His coercion theory stresses that processes that take place during family conflict cause and maintain behaviour problems. Antisocial behaviour is shaped and reinforced by thousands of episodes of conflict between family members. The difficult child learns to gain control over a chaotic or unpleasant family environment. He learns to avoid his parent's demands by persisting noisily with his own demands, whilst in the same interactions, parent and siblings learn to give in. Both parent and child are negatively reinforced for their behaviour, as they learn how to switch off the other's annoying behaviour. Over hundreds of repetitions, these interactions become over-learned and more-or-less automatic. As the child learns the success of coercive behaviour, then he may take this behaviour outside the home, and depending on the social environment (e.g. behaviour of teachers or peers), he may find his behaviour is reinforced in other settings as well.

For a negative cycle of family interaction to start and perpetuate there may need to be a combination of a temperamentally difficult child and disrupted parenting skills, although Patterson's theory gives much greater weight to parenting mechanisms. His careful (1982) observational studies in the home found that compared to non-problem families, parents of children with behaviour problems tended to be more harsh, punitive, erratic, and inconsistent in their responses to the child. Using robust measures from multiple settings and informants, Patterson et al. (1992) defined a set of 'family management' practices, including discipline, monitoring and problem solving. The discipline construct, and its psychometric properties, has been particularly well researched. Patterson defines good discipline as:

- accurately tracking and noticing problem behaviour;
- ignoring trivial transgressions; and
- having clear firm sanctions.

Poor discipline was measured in a number of ways, producing a robust reliable construct, by direct observation, daily telephone interviews and systematic observer ratings. Parent questionnaires did not correlate well with other measures of discipline, so were not used in the main analyses.

Patterson et al. (1992) found that parents of children with behaviour problems were poor at all three facets of discipline. They tended to be over-inclusive in their defining and tracking of problem behaviour, and poor at ignoring more trivial misbehaviour, instead engaging in much ineffective scolding and nagging. They tended to escalate their demands on the child, becoming more angry and threatening but lacked any effective, non-abusive back up sanctions. In three different longitudinal studies starting in middle childhood they found that poor discipline predicted the persistence of antisocial behaviour into adolescence, and accounted for a highly significant 30 per cent of the variance in antisocial outcomes, even after controlling for the stability of antisocial behaviour over time. Patterson and Forgatch's (1995) intervention study found that the magnitude of improvement in parenting skill predicted the magnitude of change in 'harder' measures of antisocial behaviour at follow up, such as reduced arrest rates and out-of-home placement, providing strong evidence from a 'dose-response' relationship (Rutter, 1994a) for the causal role of parent discipline style.

An important aspect of discipline that Patterson stresses, and which is also a core skill in effective parent-training programmes, is the need for parents to follow through consistently on their demands to the child. This doesn't mean that demands made on the child are never negotiable; rather it means that once the parent has clarified the ground rules and insisted firmly on a course of action, then they should stick to this, and not capitulate, otherwise the child learns to be coercive to get their own way. Following through on demands is central to Patterson's theory, but is not adequately defined and measured in his work. Gardner (1989) could find no evidence that children with behaviour problems are more likely to be reinforced for their difficult behaviour via the mechanism of parents failing to follow through on their demands. Thus, she set out to test whether this was the case, using a sample of 40 pre-schoolers, recruited from nurseries, half with behaviour problems, and half without. Parent-child interaction was assessed during four hour-long sessions of naturalistic home observations, using a reliable system for analysing interactions and identifying episodes of different kinds of activity, for example joint play, conflict, conversation (Gardner, 1987; 1994).

The results showed that compared to mothers in the control group, mothers of children with behaviour problems were seven times more likely to be inconsistent by failing to follow through their demands during episodes of 'angry conflict'. These episodes were defined as a mother-child dispute where one or other showed negative affect, e.g. yelling, hitting, threatening. Capitulation by mothers happened in nearly half the conflict episodes in the problem group, compared to less than a tenth in the control group. Moreover, the likelihood of the mother capitulating was significantly higher when the conflict began with a demand by the mother, compared to a demand by the child. This finding supports Patterson's theory that what children learn in highly conflictual families is to successfully avoid conforming with parental demands (known as a negative reinforcement process). Difficult children appeared to be less successful at persuading others to conform with theirs (a positive reinforcement process).

By directly observing in fine detail the interactions during mother-child conflict, this study provides an important test for Patterson's hypothesis that children with behaviour problems are more likely to be reinforced for their difficult behaviour, particularly though a negative reinforcement process. Not only was the probability of mother capitulation much higher during each conflict episode, but difficult children also experienced this process much more often, as the frequency of conflict was much higher than in the control group.

Implications

Patterson's social learning theory model has stood up very well to the most rigorous causal tests yet seen in this field, especially for the parental discipline construct. The main implications for therapy are that this strongly affirms the importance of these basic discipline skills forming the core, though not necessarily the entirety, of any parenting intervention (Webster-Stratton, 1994; 1998). These skills are very apparent in manuals for evidence-based interventions such as Webster-Stratton's (1992) which teaches parents to set consistent limits, follow through commands, ignore minor problems, and apply calm consequences such as time out. Similar principles are used in other effective interventions (Barlow, 1998, this volume; Cunningham et al., 1995; Patterson, 1982; Tremblay et al., 1995). Patterson's basic research and clinical trials suggest that parents of older children should also be taught monitoring and family problem solving skills. Of course none of these therapeutic ideas are new, but nevertheless very few children receive this kind of therapy (Webster-Stratton and Taylor, 1998, this volume) and many are offered different kinds of family and parenting interventions that have nothing like such a clear evidence base. It is important to point to the strength of the evidence in order to argue for more children getting this kind of help.

Limitations of Patterson's Approach

Firstly, although parent training has better evidence for its effectiveness than other therapies, the success rate could be higher. Patterson's data show that two-thirds of families are helped. There is some evidence that the success rate may be higher, up to 75 per cent, in some preschool samples (Webster-Stratton, 1994). There is a need to improve this success rate, for example by drawing on other areas of basic research as well as social learning theory.

Secondly, Patterson's model argues that the most important thing to do is to help families to handle conflict and difficult behaviour better when it happens, in order to help the child to decrease their problem behaviour. But until recently, very few researchers in this field have examined the nature of parent-child interactions taking place the rest of the time, when there is no conflict. These encounters make up the great majority of interactions (Gardner, 1987, 1994; Reid, 1987), and it is likely that the nature of these more positive interactions influences when and whether conflict occurs, and how it is resolved, and importantly, might give us clues as to how parents could help prevent problem behaviour from arising.

These more positive and supportive interactions may be particularly important for the development of good relationships and the prevention of problem behaviour in younger children. Much of Patterson's model has been developed using older children, and samples with very wide age ranges, drawing little on basic developmental research with younger children. This is an important limitation, as it is likely that different parenting mechanisms account for the development and maintenance of behaviour problems at age three compared to those in middle childhood.

Studies of Early Positive Interactions in the Family

I will now look at some rather different theoretical approaches to understanding parent-child interaction, that focus less on clinical disorders, and more on normal developmental processes, such as how parent and child build constructive, positive interactions. Recent studies have begun to examine how this theoretical tradition can help understand the early development of behaviour problems and their interventions (Campbell, 1995; Gardner, 1987; 1994; Gardner et al., 1998; Pettit and Bates, 1989; Pettit et al., 1997; Shaw et al., 1994a; Zahn-Waxler et al., 1990).

Playful Interactions

A number of studies have examined the influence of positive interactions such as joint play. Patterson et al. (1992) argue that these are not an important causal influence on behaviour problems, since their longitudinal studies found that parental positive behaviour accounted for little of the variance in behaviour problems. But these studies measured only a limited range of variables, and this finding is at odds with many other studies. Patterson claims that where parents and behaviour problem children have few harmonious interactions then this is a result, not a cause, of many years of problem behaviour.

A study by Gardner (1987) began to examine this question by looking at whether there were differences between behaviour problem and control groups in the nature and frequency of mother-child positive activities, even at a young age. The same sample of preschoolers described earlier were observed at home for four hours. As expected, there were large group differences in the amount of mother-child conflict. However, even in the most conflictual families this only took up a small proportion of their time, so there was plenty of room for variation in the rates of other kinds of interactions. It was found that children without behaviour problems spent three times more time playing spontaneously with their mothers and twice as much time in pleasant conversation. In contrast the children with behaviour problems spent significantly more time watching TV and doing nothing, which was defined as aimless wandering, fiddling, and engaging in very brief talk or play. These findings suggest that children with behaviour problems might be learning something different even when not engaged in conflict, as they were getting few models of cooperative, harmonious interaction with others. These low levels of positive interactions cannot easily be explained as resulting from a downhill spiral of years of conflict as Patterson (1982) suggests, since preschoolers were only at the beginning of a possible antisocial career. Further evidence for the role of joint play as a contributor to behaviour problems comes from a longitudinal study by Pettit and Bates (1989) who found in a normal sample that a lack of frequent playful interactions in the second year were better predictors of four-year-old behaviour problems than were conflictual interactions.

These studies raise the question of what aspects of interaction during joint play are important. Gardner (1994) went on to examine in detail the nature and quality of interaction during joint play. Predictions were made from the developmental literature about how the quality of play might differ in the two groups. It was found that mothers of behaviour problem children showed less warmth and more negative affect, were less responsive to their child's suggestions and questions about the play, and used less sensitive forms of control. Mothers also seemed to be less keen on playing; they were less likely to initiate play, so the child had to do this more often. In the control group, it was mothers who were more likely to initiate play. Once play had begun, mothers in the behaviour problem group seemed to be less involved; they asked fewer questions, and made similar numbers of suggestions about the game as their child. In contrast, control group mothers made many more suggestions than their child and appeared to be in charge of the game, albeit in a more sensitive, warm, responsive manner. It might be argued that these patterns of maternal behaviour during play were simply a reaction to trying to play with a negative, uncooperative child. But this seems an unlikely explanation, since the children were not especially difficult during play, and more group differences were found in mothers' behaviour than in children's. Thus children with behaviour problems, compared to control group children, did not show significantly higher rates of negative affect, and were actually more responsive to their mothers' suggestions than their mothers were to theirs. They made a good contribution to initiating and keeping the play going.

These results are at least suggestive that positive parenting qualities during play may contribute to behaviour problems, rather than simply reflecting the child's effects on the parent in that situation. Other researchers examining one or two of these variables have come to similar conclusions. Pettit and Bates (1989) found that mothers who were involved and proactive during play had children with fewer behaviour problems. Shaw et al. (1994a) found that maternal responsiveness at age one predicted fewer behaviour problems at age three in boys only. Pettit et al. (1997) in an interview, rather than observational study, found that a set of positive parenting skills at age five (including proactive teaching, warmth and involvement in the child's friendships) predicted fewer behaviour problems at age eleven.

How do these findings match up with what is taught in parent training? Work with younger children, developed by Forehand and McMahon (1981), and by Webster-Stratton (1992; 1998), focuses on intervening first through joint play, and then teaching core discipline skills. They recommend regular play sessions, using praise, sensitive commands, warmth and responding to the child's lead, just as basic research suggests. But they also place great emphasis on a style of 'responsive play' which involves exclusively following the child's lead, with mothers not directing the play at all.

In contrast, in Gardner's (1994) study, sitting back and letting the child take the lead was more characteristic of the mothers of children with behaviour problems, whilst mothers in the control group tended to take the lead a great deal. It is interesting that the therapy appears to teach a style that does not mirror that of normal parents. This raises the question of whether teaching 'responsive play' is the best strategy. Clinicians often report that this technique appears to be very effective at helping to establish warmer interactions. However, this element of the package of interventions has never been evaluated separately, so we don't know whether it is an essential component. It might be that the active ingredient is 'discipline' skill, or it might be that a different way of teaching play would work just as well. Alternatively, it could be that effective intervention strategies do not always need to mimic normal good parenting. Where the relationship has become very negative, it may be helpful to teach unusually 'positive' strategies in order to rebuild the relationship.

Positive Control Strategies

What else does developmental research identify as predictors of good social adjustment in the preschool years? Apart from playful interactions, the literature examines positive control strategies (e.g. reasoning, negotiation, distraction, use of humour, and incentives) that are thought to help prevent and resolve conflict (Reid et al., 1994; Kuczynski, 1984; Pettit et al., 1997). Some correlational and longitudinal studies and laboratory experiments have been carried out, but few have used clinical groups (Grusec and Goodnow, 1994). These control strategies may operate through a number of possible mechanisms, such as by capturing the child's interest, giving him responsibility for his own behaviour, showing the parent's interest in and appreciation of the child's viewpoint, and using a non-confrontational style (Dunn and Kendrick, 1982; Grusec and Goodnow, 1994). Kochanska and Aksan (1995) carried out an observational study of maternal control strategies in normal two- to three-year-olds. They found that a cluster of 'gentle' control strategies (e.g. reasoning, compromise, polite requests) correlated positively with child compliance and negatively with child noncompliance and resistance.

Reasoning (or induction) has been much studied as a form of positive control. It is defined as explaining to the child the consequences of their behaviour, for example the effect misbehaviour might have on others. Kuczynski's (1983, 1984) laboratory experiments show that reasoning can have powerful effects on children's behaviour, but these studies do not answer the question of whether parents' use of reasoning and other positive control strategies in natural settings helps to prevent behaviour problems.

We set out to study their contribution to preschool behaviour problems in a sample of three-year-olds drawn from the New Forest epidemiological study (Gardner et al., 1998). It was predicted that mothers of children with behaviour problems would use fewer positive kinds of control, such as reasoning, compromise, and incentives, compared to the non-problem group. We used a common task for eliciting both maternal control strategies and child noncompliance, a clearing up task. The sample consisted of 52 children, 34 with behaviour problems and 18 controls. Mother-child pairs were observed in the home at age three and followed up at age five. We found, contrary to predictions from the literature, that there were no differences in the frequency of these gentle control strategies, in fact, if anything, there was a trend for mothers to be more likely to use these strategies in the problem group.

To help interpret this finding we looked more closely at the data and found that the frequency of positive strategies was highly correlated with the frequency of child noncompliance. It might be expected that after controlling statistically for the amount of noncompliance, mothers in the control group would then show a greater tendency to use these strategies. However, after doing this, using analysis of covariance, there were still no group differences in the frequency of positive strategies. Certainly, it didn't seem that positive control strategies were something that mothers of difficult children were poor at, or needed to be taught how to do. This is of course exactly what Patterson (1982) would have predicted. He suggests reasoning during conflict simply reinforces noncompliance, and therefore the problem group mothers would be expected to do more of this. Of course, these findings are based on a small sample studied in one particular context, and need replicating. Nevertheless, these puzzling data lead us to other interesting and testable hypotheses.

Timing of Strategies

Perhaps reasoning and bargaining can be helpful strategies, but only if parents follow through on the consequences of their verbal strategies. Webster-Stratton (1992) teaches these skills, called 'natural and logical consequences'. Alternatively, maybe reasoning and other forms of gentle control are ineffective strategies to use during conflict. However, it may be that they are effective at other times, for example, before conflict and misbehaviour have started. The whole issue of how parents time their strategies seems to have been paid little attention in the literature. Particularly effective parenting might involve anticipating when a situation is likely to be difficult and taking steps to prevent conflict arising in the first place. Parent training manuals rarely make explicit mention of teaching skills for anticipating and preventing conflict, apart from one study by Sanders and Dadds (1982). Evidence to support the influence of preventive strategies comes from a study of normal children by Holden (1983) who examined parental anticipation using an elegant combination of a naturalistic observational study in a supermarket, and an experimental laboratory study (Holden and West, 1989). Both studies found that parents who took steps to prevent conflict by engaging the child before trouble occurred experienced less misbehaviour.

It appeared that there were good grounds for examining the timing of mothers' positive control and their relation to problem behaviour. Gardner et al. (1998) using the New Forest sample hypothesised that:

- mothers of children in the non-problem group would be more likely to prevent trouble in the clear-up task by offering the child a reason or incentive for clearing-up at the outset of the task, before they started to misbehave. This was called a pre-emptive strategy; and that
- mothers of children with behaviour problems would be more likely to wait until the child had refused to tidy, then start to cajole and persuade them. This was called a reactive strategy.

The results showed that although most mothers used reactive strategies, pre-emptive strategies were nevertheless used significantly more often by mothers in the control group, compared to the problem group. The authors went on to do an exploratory follow-up of half the sample to see if mothers' use of pre-emptive versus reactive strategies predicted how children turned out two years later at age five plus. These longitudunal findings need interpreting with caution as the sample size was small (n = 25). It was found that reactive strategies predicted level of behaviour problems at age five, even after controlling for level of behaviour problems at age three. Factors such as social class and maternal depression did not account for this connection between pre-emptive versus reactive strategies and behaviour problems.

The findings of this study suggest that mothers of children with behaviour problems have no difficulty using a range of positive discipline strategies to get their three-year-old to clear up. However, group differences lay not in the content and frequency of strategies, but in their timing. Mothers of children without behaviour problems were more likely to pre-empt conflict by using a helpful strategy *before* the child started to misbehave. Moreover, these parenting differences at age three predicted the course of development of problem behaviour over the next two years. Few studies have attempted to observe parents' preventive strategies and this study suggests that it is possible to measure these by setting up everyday situations in the home which the parent knows in advance are going to happen, and which are likely to provoke mild conflict. In our next study we are examining mothers' pre-emptive strategies in a wider range of common difficult situations, including several where the mother is busy, and where the child has to turn off the TV, clear up, and eat lunch. If the finding of the New Forest study about the significance of pre-emptive strategies is replicated in a wider range of situations in the home, then this would be a good argument for putting the explicit teaching of pre-emptive strategies into intervention studies. It would be important to then test whether this component of the intervention actually makes a difference, as it would not be helpful to add components drawn from basic research without also testing their clinical value, using randomised controlled trials.

Conclusions

The research reviewed in this chapter shows clearly the importance of Patterson's parental discipline skills in the development and treatment of child behaviour problems. The evidence from a very substantial body of detailed longitudinal studies and controlled therapy trials suggests that these skills need to form the core of any parenting intervention. There are however other more positive parenting skills, including play skills and positive control strategies, which recent evidence suggests may be critical, particularly in the early development of behaviour problems, and which form a component of some parenting interventions. Basic research has begun to identify some of the strategies parents use to prevent problem behaviour. These strategies may be particularly important, and warrant further testing in longitudinal studies, followed by careful testing in the context of well-controlled intervention trials. This may serve the twin purposes of helping to improve the outcome of therapy, and further testing theories about the precise parenting mechanisms which contribute to the development of these very common and serious disorders in children.

References

American Psychiatric Association (1994), *Diagnostic and Statistical Manual of Mental Disorders*, 4th edn, Washington, DC, American Psychiatric Association.

Bates, J.E., Bayles, K., Bennett, D.S., Ridge, B. and Brown, M.M. (1991), 'Origins of externalizing behavior problems at eight years of age' in Pepler, D.J. and Rubin, K.H. (eds), *The Development and Treatment of Childhood Aggression*, Hillsdale, NJ, Erlbaum.

Baumrind, D. (1967), 'Child care practices anteceding three patterns of pre-school behavior', *Genetic Psychology Monographs*, 75, pp. 43–88.

Bryant, P.E. (1985), 'Parents, children and cognitive development' in Hinde, R.A., Clermont, A. and Stevenson-Hinde, J. (eds), *Social Relationships and Cognitive Development*, a Fysson Foundation symposium, pp. 239–52.

Campbell, S.B. (1995), 'Behavior problems in pre-school children: a review of recent research', *Journal of Child Psychology and Psychiatry*, 36, pp. 113–49.

Cunningham, C., Bremner, R. and Boyle, M. (1995), 'Large group community-based parenting programs for families of pre-schoolers at risk for disruptive behaviour disorders: utilization, cost effectiveness and outcome', *Journal of Child Psychology and Psychiatry*, 36, pp. 1141–60.

Deater-Deckard, K., Dodge, K.A., Bates, J.E. and Pettit, G.S. (1996), 'Physical discipline among African American and European American mothers: Links to children's externalizing behaviors', *Developmental Psychology*, 32, pp. 1065–72.

Deater-Deckard, K. and Plomin, R. (in press), 'An adoption study of the etiology of teacher and parent reports of externalizing behavior problems in middle childhood', *Child Development*.

Dishion, T.J., French, D.C. and Patterson, G.R. (1995), 'The development and ecology of antisocial behavior' in Cicchetti, D. and Cohen, D. (eds), *Developmental Psychopathology*, Vol. 2, New York, Wiley.

Dumas, J.E., LaFreniere, P.J. and Serketich, W.J. (1995), '"Balance of power": A transactional analysis of control in mother-child dyads involving socially competent aggressive and anxious children', *Journal of Abnormal Psychology*, 104, pp. 104–13.

Dunn, J. and Kendrick, C. (1982), *Siblings: Love, Envy and Understanding*, London, Grant McIntyre.

Eaves, L.J., Silberg, J.L., Meyer, J.M., Maes, H.H., Simonoff, E., Pickles, A., Rutter, M., Neale, M.C., Reynolds, C.A., Erickson, M.T., Heath, A.C., Loeber, R., Truett, K.R. and Hewitt, J.K. (1997), 'Genetics and developmental psychopathology: 2. The main effects of genes and environment on behavioral problems in the Virginia Twin Study of Adolescent Behavioral Development', *Journal of Child Psychology and Psychiatry*, 38, pp. 965–80.

Forehand, R.L. and McMahon, R.J. (1981), *Helping the Noncompliant Child*, New York, Guilford Press.

Forgatch, M.S. (1991), 'The clinical science vortex: a developing theory of antisocial behavior' in Pepler, D.J. and Rubin, K.H. (eds), *The Development and Treatment of Childhood Aggression*, Hillsdale, NJ, Erlbaum.

Gardner, F. (1987), 'Positive interaction between mothers and children with conduct problems: Is there training for harmony as well as fighting?', *Journal of Abnormal Child Psychology*, 15, pp. 283–93.

Gardner, F. (1989), 'Inconsistent parenting: Is there evidence for a link with children's conduct problems?', *Journal of Abnormal Child Psychology*, 17, pp. 223–33.

Gardner, F. (1994), 'The quality of joint activity between mothers and their children with behaviour problems', *Journal of Child Psychology and Psychiatry*, 35, pp. 935–48.

Gardner, F. (1997), 'Observational methods for recording parent-child interaction: how generalisable are the findings?', *Child Psychology and Psychiatry Review*, 2 (2).

Gardner, F., Sonuga-Barke, E., and Sayal, K. (1998), 'Parents anticipating misbehavior: An observational study of strategies parents use to prevent conflict with behavior problem children', submitted for publication.

Grusec, J.E. and Goodnow, J.J. (1994), 'Impact of parental discipline methods on the child's internalization of values: A reconceptualization of current points of view', *Developmental Psychology*, 30, pp. 4–19.

Holden, G.W. (1983), 'Avoiding conflict: Mothers as tacticians in the supermarket', *Child Development*, 54, pp. 233–40.

Holden, G.W. and West, M.J. (1989), 'Proximate regulation by mothers: a demonstration of how differing styles affect young children's behavior', *Child Development*, 60, pp. 64–9.

Kazdin, A.E. (1993), 'Treatment of conduct disorder: Progress and directions in psychotherapy research', *Development and Psychopathology*, 5, pp. 277–310.

Kochanska, G. and Aksan, N. (1995), 'Mother-child mutually positive affect, the quality of child compliance to requests and prohibitions, and maternal control as correlates of early internalization', *Child Development*, 66, pp. 236–54.

Kuczynski, L. (1983), 'Reasoning, prohibitions, and motivations for compliance', *Developmental Psychology*, 19, pp. 126–34.

Kuczynski, L. (1984), 'Socialization goals and mother-child interaction: Strategies for long-term and short-term compliance', *Developmental Psychology*, 20, pp. 1061–73.

Loeber, R., (1990), 'Development and risk factors of juvenile antisocial behavior and delinquency', *Clinical Psychology Review*, 10, pp. 1–41.

Loeber, R. and Farrington, D.P. (1994), 'Problems and solutions in longitudinal and experimental treatment studies of child psychopathology and delinquency', *Journal of Consulting and Clinical Psychology*, 62, pp. 887–900.

Loeber, R. and Hay, D. (1994), 'Developmental approaches to aggression and conduct problems' in Rutter, M.L. and Hay, D. (eds), *Development Through Life: a handbook for clinicians*, Oxford, Blackwell.

Maccoby, E.E. and Martin, J.A. (1983), 'Socialization in the context of the family: Parent-child interaction' in Hetherington, E.M. (ed.), *Handbook of Child Psychology: Vol. 4. Socialization, personality and social development*, New York, Wiley.

Patterson, G.R. (1982), *Coercive family process*, Eugene, Or., Castalia.

Patterson. G.R. and Forgatch, M.S. (1995), 'Predicting future clinical adjustment from treatment outcome and process variables', *Psychological Assessment*, 7, pp. 275–85.

Patterson, G.R., Reid, J.B. and Dishion, T.J. (1992), *Antisocial Boys*, Eugene, Or., Castalia.

Pettit, G.S. and Bates, J.E. (1989), 'Family interaction patterns and children's behavior problems from infancy to four years', *Developmental Psychology*, 25, pp. 413–20.

Pettit, G.S., Bates, J.E. and Dodge, K.E. (1997), 'Supportive parenting, ecological context, and children's adjustment: a seven-year longitudinal study', *Child Development*, 68, pp. 908–23.

Plomin, R. (1994), 'The Emmanuel Miller Memorial Lecture 1993. Genetic research and identification of environmental influences', *Journal of Child Psychology and Psychiatry*, 35, pp. 817–34.

Plomin, R., Foch, T.T. and Rowe, D.C. (1981), 'Bobo clown aggression in childhood: Environment, not genes', *Journal of Research in Personality*, 15, pp. 331–42.

Reid, J.B. (1978), *A Social Learning Approach to Family Intervention. Vol II: Observation in home settings*, Eugene, Or., Castalia.

Reid, J.B. (1987), 'Social interactional patterns in families of abused and nonabused children' in Zahn-Waxler, C., Cummings, M. and Ianotti, R. (eds), *Altruism and aggression: Biological and Social Origins*, Cambridge, Cambridge University Press.

Reid, J.B. (1993), 'Prevention of conduct disorder before and after school entry: relating interventions to developmental findings', *Development and Psychopathology*, 5, pp. 243–62.

Reid, M.J., O'Leary, S.G. and Wolff, L.S. (1994), 'Effects of maternal distraction and reprimands on toddlers' transgressions and negative affect', *Journal of Abnormal Child Psychology*, 22, pp. 237–46.

Richman, N., Stevenson, J. and Graham, P. (1982), *Pre-school to school: A behavioural study*, London, Academic Press.

Robins, L.N. (1991), 'Conduct disorder', *Journal of Child Psychology and Psychiatry*, 32, pp. 193–212.

Rutter, M. (1978), 'Family, area and school influences in the genesis of conduct disorders' in Hersov, L.A., Berger, D. and Shaffer, D. (eds), *Aggression and Anti-Social Behaviour in Childhood and Adolescence*, Oxford, Pergamon Press.

Rutter, M. (1994a), 'Beyond longitudinal data: causes, consequences, changes, and continuity', *Journal of Consulting and Clinical Psychology*, 62, pp. 928–40.

Rutter, M. (1994b), 'Family discord and conduct disorder: cause, consequence, or correlate?', *Journal of Family Psychology*, 8, pp. 170–86.

Sanders, M.R. and Dadds, M.R. (1982), 'Effects of planned activities and child management procedures in parent training: an analysis of setting generality', *Behavior Therapy*, 13, pp. 452–61.

Sanson, A., Oberklaid, F., Pedlow, R. and Prior, M. (1991), 'Risk indicators: assessment of infancy predictors of pre-school behavioural maladjustment', *Journal of Child Psychology and Psychiatry*, 32, pp. 609–26.

Sears, R.R., Maccoby, E.E. and Levin, H. (1957), *Patterns of Child Rearing*, New York, Harper and Row.

Shaw, D.S., Keenan, K. and Vondra, J.I. (1994a), 'Developmental precursors of externalizing behavior: ages 1 to 3, *Developmental Psychology*, 30, pp. 355–64.

Shaw, D.S., Vondra, J.I., Hommerding, K.D., Keenan, K. and Dunn, M. (1994b), 'Chronic family adversity and early child behavior problems: a longitudinal study of low-income families', *Journal of Child Psychology and Psychiatry*, 35, pp. 1109–22.

Simonoff, E., Pickles, A., Hewitt, J., Silberg, J. Rutter, M., Loeber, R., Meyer, J., Neale, M. and Eaves, L. (1995), 'Multiple raters of disruptive child behavior; using a genetic strategy to examine shared views and bias', *Behavior Genetics*, 25, pp. 311–26.

Tremblay, R.E., Pagani-Kurtz, L., Masse, L.C., Vitaro, F. and Pihl, R.O. (1995), 'A bimodal preventive intervention for disruptive kindergarten boys: its impact through mid-adolescence', *Journal of Consulting and Clinical Psychology*, 63, pp. 560–8.

Webster-Stratton, C. (1992), *The Incredible Years: A Trouble-Shooting Guide for Parents of Children Ages 3-8 Years*, Toronto, Umbrella Press.

Webster-Stratton, C. (1994), 'Advancing videotape parent training: A comparison study', *Journal of Consulting and Clinical Psychology*, 62, pp. 583–93.

Webster-Stratton, C. (in press), 'Preventing conduct problems in head start children strengthening parenting competences', *Journal of Consulting and Clinical Psychology*.

Webster-Stratton, C., Kolpacoff, M. and Hollinsworth, T. (1989), 'The long-term effectiveness and clinical significance of three cost-effective training programs for families with conduct problem children', *Journal of Consulting and Clinical Psychology*, 57, pp. 550–3.

Webster-Stratton, C. and Spitzer, A. (1991), 'Development, reliability, and validity of the daily telephone discipline interview', *Behavioral Assessment*, 13, pp. 221–39.

White, J.L., Moffitt, T.E., Earls, F., Robins, L. and Silva, P.A. (1990), 'How early can we tell?: Predictors of childhood conduct disorder and adolescent delinquency', *Criminology*, 28, pp. 507–28.

Zahn-Waxler, C., Iannotti, R.J., Cummings, E.M., and Denham, S. (1990), 'Antecedents of problem behaviors in children of depressed mothers', *Development and Psychopathology*, 2, pp. 271–91.

PART III
EFFECTIVE INTERVENTIONS

5 Preschool Intervention to Prevent Behaviour Problems and School Failure

KATHY SYLVA AND PAUL COLMAN

Summary

- *Research shows that early learning experiences have immediate, measurable effects on the cognitive and social development of preschool children.*
- *Early childhood education, which is centred on active learning, can lead to lasting gains in educational performance, social adjustment and later employment. It **does** this through encouraging high aspirations, motivation to learn and feelings of social commitment, especially for children from disadvantaged backgrounds.*
- *It is suggested that early childhood education is effective because it encourages social skills and shapes the cognitions children develop about the social environment and their own role in it.*
- *From the policy point of view, those early childhood programmes whose evaluations have been rigorous and long-term are a wise investment.*

This chapter will examine the evidence which supports the widely held belief that early learning in preschool education has lasting impact on the children's social and cognitive development (Ball, 1994; Sylva, 1994a). We will concentrate on education in centre-based settings in which 'intervention' is one of the expressed objectives. This includes learning which takes place in nursery schools and classes, day nurseries or child care centres, and playgroups.

The chapter is limited to examination of *key studies* so that their methods can be discussed in some detail. Attempts are made to create a critical framework for considering the scientific rigour of various research methods.

An understanding the effects of early childhood programmes can only be achieved alongside a refining of methodological techniques. Many studies have sought to evaluate preschool education, but the validity of their conclusions is tied to their research designs. The studies to be presented here will be considered from two different angles, the nature of the intervention and methods for establishing its effectiveness. Firstly, different types of interventions must be identified and distinguished, before understanding can progress to the level of detailed causal pathways. Secondly, the issue of what is considered to be an 'outcome' in each study will assessed. Differences in theoretical frameworks can lead to divergent expectations of what would be the positive outcomes of a programme. These differences may drastically affect whether an evaluation has been seen to have been successful. We must also consider the best ways to describe and compare children's early learning experiences. Is it enough merely to state the child's presence or absence from preschool education or do we need stronger forms of experimental control?

After concluding what these studies reveal about the effect of early childhood programmes on development, specific aspects, especially curriculum, will be considered in depth to suggest how they lead to protective factors, which may prevent behaviour or educational problems. What are the ingredients of preschool education that can reduce the likelihood of long term negative outcomes such as delinquency and reading delay?

Early Research in the USA on Educational Programmes for Disadvantaged Preschool Children

The American project Head Start has received government funding for three decades in hopes it would 'break the cycle of poverty'. A simple input/output model was used in early studies on the impact of Head Start. Typically, IQ or attainment test scores of preschool 'graduates' were compared to scores of control children who had no preschool experience. Initial evaluations seriously underestimated the value of the programme (Smith and Bissell, 1970) by focusing on measures of intelligence as the main outcome. Sadly, they found that early IQ gains quickly washed out, leaving graduates of Head Start no different from control children.

Luckily, there is cause for optimism when examining research on programmes which are *not* part of Head Start. Researchers carried out a meta-analysis of the effects of a small group of preschool programmes which were of excellent quality (Lazar and Darlington, 1982). Each of this small group of programmes employed rigorous research designs and curricula based on developmental theory. The authors limited their selective meta-analysis to preschool projects with adequate sample sizes, norm-referenced assessment tests, comparison/control groups, and follow up of children well beyond school entry. By these strict criteria, the results of 11 carefully monitored programmes were entered for meta-analysis, a statistical exercise which enables researchers to compare the size of effect across many different studies. Details on educational and employment histories were compiled on a sample of more than 2,000 preschool 'graduates' and matched controls to measure the effect of early education. In addition they carried out new interviews with the (now) adolescents and their families. Results from the meta-analysis showed that participation in excellent, cognitively oriented preschool programmes was associated with later school competence and avoidance of assignment to 'special' education. Interviews carried out at age 19 showed the nursery group talked to their parents more about life in school and the parents themselves had higher aspirations for employment of their children. It appeared that the legacy of preschool lay not with IQ gains but with children's remaining in mainstream education and developing positive views of themselves and their futures.

The Perry Preschool Research: Comparing Early Childhood 'Graduates' to a Control Group

The most carefully controlled of the 11 programmes reviewed by Lazar's team was the Perry Preschool Project, which became known later as High/ Scope. This curriculum is based on Piagetian theory and includes intensive parent participation. The programme has been subjected to careful evaluation for almost 30 years and has consistently shown striking social and economic outcomes (Berrueta-Clement, Schweinhart, Barnett, Epstein, and Weikart, 1984; Schweinhart and Weikart, 1993). The study is one of the few preschool evaluations following an experimental paradigm with random assignment of children to the 'treatment' (i.e. early childhood education) or 'control' (i.e. home) groups. The results showed an initial IQ advantage for preschool graduates which disappeared by secondary school.

At the time of the early evaluations of early childhood programmes, raised IQ was viewed as the means of bridging the gap between the individual and her later success. Therefore raising IQ became the means by which success was judged. As developmental psychology advanced and broadened, so did ideas and aspirations of early education programmes. The High/Scope evaluators widened their scope to include social and economic outcomes. They found startling differences in social adjustment and community participation between the children who attended the programme and the control group who had remained at home.

Jean E. Dumas, Ph.D.

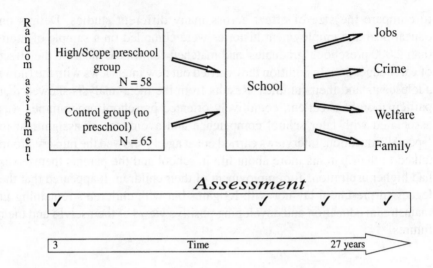

Figure 5.1   The Perry Preschool evaluation study

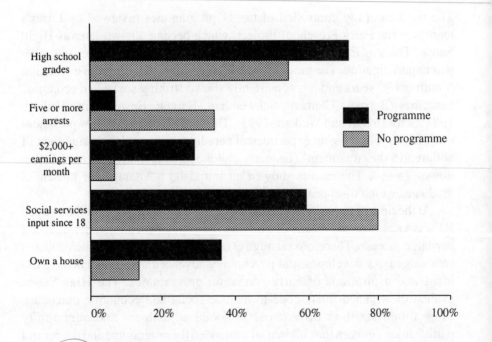

Figure 5.2   The Perry Preschool outcomes

Jean E. Dumas, Ph.D.

Results from follow-up at age 27 appear in Figure 5.2. This broad range of positive outcomes is confirmed in other research, especially with regard to delinquency, by Larry, Mangione and Honig (1988) who found that preschool attendance lowered the rate of antisocial behaviour.

Schweinhart and Weikart (1993) carried out a cost-benefit analysis which shows that for every $1,000 that was invested in the preschool programme, at least $7,160 (after adjustment for inflation) has been or will be returned to society. These calculations were based on the financial cost to society of juvenile delinquency, remedial education, income support, and joblessness – set against the running costs of an excellent preschool programme. The economic analysis also estimated the return to society in taxes from the higher paid preschool graduates who, incidentally, often owned two cars.

There have been two other cost benefit analyses carried out on preschool interventions, both in the US. Barnett and Escobar (1990) present data from a preschool language intervention curriculum studied by Weiss and a comprehensive early day care programme for disadvantaged families studied by Seitz. Both studies showed that the costs of the programmes were more than offset by the savings later on in the children's schooling and medical care.

With increasingly high uptake of early education, fuelled by a government commitment to preschool education for all who wish it, the opportunity for this type of randomised control experiment becomes impractical if not unethical. Children cannot be deprived of preschool education for the purpose of science. As 'home' children naturally diminish, it is increasingly difficult to look at the effect of 'no intervention'. An alternative, if less ideal design, is to compare the effects of different kinds of early education programmes while accounting for baseline measures. Although this will not inform us of the effect of early education per se, it enables us to pinpoint which kinds of preschool programme are the most effective in promoting educational and social gains. In addition, comparing the effects of different kinds of early education will provide clues as to the mechanisms which might bring about change in children's lives.

High/Scope Research: Comparing the Effects of Different Curricula

It is clear that some, but certainly not all, preschool interventions put children on the path to greater school commitment, better jobs and lower rates of antisocial behaviour. In a later study, Schweinhart, Weikart and Larner (1986) compared the effects of three different curricula: High/Scope (the 'active learning' curriculum used in the Perry Preschool Project), formal skills (didactic instruction) and traditional nursery (curriculum centred on free play). At the point of entry to school, they found that children from all three programmes had increased IQs. However, follow-up at the age of 15 showed that children who had attended the formal programme had higher rates of antisocial behaviour and had lower commitment to school than those who attended the two programmes based on active learning and play. Thus, raised IQ at school entry does not necessarily put children on the path to educational and social success. Only the children who experienced active learning programmes before school retained the advantage of their early education, an advantage they demonstrated by pro-social behaviour and higher confidence when interviewed as adolescents.

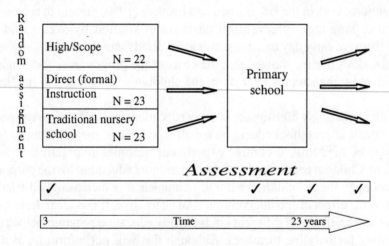

Figure 5.3   The three curricula comparison group

A later follow up of the same cohort in 1997 (Schweinhart and Weikart, 1997) investigated the impact of the three different curricula on adult social and economic outcomes. By the age of 23 the graduates of High/Scope and the traditional nursery programmes were better off in important ways compared to those whose preschool education was formal in the direct instruction group. Those who had experienced a formal programme had more arrests (over the lifetime), both felony and misdemeanour (see Figure 5.4), more years of special education, and less adult involvement in community activities. More of the graduates of the active learning programmes were living with a spouse and they had fewer suspensions from work for discipline problems. Intriguingly, in depth interviews revealed that the High/Scope graduates had significantly lower rates of all round irritation. They were particularly less likely to report that friends or family were 'giving them a hard time', suggesting a more positive view of their immediate social environment. The children who had experienced a formal, skills-orientated programme before entering school grew up to be hostile to authority and also towards their peers.

This rigorous longitudinal study with random assignment supports the claim that early childhood curricula in which children initiate their own learning activities are superior to programmes of didactic instruction. It may be that children learn to direct and control their own behaviour when they attend 'progressive' schools which provide opportunity for collaborative and exploratory play. Alternatively it may be that the social skills developed during the freer programmes were useful later on.

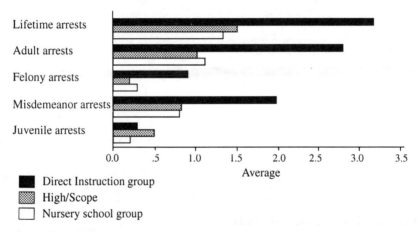

Figure 5.4 Mean arrests at age 23 by curriculum group

The Portuguese Comparative Study of Curricula

The previous study is not alone in demonstrating that formal education in the preschool years impedes later progress. It is supported by several studies in the US and a recent study by Nabuco (1996) carried out in Portugal. In this European study, the outcomes of three preschool curricula were researched throughout the first year of primary school. Children were studied in their nurseries (High/Scope, formal skills or progressive/free play) and followed through the first year of primary school where they were matched with a comparison group of children who entered school direct from home.

Altogether, 219 children were tested in September and June on a range of measures. In the absence of random assignment to group, the pre- and post-testing design allowed the researchers to measure the contribution to developmental progress in Year 1 of primary school of the type of preschool curriculum the children had experienced (see Figure 5.5).

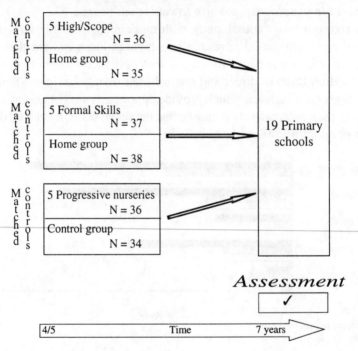

Figure 5.5   The Portuguese study

Nabuco's findings were consistent with the American research reported previously (Nabuco, 1996; Sylva and Nabuco, 1996); children benefited more from programmes focused on active learning than those which centred on formal lessons. The High/Scope group outperformed the other groups in reading (Figure 5.6) and also in writing. Sadly, the formal skills group had higher anxiety scores (Figure 5.7) and lower self-esteem (Figure 5.8) than the other two groups. This European study mirrors the previous American one in that the formal curriculum hindered progress later on and was associated with poor academic attainment and with personal difficulties which included low self-esteem and higher anxiety.

In Nabuco's short-term longitudinal design, children were too young for full-blown delinquency; however, it confirms the work of Schweinhart and

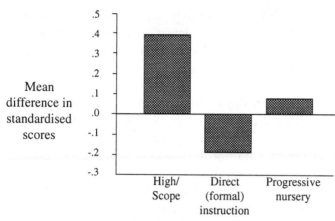

Figure 5.6   Effect of curriculum on reading

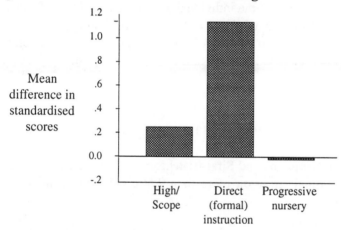

Figure 5.7   Effect of curriculum on anxiety

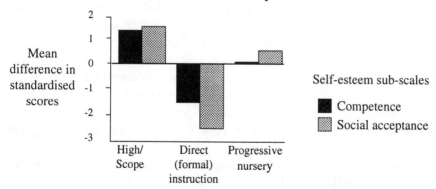

Figure 5.8   Effect of curriculum on self-esteem (self-report)

Weikart (1997) showing that a very formal preschool programme led to social difficulties. On the whole, early education is advantageous; however, too formal a curriculum may present hidden dangers especially for children's future social skills and adjustment, and social representations of their immediate environment.

This Portuguese quasi-experimental design is based on existing populations and so avoids the ethical and practical problems posed by random assignment to a control group. However, this design is only suitable in countries where a fair proportion of families do not have access to preschool education. Comparing groups can inform us about the effects of various curricula and these can be contrasted to a control ('home') group. Although an early education programme involving active learning may result in improved outcomes overall, it may be useful to look deeper. Designs presented so far will not reveal differences at the individual level nor at the level of specific school. Individual factors may play a large part in mediating the effects of early intervention and certain pre-schools may be more effective than others. Exploring the effects of child level and centre level characteristics will require far more advanced methods.

The Effective Provision of Preschool Education Project in the UK

Sylva, Melhuish, Sammons and Siraj-Blatchford (1996) are carrying out a five-year longitudinal study on more than 2,500 children to answer the following questions:

- Are some preschool centres more effective than others in promoting academic competence and social skills? If so, what are their characteristics?
- What are the effects of differing curriculum/management/parent involvement/resources to positive child outcomes?

Recruitment and baseline assessment begin at age three, there is interim assessment at school entry, and final outcomes are measured at age seven via standardised tests of reading and maths, rigorous assessment of social and emotional skills, and self report on pupil's attitudes towards learning and school.

This complex design is based upon multilevel modelling and will result in conclusions at three levels:

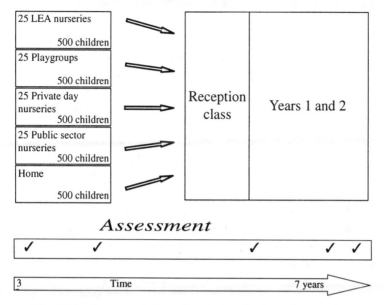

Figure 5.9 Effective provision of preschool education study

- the programme level – to compare the effects of various types of early education;
- the centre level – to identify individual centres which lead to positive or negative outcomes; and
- the child level – to look for characteristics of the child which influence later development and may interact with the type and quality of educational provision.

Each of these levels can be looked at independently, e.g. which type of children benefit from early education, which type of programme is most effective and for which children? Such designs require extensive effort and funds as well as precise levels of measurement; for multilevel modelling to work, large groups are required. This large government funded study will end in 2001, but we already know a great deal about variation in provision in the UK. The final results will show if and how differences in provision in the UK lead to differences in outcomes for children.

The Social Consequences of Early Childhood Education

If we were to make evidence-based decisions for preventing behaviour problems, we would recommend universal early childhood education. Furthermore, on the basis of evidence presented here, the educational practice would be shifted away from the current stress in the UK on formal academic preparation and towards the development of social skills and commitment (Sylva, 1997). One reason for the imbalance is the mistaken view that it is more important to teach cognitive skills than social ones. It is the social domains of development that early childhood education has been shown to enhance.

In 1985, Michael Rutter reviewed the literature on the effects of education on children's development and concluded that: 'The long term educational benefits stem not from what children are specifically taught but from effects on children's attitudes to learning, on their self esteem, and on their task orientation'. More than a decade later we can put in place some of the pieces unavailable when Rutter wrote his classic review (Sylva, 1994b). The most important impact of early education appears to include: children's aspirations, motivations and social adjustment. These are moulded through active learning experiences in the preschool centre which enable children to enter school with a positive self-esteem and begin a school career of commitment and social responsibility.

The Mechanism of Influence

If early education is better than home, and certain curricula superior to others, we should be seeking the mechanisms responsible for such an effect. It has been shown that curricula based on active learning lead to the most lasting benefits. In active learning children are freer to organise the social and intellectual frameworks of their interactions. Whilst being placed in a group with other children requires pro-social cooperative skills, having to form and regulate these groups themselves requires children to develop a level of social functioning which includes planning and social representations along with actual behaviours.

Being able to organise oneself within a structured environment may help develop qualities necessary for social inclusion. The key benefit of the active learning approach is that it encourages identification with the group and empowerment to contribute. The self-initiated learning absent in formal programmes may be encouraging withdrawal from collaborative learning and the attraction of alternative deviant pathways.

Positive group experience can affect the representations of both the self and the other. Through successful experiences and encounters, children learn their own self-worth and develop a positive self-esteem. Complementing this, children may be constructing representations of social interactions; building up cognitions of other people as friendly, prosocial creatures. (Recall the finding of Schweinhart and Weikart (1997) that children from the formal programme grew up to be distrustful and irritable in their social environment.) It is proposed here that positive social adjustment did not spring from an imposed social contract, but rather it developed in the framework of a peer community. The child's social world develops away from the dyadic interactions of infancy towards the integrated structure of the preschool, then slowly towards the social structures of adulthood.

Perhaps preschool can promote this process by providing a midway, a gentle initiation into hierarchical social structures. If these formal school structures are imposed too abruptly, or too soon, they can alienate children not only from figures of authority, but also from their peers. Prosocial interactions require a certain safety and security. The absence of appropriate prosocial behaviour may leave the child open to peer rejection, which has been shown to lead to poor social, emotions and academic adjustment (Parker and Asher, 1987; Parker, Rubin, Price and DeRossier, 1995). If early education can encourage inclusion, then it's likely that these social gains will outweigh the direct cognitive benefits related to school-like skills.

References

Ball, C. (1994), *Start right, The importance of early learning*, London, Royal Society for the Arts, Manufacturing and Commerce.

Barnett, W.S. and Escobar, C.M. (1990), 'Economic costs and benefits of early intervention' in Meisels, S.J. and Shonkoff, J.P. (eds), *Handbook of Early Childhood Intervention*, Cambridge, Cambridge University Press.

Berrueta-Clement, J.R., Schweinhart, L.J., Barnett, W.S., Epstein, A.S. and Weikart, D.P. (1984), *Changed lives: the effects of the Perry pre-school programme on youths through age 19*, Ypsilanti, Michigan, The High/Scope Press.

Larry, J.R., Mangione, P.L. and Honig, A.S. (1988), 'Long-term impact of an early intervention with low-income children and their families' in Powell, D.R. (ed.), *Parent education as early childhood intervention: emerging directions in theory, research and practice*, Vol. 4, Hillsdale, N.J., Ablex.

Lazar, I. and Darlington, R. (1982), 'Does Head-Start work?. A 1-year follow up comparison of disadvantaged children attending Head-Start, no preschool, and other preschool programmes', *Developmental Psychology*, 24 (2), pp. 210–22.

Nabuco, M.E. (1996), 'The effects of three early childhood curricula in Portugal on children's progress in the first year of primary school', thesis submitted for degree of Doctor of Philosophy at the Institute of Education, University of London (unpublished).

Parker, J. and Asher, S.R. (1987), 'Peer relations and later personal adjustment: Are low-accepted children at risk?', *Psychological Bulletin*, 102, pp. 375–89.

Parker, J., Rubin, K.H., Price, J. and DeRossier, M. (1995), 'Peer relationships, child development, and adjustment: A developmental psychopathology perspective' in Cicchetti, D. and Cohen, D. (eds), *Developmental Psychopathology: Vol. 2 Risk, disorder and adaptation*, New York, Wiley.

Rutter, M. (1985), 'Family and school influences on cognitive development', *Journal of Child Psychology*, 26 (5), pp. 683–704.

Schweinhart, L.J., Weikart, D., and Larner, M. (1986), *Consequences of three pre-school curriculum models through age 15. Early Childhood Research Quarterly*, (1), pp. 15–45.

Schweinhart, L.J. and Weikart, D.P. (1993), *Significant benefits: The High Scope Perry pre-school study through age 27*, Ypsilanti, Michigan, High Scope UK.

Schweinhart, L.J. and Weikart, D.P. (1997), *Lasting Differences, The High/Scope preschool curriculum comparison through age 23*, Ypsilanti, Michigan, High Scope Press.

Smith, M.S. and Bissell, J.S. (1970), 'The impact of Head Start: The Westinghouse-Ohio Head Start evaluation', *Harvard Educational Review*, 40, pp. 51–104.

Sylva, K. (1994a), 'The impact of early learning on children's later development' in Ball, C. (ed.), *Start right, The importance of early learning*, London, Royal Society for the Arts, Manufacturing and Commerce.

Sylva, K. (1994b), 'School influences on children's development', *Journal of Child Psychology and Psychiatry*, 35 (1), pp. 135–70.

Sylva, K. (1997), *Developing the primary school curriculum: the next steps*, London, School Curriculum and Assessment Authority.

Sylva, K., Melhuish, E., Sammons, P. and Siraj-Blatchford, I. (1996), *Effective Provision of Pre-School Education*, London, Institute of Education.

Sylva, K. and Nabuco, M.E. (1996), 'Children's learning in day care: How shall we study it?', paper presented at the ISSBD international Conference of Behavioural Development XIVth Biennial Meeting, Quebec City, Canada, 12–16 August.

6 Parent-training Programmes and Behaviour Problems: Findings from a Systematic Review

JANE BARLOW

Summary

- *Behaviour problems in children constitute an important public health issue and the implications of such behaviours are wide-ranging, including problems for families, schools and society in general. Effective interventions for behaviour problems are now required.*
- *To date there has been very little systematic evidence of the effectiveness of treatment programmes for behaviour problems, but 'parent-training programmes' appear to represent a promising intervention.*
- *This chapter reports on a systematic review of the published literature between 1970–1996 on the effectiveness of parent-training programmes in improving behaviour problems in children between the ages of 3–10 years.*
- *Results of this review showed that group-based parent-training programmes are remarkably effective in helping these children*
- *Group behaviour modification programmes appeared to be the most successful in improving behaviour problems and produced the largest effect size.*
- *This review highlights the present paucity of methodologically rigorous research on parent-training programmes and directions for future research are discussed.*

Introduction

During the last decade, there has been an increasing interest in parent-training programmes in the UK on the part of both parents and professionals in clinical and public health settings. However, the burgeoning of programmes in this country has not, so far, been paralleled by a similar interest in their evaluation. The result of this is a paucity of high quality studies on the effectiveness of parent-training programmes in this country. A recent survey of 38 group-based parent-training programmes being run in the UK showed that while there was considerable anecdotal evidence concerning the success and effectiveness of all the programmes in the survey, written or published evaluation reports were available for less than half of these programmes (Smith, 1996). Only nine programmes had been 'externally' evaluated, and most of these evaluations were based on findings from fewer than 50 parents. Only four studies had used a control group (ibid.).

This chapter begins with a discussion of the nature of behaviour problems in terms of their prevalence and long-term outcomes, and the relationship between behaviour problems and parenting management skills. It goes on to present the findings of a systematic review of the effectiveness of parent-training programmes in improving the behaviour of children between the ages of 3–10 years. The chapter concludes with a discussion of a new model of parent-training – the home/school linked parent-training programme – which addresses the risks arising from two primary pathways, the home and the school. It is suggested that this model is based on a 'population' as opposed to a 'high-risk' approach, and in a number of respects represents an important advance on the basic model of parent-training.

Behaviour Problems

Behaviour problems are now the most important cause of disability in childhood (Bone and Meltzer, 1989). The estimated prevalence in preschool children using clinical criteria is approximately 10–15 per cent (Campbell, 1995). Current estimates of prevalence, however, underestimate the full extent of the problem. Prevalence data based on the use of clinical criteria in which an arbitrary threshold has been set to define a group of children in need of treatment, actually excludes large numbers of children who do not require professional intervention, but who nevertheless, may have a range of problems which interfere with their own development and that of other children. Thus, self-reported prevalence of behaviour problems is much higher than clinical estimates (Offord, Alder and Boyle 1986; Kazdin 1996). Kazdin (1996, p. 6) notes:

> Among youths aged 13–18 years, more than 50% admit to theft, 35% admit to assault, 45% admit to property destruction, and 60% admit to engaging in more than one type of antisocial behaviour, such as aggressive acts, drug abuse, arson and vandalism.

Aggressiveness, conduct problems and antisocial behaviours are also the most frequent cause of child and adolescent clinical referral encompassing between one-third to one-half of all child and adolescent clinic referrals (Kazdin, Siegel and Bass, 1990; Robins, 1981).

In addition to having a high prevalence, behaviour problems are extremely stable over time (Robins, 1981; Robins and Rutter, 1991; Stewart, 1985; Farrington, 1991; Moffit et al., 1996; Rutter, 1996; Loeber and Hay, 1997). In the Dunedin study for example, antisocial behaviour at age 13 was predicted by externalising behaviour at age three and behaviour problems at age five (Robins, 1991). In a further 22-year follow-up study, peer-rated aggression at age eight predicted the number of convictions by age 30, as well as the seriousness of the crimes (Eron and Huesmann, 1990). There are, however, important sex differences in the stability of behaviour problems, boys being much more likely than girls to continue exhibiting problem behaviours (Quinton, Rutter and Gulliver, 1990).

Behaviour problems are not only stable across time *within individuals* but also *within families,* and the continuity is evident across multiple generations. Both parental and grandparental factors predict the level of aggression shown in the next generation of children (Patterson, DeBaryshe and Ramsey, 1989).

It follows from the stability of the problem that the prognosis is poor, and behaviour problems in childhood predict a range of deleterious outcomes (Moffit et al., 1996; Rutter, 1996; Champion, Goodall and Rutter, 1995; Offord and Bennett, 1994). The costs to the individual include delinquency and criminal behaviour, alcoholism, drug abuse, poor work and marital outcomes, and a range of psychiatric disorders. The costs to society include both the trauma, disruption and psychological costs wrought by behaviour problems in homes, schools and communities, and the financial costs of services to deal with these problems including community youth justice, courts, social workers, psychiatric services, and foster homes.

The need for early intervention is indicated by both long-term outcome studies which show that interventions with antisocial youth produce at best, short-term effects that are lost within a year or two (Kazdin, 1993), and research which shows that the *early* onset of behaviour problems is associated with poorer long-term outcomes (Moffit et al., 1996).

Parenting Practices and Child Behaviour

It is now recognised that there are a number of 'disruptors' to effective parenting (Patterson, DeBaryshe and Ramsey, 1989). 'Disruptors' refer to any factors which either predispose the parents to child management problems or that make the management of children more difficult. These include parental and grandparental traits or psychopathology such as their own history of antisocial behaviour, demographic factors such as income, level of parent education, ethnicity, neighbourhood, or other family stressors such as unemployment, marital conflict and divorce.

There is now a number of empirically validated models depicting the developmental progression for conduct and behaviour problems. These show a clear association between parenting practices characterised by harsh and inconsistent discipline, little positive parental involvement with the child, poor monitoring and supervision, and behaviour and conduct problems in early childhood (McCord, McCord, and Howard, 1963; Loeber and Dishion, 1983; Patterson, Debaryshe, and Ramsey, 1989; Patterson, Dishion and Chamberlain, 1993). Patterson's 'escalation' model shows how poor parenting practices in early childhood very often lead on to academic failure and rejection by normal peers in middle childhood, the long-term result being a commitment to deviant peer groups and delinquency in late childhood and adolescence (Patterson, Dishion and Chamberlain, 1993).

The importance of parenting skills has been confirmed by recent work using structural equation models which showed that parenting and family interaction variables accounted for as much as 30–40 per cent of the variance in child antisocial behaviour (Patterson, DeBaryshe and Ramsey, 1989).

This raises the question as to what the particular mechanism or relationship is between parenting practices and child behaviour. Possibly some of the best empirical evidence concerning this issue has been based on the behavioural and social learning theory model. Within this framework, poor parental child management skills refer to the ways in which family members *inadvertently* develop and sustain antisocial and aggressive patterns of behaviour in children through the use of 'faulty contingencies', or actions which are not contingent on the child's behaviour. One of the ways in which family members may develop and sustain particular patterns of behaviour in children is the 'positive reinforcement' of bad behaviour. This occurs when a child engages in a disruptive behaviour in order to obtain a desired end. In the absence of more effective methods of dealing with this behaviour, the parent concedes what is being demanded, thereby inadvertently rewarding the child for his/her poor behaviour.

The 'negative reinforcement' of bad behaviour is an even more potent means of developing and sustaining aggressive behaviour in particular, in children. This occurs when a parent initiates an aversive interaction with a child and then backs off following a counterattack from the child. From this set of interactions the child learns that aversive reactions produce pay-offs. Escalation into more severe coercive interchanges occur as the child increasingly uses aversive behaviours to 'terminate aversive intrusions by other family members' (Patterson, DeBaryshe and Ramsey, 1986, p. 330). The absence of 'positive reinforcement' of pro-social behaviours further contributes to an overall pattern of interactions between parent and child from which poor behaviour and inadequate social skills in the child both at home and at school, may result.

Research shows that aggressive and antisocial children are more likely to interpret the intentions and actions of others as hostile and that they are more likely to include physical force and aggression as a solution to interpersonal problems (Offord and Bennett, 1994). The problem-solving skills of aggressive and antisocial children are on the whole poor, and they are deficient with regard to their 'behavioural response repertoire' (ibid.).

While this model very clearly depicts one type of mechanism by which poor behaviour in children is developed and sustained, it has nevertheless been argued that it gives insufficient emphasis to a whole range of factors which play a significant role in the development of childhood behaviour problems. Griest and Wells (1983) advocate an expanded behavioural family therapy model which includes not only child management factors, but cognitive parent variables such as parental perceptions of the child's behaviour, psychological parent variables such as the presence of maternal depression or anxiety, marital variables which take into account the presence of marital discord and divorce, and social variables such as the presence of an extended family, and supportive community relations. This is consistent with more recent research which shows the importance of a range of risk factors in the development of conduct and behaviour problems (Campbell, 1995; Yoshiwaka, 1994; Pepler and Rubin, 1991; Robins and Rutter, 1990).

Parent-training Programmes

Most parent-training programmes irrespective of theoretical orientation, are based on the assumption that child behaviour is a function of the contingencies occurring in the family between the parent and the child, and that the basic process contributing to child behaviour problems, is a parenting skills deficit (Griest and Wells, 1983). As such, the main goal of many parent-training programmes is the development of a range of skills, and parents are helped to identify, define, observe and respond to problem behaviour, in new ways.

In programmes based on behavioural principles, the emphasis is on promoting change in children's behaviour using social learning techniques, including positive reinforcement, finding alternatives to punishment such as the use of time-out or loss of privileges, and the use of negotiation and contingency contracting. Group sessions provide opportunities for parents to see how these techniques are implemented, and the opportunity to practice newly acquired skills.

The behavioural type of parent-training programmes have now been paralleled by a range of parenting programmes which Smith (1996) in her review of parent-training programmes refers to as 'relationship' programmes. These have a greater emphasis than the behavioural programmes on interpersonal relationships within the family, and are very often based on humanistic, communications, Adlerian and family systems theory rather than behavioural/social learning principles. The aim of these programmes is to provide the parent with new skills in listening and communicating with children, for example by using 'I' rather than 'You' statements, and through the negotiation of problems in a way which permits both parents and children to 'win'. Many parent-training programmes, however, are eclectic, and draw on a range of both behavioural and relationship theories and practices. Figure 6.1 shows some examples of the content of both the behavioural and relationship programmes.

- *Helping parents to help children to recognise, name and deal with their feelings*
- *Learning how to engage a child's cooperation*
- *Finding alternatives to punishment*
- *Helping parents to encourage the child to be autonomous and take responsibility*
- *Freeing children from playing roles*
- *Using praise*
- *Negotiating with children using choices and consequences*
- *Becoming more effective listeners*
- *Helping parents reflect on their own experiences of being parented and the ways in which these influence their present parenting practices*

Figure 6.1   Content of parent-training programmes

The Effectiveness of Parent-training Programmes

In order to examine the effectiveness of parent-training programmes in improving behaviour problems in young children, a systematic review was recently undertaken of published literature between 1970 and 1996 (Barlow, 1997). A number of strict inclusion criteria were established in order to identify rigorous quantitative studies, which had used both randomisation and a no-treatment or waiting-list control group. The research question was 'how effective are parent-training programmes in improving behaviour problems in young children between the ages of 3–10 years'? The search strategy was aimed primarily at the identification of overviews, and secondarily at the identification of first-order evidence in the form of randomised controlled trials. In the case of overviews, only quantitative studies were included in the review. In the case of randomised controlled trials (RCTs) the study design had to include randomisation of participants to an experimental and control group, the latter being either a waiting-list, no-treatment or a placebo group. Studies comparing two different therapeutic modality groups, without a control group, were excluded from the review.

The review included only those studies focusing on children between the ages of 3–10 years. The primary problem of participants in both the experimental and control groups, was behaviour problems characterised by at least one externalising problem, i.e. temper tantrums, aggression, noncompliance, etc. Studies in which the primary disorder was an internalising problem were excluded from the review, i.e. autism, anxiety disorders, depression, etc.

Studies had to include at least one 'group-based' parent-training programme, all group-based programmes being eligible for inclusion irrespective of the theoretical basis underpinning the programme. This included parent-training groups based on psychoanalytic, family systems, Adlerian, humanistic, and behavioural theories. Studies using joint techniques, i.e. behavioural parent-training *and* problem-solving skills, were also included in the review.

No restrictions were placed on the language of the studies to be included in the review, and the years searched ranged from 1970–97. Studies predating 1970 were excluded from the review. Studies had to include at least one standardized child behaviour outcome measure such as parent or teacher written or verbal reports, or independent observations using standardized coding schemas.

A total of 255 studies were identified but only three meta-analyses and

18 RCTs met all the inclusion criteria and were therefore included in the review.

Findings of the Systematic Review

The results of this review were largely positive and showed that group-based programmes improved the behaviour of young children, compared with no-treatment or waiting-list control groups, as measured by both parent-reports and independent observations of children's behaviour. The effect sizes ranged from 0.3–1.8 for parent-reported child behaviour outcome measures. Independent observations of children's behaviour produced marginally lower effect sizes ranging from 0.2–0.9. In two studies, independent observations failed to confirm the improvements in children's behaviour reported by parents (Cunningham et al., 1995; Firestone et al., 1980).

Long-term follow-up of parent-training programmes to assess whether changes in behaviour were maintained over time, was limited to three years. Studies in which long-term follow-up was conducted ranged from six months (Cunningham et al., 1995; Scott and Stradling, 1987; Spaccarelli et al., 1992) to one year (Webster-Stratton et al., 1982, 1989), two years (Bernal et al., 1980) and three years (Webster-Stratton, 1990b; Daly et al., 1985). The findings from these studies showed that the effects of parent-training programmes on children's behaviour were enduring over time. However, in a number of studies between 25–45 per cent of parents continued to experience problems with their children's behaviour. One study showed that the families who continued to have problems were characterised by single parent status, increased maternal depression, lower social class status and a family history of alcoholism and drug abuse (Webster-Stratton, 1990b).

Only two studies assessed the cost-effectiveness of parent-training programmes (Cunningham et al., 1995; Webster-Stratton et al., 1988). One study showed that community group-based programmes were six times more cost-effective than individual clinic-based programmes, and possibly more acceptable to many parents (Cunningham et al., 1995). The effectiveness of this study, however, was based on parent-reports only, of improvement in children's behaviour. A further study showed that while both group-based and individual programmes produced similar changes in parental attitudes and child behaviour, the group-based programme used only 48 hours of therapist time compared with 251 hours for a similar number of parents receiving individual therapy (Webster-Stratton et al., 1988). The group-based programme was again significantly more cost-effective.

The findings of this review also showed that behavioural programmes consistently produced the largest effect sizes. This may, however, reflect the absence of more rigorous studies of the 'relationship' type programmes. The only relationship type parent-training programmes which had been sufficiently rigorously evaluated to be included in the review, were Parent Effectiveness Training (PET) and Adlerian programmes. None of the studies comparing these with behavioural programmes showed any significant differences in child behaviour outcomes between the two types of programme (Frazier and Matthes, 1975; Bernal et al., 1980; Pinsker and Geoffroy, 1981). Many of the existing evaluations of both PET and Adlerian programmes have focused on changes in parental attitudes and behaviour, rather than changes in child behaviour outcome measures, and rigorous evidence of their effectiveness in producing behavioural changes in children, is still needed.

These findings have recently been confirmed by a systematic review conducted by the NHS Centre for Reviews and Dissemination at York, in which it was concluded that school-based interventions and parent-training programmes for children with behavioural problems can improve conduct and mental well-being in children (NHS Centre for Reviews and Dissemination, 1997).

A number of problems emerged with the studies included in this review. The main methodological problem encountered was that most studies provided insufficient data with which to calculate effect sizes, thereby limiting the possibility of comparing the findings across studies. In addition, two studies which included independent observations failed to confirm the parent-reports of changes in children's behaviour (Cunningham et al., 1995; Firestone et al., 1980). The Firestone et al. (1980) study, which was one of only two studies to include teacher-reports, showed that teachers do not always confirm the improvements in children's behaviour reported by parents. This suggests that changes in children's behaviour at home, are not necessarily generalisable to other settings, such as the school, and points to the importance of including teachers in parenting programmes. Finally, long-term follow-up is at present limited to three years, and as a result of the use of waiting-list control groups, there is no long-term comparison between experimental and control group available to date, or evidence concerning the relationship between the duration of the programme and the maintenance of effects over time.

Overall, it was difficult to determine which programme appeared to be best supported by the evidence because of insufficient data. The only programme which had been systematically evaluated in a number of trials was the Webster-Stratton programme based on the use of video-tape modelling. A series of studies were conducted which showed that a video-tape modelling programme using a group-discussion format, a group-discussion with video-tape modelling format, and an individual video-tape modelling format, all led to reliable and sustained improvements in children's behaviour for up to one year, for two-thirds of the sample (Webster-Stratton, 1982, 1984, 1989, 1990a; Webster-Stratton et al., 1988, 1989). The group discussion with video-tape modelling format, however, produced higher ratings on consumer satisfaction. Subsequent research by Webster-Stratton showed that the most stable improvements at three-year follow-up were produced by the combined video-tape modelling with therapist-led group discussion format (Webster-Stratton, 1990b).

Webster-Stratton's series of research studies based on children with clinically defined behaviour problems from high-risk backgrounds, undoubtedly shows that this video-tape modelling programme is effective in changing children's behaviour using both individual and group-based methods. The effectiveness of this programme is now being evaluated in the UK context, at the Maudsley Hospital, London.

Further comparison between studies was difficult due to the fact that while many of the programmes reviewed, might broadly be referred to as 'behavioural', there was nevertheless, considerable variety in the structure and process of most programmes. Thus, while many programmes relied solely on the teaching of behavioural skills, a small number combined the teaching of basic behavioural skills with problem-solving or child-management skills. Furthermore, a variety of techniques were used to teach these programmes, ranging from verbal instruction supplemented by the use of manuals and pamphlets, to the use of more technologically advanced methods such as Webster-Stratton's video-tape modelling.

Who Benefits from Parent-training Programmes?

While the results of this review show that parent-training programmes are remarkably effective in improving behaviour problems in young children, some caution should, nevertheless, be exercised before these findings are generalised to other parents in the population. Very little information was provided in a number of studies regarding the personal or socio-demographic characteristics of participating parents, and the results of many studies were based on the findings from parents who had volunteered to take part in the study. However, four studies used samples of children with clinically defined behaviour problems (Webster-Stratton, 1984, 1990b; Webster-Stratton et al., 1988, 1989) and a further three studies were based on samples which were described as being at least one standard deviation above the mean for age and sex on a standardised behaviour outcome measure (Bernal et al., 1980; Sheeber and Johnson, 1994; Cunningham et al., 1995). In addition, a number of studies involved samples comprised of referred families from high-risk backgrounds – single parents in receipt of social security benefit (Scott and Stradling, 1987), mothers reporting depression and spouse/childhood abuse, alcoholism and drug abuse, and parents with prior involvement with the child protective services (Webster-Stratton, 1984, 1990b; Webster-Stratton et al., 1988, 1989).

The dropout rate in one of these studies was as high as 41 per cent (Scott and Straddling, 1987), although the average dropout rate conformed to the more usual level of about 28 per cent (Forehand et al., 1983). Only one study provided data on the parents who dropped out of the programme and this revealed no significant differences between 'completers' and 'dropouts' in terms of the number of children at home, parental education, perceived social support, maternal depression, family functioning or behaviour problems at home (Cunningham, Bremner and Boyle, 1995). However, other research has shown that premature termination from treatment among families with children referred for antisocial behaviour is associated with more severe conduct disorder symptoms and more delinquent behaviours; mothers reporting greater stress from their relations with the child, their own role functioning, and life events; and families being at greater socioeconomic disadvantage (Kazdin, 1990). Other studies have also identified individuals more likely to drop out as including those from a lower social class (McMahon et al., 1981; Strain et al., 1981; Holden et al., 1990) or an ethnic minority, and those children with a greater number of presenting problems (Holden et al., 1990).

In addition, there are many different paths into conduct disorder – physical and sexual abuse, fostering and adoption, learning disabilities and pervasive developmental disorder. There appears to be very little evidence at the present time of the effectiveness of parent-training programmes with these subgroups of children.

Finally, we still do not know whether particular types of programmes are more suited to particular groups of parents than others. The recruitment of parents to programmes at the present time reflects the assumption that all parents can benefit from whichever programme is on offer, with the result that parents who drop out may be blamed for their failure to complete the programme. The identification of particular personal and socio-demographic characteristics of parents who drop out of parenting programmes may help to identify groups of individuals who are not benefiting from particular programmes, but this will not resolve problems arising from the way in which parents are currently recruited to programmes, irrespective of individual differences and preferences.

Directions for Future Research

This systematic review of the effectiveness of parent-training programmes has highlighted the need for more research in a number of areas. Parent-training programmes appear to be remarkably effective in producing change in children's behaviour compared with no-treatment or waiting-list control groups, and there is a broad literature pointing to the effectiveness of behavioural interventions more generally. However, we still know very little about many elements of the *process* known as 'parent-training', and the role that each of the component parts plays in producing improvements in child and parental well-being.

There is also a need for more research on the relationship type programmes. This would involve some evaluation of the effectiveness of more unstructured or open type training formats which offer participating parents the opportunity to explore their personal feelings about parenting, their own experiences of being parented, and the nature of the relationships within their own families, in terms of the effects of such factors on their current parenting practices. Future research should also address the importance of skilled leadership or facilitation with regard to outcomes such as parent recruitment and retention.

Further research is needed on the generalisability of parent-training programmes with particular attention to children's behaviour in school as well as at home. The combination of information from different sources is also necessary, reflecting the fact that the 'accurate assessment of children's functioning must take account of variations in their behaviour across situations and interaction partners' (Achenbach, 1985 in Verhulst and Koot, 1992, p. 75). Multiple measures are required that 'encompass multiple methods of assessment i.e. paper and pencil tests and direct observations, multiple sources of information i.e. child, parent and teacher, and child performance in multiple settings i.e. home, school and the community' (Kazdin, 1993, p. 294).

The use of other clinically relevant outcome measures is also needed, including measures of cost-effectiveness. Evidence concerning the cost-effectiveness of group-based parent training programmes compared with individual clinic-based programmes is still limited to a small number of studies. In addition, the impact of treatment might be assessed using broader social outcomes such as mental health and medical services utilisation, hospitalisation, and incarceration, use of illegal substances and conviction rates (ibid.). Measures of quality of life would also add an important domain to treatment evaluation for children and adolescents (ibid.).

This review focused explicitly on child behaviour outcome measures, which is only a very small, albeit important part of the story about the effectiveness of parent-training programmes. Other reviews are now needed to collate evidence from rigorous studies concerning the effectiveness of parent-training programmes in improving other aspects of child and parental well-being. For example, is there sufficient rigorous evidence to show that parent-training programmes produce improvements in maternal well-being, and what is the relationship between such improvements and subsequent changes in children's functioning? Reviews are also now needed of the effectiveness of parent-training programmes for children aged 0–3 years and indeed, for adolescents.

Finally, the public health benefit of parent-training programmes has received very little attention to date, or their use as primary preventative health measures. Evaluation is now needed of the extent to which parent-training programmes are useful in lowering the population mean on child behaviour outcome measures.

Where to Now?

Offord (1994) suggests that:

> [t]here is now a need to conceptualise the primary and secondary prevention of behaviour problems as an ongoing process that begins in early childhood and continues throughout adolescence and beyond. Time-limited interventions offered at one point in a child's life, and to just a few children, are unlikely to produce long-term changes in present levels of antisocial behaviour and conduct disorder, or to prevent subsequent behaviour problems. (Offord and Bennett, 1994, p. 1076)

This quotation points to the need for more systematic and comprehensive approaches to the issue of behaviour problems. This is necessary for a number of reasons. First, evidence now shows the importance of the 'cumulative' effect of 'multiple risk factors' in the development of childhood

⋋ psychopathology. The multiplicative or synergistic relationship between risk factors was demonstrated by Rutter in his 1979 Isle of Wight Study (Rutter, 1977) in which he identified six family variables which were significantly associated with psychiatric disorder in his study children. Rutter showed that children with only one of these risk factors were actually at no more risk of disorder than children with no risk factors. However, children with two risk factors were found to be as many as four times as likely to develop disorders as those with one or no risk factors (Yoshikawa, 1994). With the further accumulation of more risk factors, the likelihood of disorder climbed several times further still. This suggests that risk factors interact, or as Rutter refers to the process, 'potentiate' each other, and as such, it may be that programmes targeting just one risk factor, are insufficient to either prevent or reduce current levels of antisocial behaviour and conduct problems (ibid.).

In addition to the cumulative and synergistic relationship between risk factors, there is now evidence to suggest that some of the most important risks for behaviour problems are mediated via two primary pathways (ibid.). The first pathway indicates that the principle effects of early risks for behaviour problems are mediated via processes that are located within the family context. The second pathway points to the principle effects of early risks being mediated via processes which are located to a greater extent within the school i.e. the child's cognitive development and school achievement. The implications of a model with two mediating pathways of this nature are the need for programmes which address the problems associated with each independent pathway – the home and the school – and which transcend many of the traditional divides in terms of which care is usually provided i.e. health, education and social services.

One such intervention is the home-school linked parent-training programme. This provides a comprehensive model of parent-training which straddles both the family and child-centred domains, and which addresses risks arising from both primary mediating pathways. The curriculum content of home-school linked parent-training programmes, which involves the teaching of values and emotional literacy in schools, is primarily an educational activity, while the parallel programme for parents is a preventative child-welfare and parent-support programme with implications for both the social and health services. This is one of a number of new approaches to parent education which links work carried out in the schools with work carried out with parents (Audit Commission, 1994).

The limited evidence available to date on home-school linked programmes, suggests significant advances on the type of basic parent-training programme directed at parents alone, which formed the basis of the systematic review discussed above. Webster-Stratton and Hammond's (1997) recent study shows that a programme directed at both parents and children can produce more significant changes in children's behaviour at one-year follow-up, than either the parent or child-centred programme alone.

An evaluation of a home-school linked programme is now being conducted in the UK. The Family Links Nurturing Programme is based on the Nurturing Programme developed and evaluated by Dr Stephen Bavolek for use in the treatment and prevention of child abuse and neglect (Bavolek, 1986). In the USA and Mexico, where this programme was developed, about two million families have taken part in the Family Programmes since 1981. A schools programme began in the USA in the early 1990s and approximately 700 schools in the USA are now using this programme. In the UK, the programme was originally run by the Family Nurturing Network. This charity began in 1993 and has since delivered 15 programmes in Oxford City and County to over 150 parents and 450 children. Family Links was established as a separate charity in 1997 to develop this fast-growing and innovative method of disseminating the Nurturing Programme in schools. In two years, this method of delivering the programme has reached over 3,000 children, over 162 parents, and 225 teachers (plus school support staff).

The theoretical basis of the Family Links Nurturing Programme is eclectic, using cognitive (knowledge-based) and affective (feelings-based) activities to promote positive relationships between parents and children, develop self-awareness and self-esteem, and to teach children values (this aspect of the programme is linked into the School Curriculum and Assessment Authority (SCAA) teaching of Values in Education and the Community). The programme is run for up to two hours each week with all four to seven-year-old children in the school, every term. A similar programme consisting of ten two-hour sessions, conducted over the course of ten weeks, is offered to all parents. The content of the two programmes parallel one another so that parents, children and teachers develop a common language and consistent approach with regard to discipline, behaviour, and feelings. Figure 6.2 shows the content of the programme for children, which has become known as the children's 'Special Time'. Figure 6.3 shows the content of the parent programme, which includes many similar sessions to the children's programme.

One of the aims of the home-school linked programme is the promotion of positive relationships between parents and children, and an improvement in the links between the home and school. One of the more specific aims for children is the development of emotional literacy and health, in order to

- *The use of boundaries and rules*
- *The use of praise and criticism*
- *Personal power and taking responsibility*
- *Anger and how to deal with it*
- *Choices and consequences*
- *Hurting touch and gentle touch*
- *Telling others/keeping secrets*
- *Praising ourselves and celebrating differences*

Figure 6.2　Content of the Nurturing Programme for children – 'Special Time'

- *The use of positive discipline, praise and time out*
- *The need for boundaries and family rules; rewards and penalties*
- *The use of personal power and choices and consequences*
- *Hurting touch and wounding words, handling anger, and the use of I and You statements*
- *Ages and stages in child development*
- *Helping children to say no and stay safe*
- *When to ignore and how to deal with troublesome feelings*
- *The use of problem solving and negotiating and how to guide children without criticising*
- *The use of negative and positive labels*

Figure 6.3　Content of the Nurturing Programme for parents

improve concentration and help children to achieve their full academic and psychosocial potential. The programme also aims to develop an increase in children's self-awareness and self-esteem, an increase in their communication and social skills, a reduction in levels of bullying and problem behaviour, and the development of positive value systems.

The specific aims for parents are an increase in their knowledge of behaviour management and age-appropriate developmental expectations, and an increase in knowledge concerning their own and their children's needs, and how to meet them. The programme aims to bridge the gap between school, home and the community. The long-term aims of the programme are a reduction in child abuse, truancy, antisocial behaviour, juvenile crime, and the breakdown of family life.

Schools which have received this programme to date, report better discipline, more cooperation, increased concentration in class, and kinder behaviour in the playground, with peers being less rejecting of children with problems. The programme also aims to provide benefits in terms of the teacher/child relationship and thereby, to improve children's learning. The whole-school approach aims to increase consistency and teamwork within the school, and to improve morale amongst the staff. The programme also has potential benefits in terms of the relationship between teachers and parents. The Ofsted report of one local school (1997) stated that 'The Nurturing Programme's principles of praise and encouragement underpin teaching and successfully raise confidence and self-esteem in pupils', and that this 'helps children to develop positive attitudes to learning and behaviour'. Anecdotal reports from parents who have received the programme to date, suggest that increases in levels of parental confidence result in parents replacing strategies such as smacking and shouting, with the development and use of clear boundaries, praise and consistency. An initial evaluation reported significant changes in attitudes amongst those children who had taken part in the programme (Layton, 1996).

This home-school linked programme represents a population-based, preventative approach to parent-training. In contrast with high-risk programmes, it aims to reduce the *population* mean on child behaviour outcome measures, and thereby improve the behaviour of *all* children, irrespective of the severity of their problems on behaviour outcome measures (see chapter 1). This is consistent with the fact that behavioural attributes as measured by child behaviour inventories, are 'normally distributed' with no clear cutoff point between normal and abnormal populations. Children who are well below the clinical cutoff point used on such measures, very often display a range of behaviour problems, which may benefit from an intervention directed at all children in school. If, as has been suggested by a number of epidemiologists, conduct and behaviour problems are 'secondary phenomena whose underlying explanation must be sought among the population as a whole' (Rose and Day, 1990, p. 1034), then it seems likely that a population approach will be necessary to reduce the current prevalence of these problems.

Conclusion

Behaviour problems in children are now an important social, educational and health issue. The prevalence of this problem, its stability over time, its poor prognosis, the need for an early intervention and the costs to both the individual and society which were referred to at the beginning of this chapter, all point to the need for early effective interventions.

The results of a recently conducted systematic review show beyond doubt that parent-training programmes are effective in improving behaviour problems in young children. Future interventions such as home-school linked programmes, must tackle a range of risk factors, and may well need to transcend the traditional divides in terms of which many interventions are currently provided i.e. education, health and social services. Home-school linked parent-training programmes offer a number of important advances on programmes directed at parents alone, and may well represent the way forward for parent-training.

References

Achenbach, T.M. (1985), *Assessment and Taxonomy of Child and Adolescent Psychopathology*, Beverly Hills, Ca., Sage.

Audit Commission (1994), London, *Seen but not Heard*, HMSO.

Barlow, J. (1997), *Systematic Review of the Effectiveness of Parent-Training Programmes in Improving the Behaviour of 3–7 Year Old Children*, Oxford, Health Services Research Unit.

Bavolek, S.S. (1996), *Research and Validation Report of the Nurturing Programs. Effective Family-Based Approaches to: Treating and Preventing Child Abuse and Neglect*, Family Development Resources Inc, USA.

Bernal, M.E., Klinnert, M.D. and Schultz, L.A. (1980), 'Outcome evaluation of behavioral parent-training and client-centered parent counseling for children with conduct-problems', *Journal of Applied Behavior Analysis*, 13 (4), pp. 677–91.

Bone, M. and Meltzer, H. (1989), *The prevalence of disability among children, OPCS Surveys of disability in Great Britain*, London, Report 3, HMSO.

Campbell, S.B. (1995), 'Behavior Problems in Preschool children: A Review of Recent Research', *Journal of Child Psychology and Psychiatry*, 36 (1), pp. 113–49.

Champion, L.A., Goodall, G. and Rutter, M. (1995), 'Behaviour problems in childhood and stressors in early adult life: 1. A 20 year follow-up of London school children', *Psychological Medicine*, 25 (2), pp. 231–46.

Cunningham, C.E., Bremner, R. and Boyle, M. (1995), 'Large group community-based parenting programs for families of preschoolers at risk for disruptive behaviour disorders: Utilisation, cost-effectiveness, and outcome', *Journal of Child Psychology and Psychiatry and Allied Disciplines*, 36 (7), pp. 1141–59.

Daly, R.M., Holland, C.J., Forrest, P.A. and Fellbaum, G.A. (1985), 'Temporal generalization of treatment effects over a 3-year period for a parent-training programme – directive parental counseling (dpc)', *Canadian Journal of Behavioural Sciences-Revue*, 17, pp. 370–88.

Eron, L.D. and Huesmann, L.R. (1990), 'The stability of aggressive behavior – even into the third generation' in Lewis, M. and Miller, S.M. (eds), *Handbook of Developmental Psychopathology*, New York, Plenum Press.

Farrington, D.P. (1991), 'Childhood aggression and adult violence: Early precursors and later life outcomes' in Peper, D.J. and Rubin, K.H. (eds), *The development and treatment of childhood aggression*, Hillsdale, N.J., Lawrence Erlbaum.

Firestone, P., Kelly, M.J. and Fike, S. (1980), 'Are fathers necessary in parent-training groups?', *Journal of Clinical Child Psychology*, 9 (1), pp. 44–7.

Forehand, R., Middlebrook, J., Rogers, T. and Steffe, M. (1983), 'Dropping out of parent-training', *Behaviour Research and Therapy*, 21 (6), pp. 663–8.

Frazier, F. and Matthes, W.A. (1975), 'Parent education: A comparison of Adlerian and behavioral approaches', *Elementary School Guidance and Counselin,g* 10, pp. 31–8.

Griest, D.L. and Wells, K.C. (1983), 'Behavioral family therapy with conduct disorders in children', *Behavior Therapy*, Vol. 14 (1), pp. 37–53.

Holden, G.W., Lavigne, V.V. and Cameron, A.M. (1990), 'Probing the Continuum of Effectiveness in Parent Training: Characteristics of Parents and Preschoolers', *Journal of Clinical Child Psychology*, 19 (1), pp. 2–8.

Kazdin, A.E. (1990), 'Premature Termination from Treatment among Children referred for Antisocial Behaviour', *Journal of Child Psychology and Psychiatry*, 31 (3), pp. 415–25.

Kazdin, A.E. (1993), 'Treatment of conduct disorder: Progress and directions in Psychotherapy research', *Development and Psychopathology*, 5, pp. 277–310.

Kazdin, A.E. (1996), *Conduct Disorders in Childhood and Adolescence*, Beverly Hills, Ca., Sage Publications.

Kazdin, A.E., Siegel, T. and Bass, D. (1992), 'Cognitive problem-solving skills training and parent management training in the treatment of antisocial behaviour in children', *Journal of Consulting and Clinical Psychology*, 60, pp. 733–47.

Layton, M. (1996), 'An Evaluation of the Effectiveness of the School and Family Links Programme', MA dissertation, Brookes University, Oxford.

Loeber, R. and Dishion, T.J. (1983), 'Early predictors of male delinquency: A review'm *Psychological Bulletin*, 94, pp. 68–99.

Loeber, R. and Hay, D. (1997), 'Key issues in the development of aggression and violence from childhood to early adulthood', *Annual Review of Psychology*, 48, pp. 371–410.

McCord, W., McCord, J. and Howard, A. (1963), 'Familial correlates of aggression in nondelinquent male children', *Journal of Abnormal and Social Psychology*, 62, pp. 72–93.

McMahon, R.J., Forehand, R., Griest, D.L.L. and Wells, K.C. (1981), 'Who drops out of treatment during parent behavior training', *Behavioral Counseling Quarterly*, 1, pp. 79–85.

Moffit, T.E., Caspi, A., Dickson, N., Silva, P. et al. (1996), 'Childhood-onset versus adolescent-onset antisocial conduct problems in males: Natural history from ages 3 to 18 years', *Development and Psychopathology*, 8 (2), pp. 399–424.

NHS Centre for Reviews and Dissemination (1997), *Effective Health Care. Mental Health Promotion in High Risk Groups*, Vol. 3, No. 3, York University.

Offord, D.R., Alder, R.J., and Boyle, M.H. (1986), 'Prevalence and sociodemographic correlates of conduct disorder. Special Issue: Psychiatric epidemiology', *American Journal of Social Psychiatry*, 6 (4), pp. 272–78.

Offord, M.D. and Bennett, K.J. (1994), 'Conduct disorder: Long-Term Outcomes and Intervention Effectiveness', *Journal of the American Academy of Child and Adolescent Psychiatry*, 33 (8), pp. 1069–78.

Patterson, G.R. (1986), 'Performance Models for Antisocial Boys', *American Psychologist*, 41, pp. 432–44.

Patterson, G.R., DeBaryshe, D. and Ramsey, E. (1989), 'A Developmental Perspective on Antisocial Behavior', *American Psychologist*, 44 (2), pp. 329–35.

Patterson, G.R., Dishion, T.J. and Chamberlain, P. (1993), 'Outcomes and Methodological Issues Relating to Treatment of Antisocial children' in Giles, T.R. (ed.), *Handbook of Effective Psychotherapy*, New York, Plenum Press.

Pepler, D.J. and Rubin, K.H. (eds) (1991), *The development and Treatment of childhood aggression*, Hillsdale, N.J., Erlbaum.

Pinsker, M., and Geoffroy, K. (1981), 'A Comparison of Parent-Effectiveness Training and Behavior-Modification Parent-Training', *Family Relations*, 30 (1), pp 61–8.

Quinton, D., Rutter, M. and Gulliver, L. (1990), 'Continuities in psychiatric disorders from childhood to adulthood in the children of psychiatric patients' in Robins, L.N. and Rutter, M. (eds), *Straight and devious pathways from childhood to adulthood*, Cambridge, Cambridge University Press.

Robins, L.N. (1981), 'Epidemiological approaches to natural history research: Antisocial disorders in children', *Journal of the American Academy of Child Psychiatry*, 20, pp. 566–680.

Robins, L.N. (1991), 'Conduct Disorder',*Journal of Child Psychology and Psychiatry*, 32 (1), pp. 193–212.

Robins, L.N. and Rutter, M. (eds) (1990), *Straight and devious pathways from childhood to adulthood*, Cambridge, Cambridge University Press.

Rose, G. and Day, S. (1990), 'The population mean predicts the number of deviant individuals', *British Medical Journal*, 301, pp. 1031–4.

Rutter, M. et al. (1977), 'Isle of Wight Studies 1964–1974', *Annual Programme in Child Psychiatry and Child Development*, pp. 359–92.

Rutter, M. (1996), 'Connections between child and adult psychopathology', *European Child and Adolescent Psychiatry*, 5 (Suppl. 1), pp. 4–7.

Scott, M.J. and Stradling, S.G. (1987), 'Evaluation of a group programme for parents of problem children', *Behavioural Psychotherapy*, 15, pp. 224–39.

Sheeber, L.B. and Johnson, J.H. (1994), 'Evaluation of a Temperament-Focused, Parent-Training Program', *Journal of Clinical Child Psychology*, 23 (3), pp. 249–59.

Smith, C. (1996), *Developing Parenting Programmes*, NCB.

Spaccarelli, S., Cotler, S. and Penman, D. (1992), 'Problem-solving skills training as a supplement to behavioural parent-training', *Cognitive Therapy and Research*, 16, pp. 1–18.

Strain, P.S., Young, C.C. and Horowitz, J. (1981), 'Generalised behavior change during oppositional child training', *Behavior Modification*, 5, pp. 15–26.

Stewart, M.A. (1985), 'Aggressive conduct disorder: A brief review. Sixth Biennial Meeting of the International society for Research on Aggression', *Aggressive Behavior*, 11 (4), pp. 323–31.

Verhulst, F.C. and Koot, H.M. (1992), *Child Psychiatric Epidemiology: Concepts, Methods, and Findings*, Sage Publications.

Webster-Stratton, C. (1984), 'Randomised trial of two parent-training programs for families with conduct-disordered children', *Journal of Consulting and Clinical Psychology*, 52 (4), pp. 666–78.

Webster-Stratton, C. (1989), 'Systematic comparison of consumer satisfaction of 3 cost-effective parent-training programs for conduct-problem children', *Behavior Therapy*, 20, pp. 103–15.

Webster-Stratton, C. (1990a), 'Enhancing the effectiveness of self-administered videotape parent-training for families with conduct-problem children', *Journal of Abnormal Child Psychology*, 18, pp. 479–92.

Webster-Stratton, C. (1990b), 'Long-Term Follow-Up of Families with Young Conduct-Problem Children: From Pre-school to Grade School', *Journal of Clinical Child Psychology*, 19 (2), 144–9.

Webster-Stratton, C. (1994), 'Advancing videotape parent-training: A comparison study', *Journal of Consulting and Clinical Psychology*, 62 (3), pp. 583–93.

Webster-Stratton, C., Kolpacoff, M. and Hollinsworth, T. (1988), 'Self-administered videotape therapy for families with conduct-problem children: Comparison with two cost-effective treatments and a control group', *Journal of Consulting and Clinical Psychology*, 56 (4), pp. 558–66.

Webster-Stratton, C., Hollinsworth T. and Kolpacoff, M. (1989), 'The long-term effectiveness and clinical significance of three cost-effective training programs for families with conduct-problem children', *Journal of Consulting and Clinical Psychology*, 57 (4), pp. 550–3.

Webster-Stratton, C. and Hammond, M. (1990), 'Predictors of treatment outcome in parent-training for families with conduct-problem children', *Behavior Therapy*, 21, pp. 319–37.

Webster-Stratton, C. and Hammond, M. (1997), 'Treating Children With Early-Onset Conduct Problems: A comparison of Child and Parent Training Interventions', *Journal of Consulting and Clinical Psychology*, 65 (1), pp. 93–109.

Yoshikawa, H. (1994), 'Prevention as Cumulative Protection: Effects of Early Family Support and Education on Chronic Delinquency and its Risks', *Psychological Bulletin*, 15 (1), pp. 28–54.

7 Parents and the Community: Parents' Views and Mapping Need

TERESA SMITH

Summary

- *This chapter discusses the role of family centres in supporting parents in disadvantaged communities and demonstrates how those communities that may need extra support can be identified. Since children living in such communities may be at high risk of emotional and behavioural difficulties, this is a valuable approach.*
- *Three studies are reported – one on family centres and two on mapping needs and services.*
- *The focus is not solely on the findings of the research. The aim is also to illustrate some of the problems with the concepts and methods involved.*
- *The chapter draws on a study carried out between 1988 and 1992 of six family centres run by The Children's Society (Smith, 1996), and recent work on mapping needs and services for children and families in a number of local authorities (Noble and Smith, 1994; Platt and Smith, 1998).*

Family Centre Research – a Sketch

Do family centres 'work'? Are they effective? Family centres were described as 'official' for the first time in the Children Act 1989 as part of 'family support' or 'preventive' services, but there is little agreement on definition or type, objectives and clientele. Yet, interest in the effectiveness of family centres continues to grow.

One reason is that they are perceived as an important vehicle for preventive or community-based services for both parents and children in severely disadvantaged neighbourhoods (Sinclair, Hearn and Pugh, 1997; Lloyd, 1997). Centres potentially provide a very flexible range of services for both children and parents. They may have started out as nursery classes, day nurseries, playgroups, residential children's homes, or community centres. They offer, in different combinations, educational programmes for children, adult

110

education for parents, a drop-in for parents to see the local social worker or health visitor, day care for preschool children, a base for the local playgroup, a parent and toddler group, after school clubs or youth groups, credit unions, food cooperatives, employment training and opportunities, and practical resources such as a toy library, buggies and stair gates on loan, and a telephone and washing machine. They can be very flexible – ranging from 'open access' services or facilities for all local parents and their children who wish to come, to focused work with highly stressed families, who may have a child on the child protection register, and are referred by social workers. Principles of accessibility, flexibility, non-stigma, and participation are played out in different ways in different types of centre. Current government interest in 'centres of excellence' – multi-agency early years centres (Makins, 1997; Whalley, 1994) – will keep this combination high on both policy and research agendas.

Underpinning this interest in prevention is the current concern with costing services (Holtermann, 1997; Hallam and Knapp, 1997). Here a hopeful development is the inclusion of family centres in the longitudinal study of the effectiveness of different preschool programmes funded by the Department of Education and Employment (Sylva, see chapter 5). Yet the question of who uses services, and who does not, for whatever reason, remains crucial to the evaluation of effectiveness.

So far, however, research on effectiveness or outcomes in family centre work is very limited. Family centres and family projects hardly feature (although family education or family training programmes do appear) in overviews of 'what works in the early years' (Macdonald and Roberts, 1995). Why should this be so?

One explanation lies in the diversity of work and objectives sailing under the 'family centre' flag. Another lies in the ambiguity of the word '*effective*'. We should ask '*effective at what for whom*?' A distinction has to be drawn between the *nature* of the programme (the service provided), *process* (how is it made accessible and for whom), and *product* (effective outcomes). Services may be 'effective' to the extent that they reach people in the 'target group' (for example, the percentage of the preschool age group catered for in the United Kingdom in comparison with our European partners) or in relation to changing the behaviour of a 'target group' (for example, parents helping their children to read, or children's long term educational achievement). A third problem is the difficulty of securing a good research design. Before researchers can embark on experimental or comparative work on outcomes (whether randomised control trials, matched controls design or action-research;

experimental or 'post hoc') they have to be confident about the stability of the programme or the curriculum they propose to investigate, and about the 'clientele'. But frequently there can be no certainty about either. Before research on the effectiveness of a service can be undertaken, we have to establish: 1) what is the 'content' or 'curriculum' or 'programme' of the service; 2) who uses, or (as important) does not use, the service and why; 3) the location of services; and 4) the relationship between location, take up, and need. Studies of this kind provide us with different information from outcome studies – and require different methods – but are equally relevant for judging the effectiveness of services.

When work on the family centre study reported in this chapter (Smith, 1996) was under way in the late 1980s and early 1990s, there was very little research on family centres – although there were some good social policy critiques (e.g. Cannan, 1992), and some good typologies of family centres and preventive work which broke down examples into 'client-focused', 'neighbourhood based', and 'community development' types (De'Ath, 1988; Gibbons, 1990; Holman, 1988). A number of descriptive case studies provided good accounts of how centres were established, the types of neighbourhoods they served, the activities they ran (for example, Daines, Lyon and Parsloe, 1990; Ferri and Saunders, 1991; Higginson, 1990; MacFarlane, 1989; Phelan, 1983; Shinman 1986, 1988). Some studies throw light on important questions such as flexible staff roles (Fogell, 1986) or concepts such as 'accessibility' (Statham, 1994). A handful have been more rigorous in observing activities or adult-child interactions or adult behaviour, or analysing users' views (Leeming, 1985; Calam and Franchi, 1987; Cigno, 1988). Very few have compared different types of centre; Ferri et al. (1981) is still the best example here, even if the focus was on 'combined centres' integrating childcare and education, rather than family centres as such. Most studies are small scale (Holman, 1992), perhaps reflecting the variety of provision.

Focusing on Process

Research is often presented as a coherent and logical progression. It starts by framing a research question, defining a hypothesis, working out a research design, locating 'target' and 'control groups', moves on to administering questionnaires, conducting observations and carrying out interviews, and ends with analysing the data, writing up the results and discussing their implications for policy and practice. What most people wish to know is the findings: for example, the claim that the High/Scope preschool programme from Ypsilanti, Michigan (Schweinhart et al., 1993) is cost effective to the tune of $1:7 in producing literate, high achieving, employable adults who are more likely to pay their taxes and keep out of trouble with the law, than those who did not benefit from the programme.

From another perspective, however, evaluation is about working backwards. Research is usually messy, a forwards and backwards business, which involves negotiating access to data or to people willing to be interviewed or observed, and thinking and rethinking different ways of acquiring and analysing information. And it almost always involves rethinking a first set of questions or assumptions, which turn out to be either unrealistic or poorly articulated.

Thus, for example, in the family centre study the apparently simple question 'are family centres *effective*?' had to be broken down into prior questions such as 'what do family centres *do*?' This in turn had to be rephrased into 'what do the users/ staff/ funders think they are doing?' and indeed 'what do the users/ staff/ funders think they *should be* doing?' as well as 'what do researchers observe family centres (that is, staff and users) doing?' This 'unpacking' of the original question took us down the 'who did what?' route. Another route unpacked 'effectiveness', which may mean one set (or many sets) of things for users (who could be asked and/or observed) and another for people who did not use the centre or who used it for a time and then stopped. A third route asked 'what does effectiveness mean in the first place?' and considered how it might be measured or assessed.

The second example from the family centre study illustrates some of the problems of method. 'Effectiveness' requires either a 'before and after' design (checking the initial position and then testing out whether a new programme or intervention or treatment brought about any change in that position) or a comparative design (checking that a number of locations or sites were similar and then testing out the impact of an intervention). The funders of the study asked for a comparative design. But it would be difficult to achieve a comparative sample of family centres, given the variation in styles and objectives. And negotiations in the real world demonstrate that external researchers may be perceived as threatening, rather than a resource, when funding itself is under threat. 'Getting the visa' (Bruner, 1980) is a real and sensitive part of the research agenda.

The study created a sample of users, rather than centres, by pooling the users of the six centres in the analysis. This, however, produced further problems. How to create a user sample? All methods had their drawbacks.

Talking to groups in the centres might omit individual users; sampling the register was impossible when many groups and activities kept no register; asking for volunteers would advantage the confident and might introduce staff bias. The method finally selected – 'sitting on the door' and sampling a week's users in each centre – avoided these problems. But it produced a sample that probably gave too much weight to work done in the project's own building and too little weight to work done elsewhere in the neighbourhood or with other organisations. The sample probably over-represented activities with large numbers of users, and under-represented activities that had few users but carried an intense workload.

'Getting the visa' does not simply represent a difficulty with method. It is a far more fundamental problem about the nature of research. Research, even if it is justified by the importance of the end in view, and governed by rules of ethical behaviour, confidentiality and consent, is often seen as something external, carried out by one set of people to or about other people. The family centre study could not be described as participatory research, or even a partnership, although considerable effort was put into meeting the funders' and the centres' views as to the content and the organisation of the study. This was not 'research from the underside' (Holman, 1986). Perhaps it should have been: some centres clearly wanted help in designing and carrying out their own research – rather than being part of an external researcher's study – but this might have become more a piece of consultancy than a comparative enquiry. The process and the conclusions did, however, prompt a fresh look at both objectives and styles of work in the family projects. As one of The Children's Society officers commented, 'research is a change agent rather than a judgment'.

The Family Centre Study – Users' Views on Their Needs and Projects' Effectiveness

It changed my life. It helped me to be more patient with my children, and to be more assertive ...

There's nothing like that round here, so it's made a big difference. There's no other meeting place for mothers and children.

It's not only me that's got little monsters! Everybody's got little monsters. I think if you see lots of other children as well, you can understand your own better. They've all got their naughty points and their good points. It's not just your children that are little angels or little demons. I think it helps get things in perspective.

It's got him used to being with other children and he's learnt that he's got to share things ... He did go through a stage of clinging to me all the time, but now he's good, he'll stay with anyone ... His speech has changed; he was very slow at talking, because he had problems with his ears; but listening to the other children has helped him to catch up very quickly.

We wouldn't have had a holiday this year except for the women's group.

It's opened up new ideas for myself (Smith, 1996).

These quotations come from the 125 parents (almost all of them mothers) interviewed between 1988 and 1992 in six family projects run by The Children's Society. The research set out, first, to draw an accurate picture – largely through the eyes of the users – of work done with children under five and their families who made use of family centres or family projects, and secondly, to explore what was meant by 'effectiveness' and 'need', again through users' eyes. We investigated mothers' views on bringing up young children in the six areas, the support they needed, their reasons for using the centres, and their views on the aims and impact of the projects as well as the benefit for their children and themselves. We also interviewed staff, and spent time observing in the projects. One method of assessing the effectiveness of a service is to ask the users. However, this study did not claim to describe or evaluate the effectiveness of family centres in general (compared, say, with playgroups, day nurseries or nursery classes), or even the whole of these six centres' work. It represents one perspective.

The six centres were heavily used – nine in ten mothers in the survey came once a week or more. The centres depended on local networks for publicity (nearly half the users had heard of the centres from friends or relatives) as well as referral by professionals. They were meeting mothers' needs for social contact and sharing problems, helping the most vulnerable to gain confidence and learn to cope with their children, meeting children's needs for safe play space and social development, providing scarce resources in neighbourhoods with few facilities, and helping to create and sustain a sense of community.

The users themselves were a highly disadvantaged group. One hundred and twenty-two of the 125 were mothers. Twenty-six per cent were lone parents. Sixteen per cent had been referred to the centres by social workers.

One-fifth said they (or their partners) were unemployed; three-quarters (unemployed or low waged) reported financial difficulties. Forty-six percent reported health problems in the family, whether adult or child. Lone parents did particularly badly. They were much less likely than couple parents to have a wage coming in, and more likely to be in financial difficulties and to have children with health problems. Health problems and financial problems seemed to go together: 93 per cent of the lone parent households with health problems also had financial difficulties, compared with only 71 per cent of the couple households.

Table 7.1   A user profile: summary of the circumstances of respondents (n = 125)

	Total	Lone parent households	Couple households
Respondents	125	33 (26%)	92 (74%)
Number of children	281	71 (25%)	210 (75%)
Number of children aged <5	186	45 (24%)	141 (76%)
'Waged'	64%	26%	79%
'Always/sometimes in financial difficulties'	75%	88%	70%
Child health problems in household	35%	49%	30%

What did users think was important when bringing up young children? They talked about the importance of safe neighbourhoods, the difficulty of 'making ends meet', depression and health problems, difficulties of bringing up children on your own, the need for day care so people could go out to work, the importance of free time, their desire to learn about child development, the value of social contact, the importance of support networks – friends, family, baby sitting.

Ninety-four per cent said it was important to have 'somewhere to go for children to be with other children'. Ninety-four per cent said it was important to have 'other adults to talk to'. This was not simply a social occasion, but an opportunity to share experiences and problems, check out perceptions, consult other parents as well as staff, ask for or give advice, learn new ways of handling difficult behaviour, make friends, help to organise groups and activities.

Were the centres effective in meeting these needs? Eight out of ten mothers said their children had learned to mix and share, communicate, make friends, gain confidence and independence, and generally become more 'sociable'. Eight out of ten said they themselves had made friends. This was about sharing experience, reducing isolation, checking out problems, learning and sharing practical information, learning that it was 'normal' to have problems in bringing up young children, and building friendships that continued beyond the centre. Figure 7.1 presents the data on parents' views about their needs in bringing up young children and the centres' contribution to meeting these needs.

But we have to distinguish between different outcomes in different types of centre. Two of the six centres in this study could be described as 'open access', two as 'client referred', and two as 'neighbourhood centres'. Centres working with clients referred by social workers were more likely to be seen by the users to concentrate on 'checking on families with problems' and helping mothers to understand and cope with their children's behaviour. Users in the more neighbourhood-based projects were more likely to say they gained self-confidence, information and new skills, particularly in centres with an adult education approach. Table 7.2 presents the activities, approaches and outcomes in the six centres.

There was no doubt that users thought the centres were effective. Almost all of those interviewed said they would recommend the centre to someone else. Eighty-six per cent said the centre had made a difference to them, and 84 per cent to their children. But there were some serious discrepancies between what users looked for in the way of support and what they thought the centres were actually were providing. The biggest gaps here were in finance ('money to spend on the children') and day care ('nurseries for working parents'). This was not surprising given the levels of disadvantage and stress experienced by the mothers we interviewed.

Users' views in this study of family centres provide us with a clear picture of how they defined their own needs in bringing up young children and the extent to which they thought those needs were met by the projects. Clearly, there were differences in aims and ethos between projects of different types, reflected in different views from the users as to projects' effectiveness in meeting their needs. The clearest message from this study is the importance of listening to what users/clients have to say. Users' views constitute one direct outcome measure. But they are also a process measure, which might help us to understand other outcome measures. For instance, what users or clients have to say about their children might help us to understand our direct observations or ratings of children's behaviour.

We also constructed an independent measure of need. We compared the neighbourhoods served by the six centres on a range of indicators drawn from census data – lone parent status, children under five, young parents, size of family, employment and unemployment, housing tenure and overcrowding,

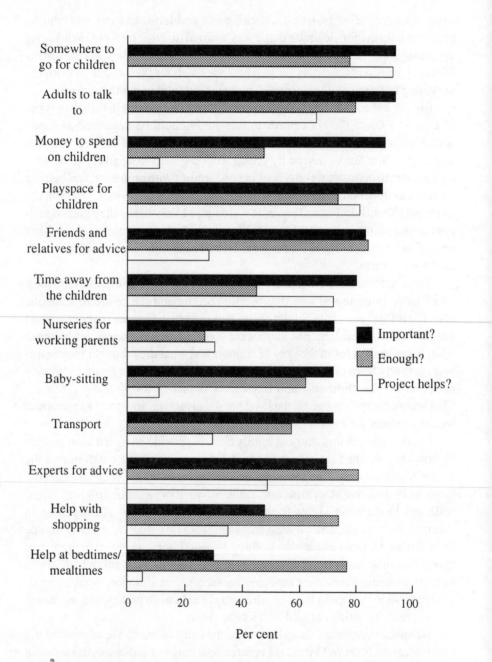

Figure 7.1 Parents' views on role of family project in bringing up children

Table 7.2   Activities, role of worker, objectives and impact by type of centre

	Type of project	Type of service	Type of activities	Role of workers	Objectives	Impact
Leicester	Open access	Mixed open and targeted	Counselling Drop-in Activity groups Playgroups Creches	Neighbourhood work	Community Learning new skills	Adult education Moving into jobs Friendship networks Confidence
Milton Keynes	'Client focused'	Direct services for targeted group	Social work Counselling Access Play sessions Budgeting Parent skills	Professional/ client	Statutory child protection and monitoring	Friendship networks Ideas for child play Understand children's behaviour
Newton-le Willows	Open access	Services for local community	Premises for local groups Liaison Helping local people identify issues	Community development Catalyst/enabler	Community Learning new skills	Friendship networks Ideas for child play Part of community
Shoebury-ness	Open access	Mixed open and targeted	Counselling Drop-in Activity groups Playgroups Creches	Neighbourhood work	Community Learning new skills	Friendship networks Part of the community/ Community supports
South Bank	Open access	Services for local community	Premises for local groups Liaison Helping local people identify issues	Community development Catalyst/enabler	Community Learning new skills	Gaining confidence Learning new skills Adult education Job entry
Telford	'Client focused'	Direct services for targeted group	Social work Counselling Access Play sessions Budgeting Parent skills	Professional/ client	Statutory child protection and monitoring	Friendship networks Time off from child Understand children's behaviour

car ownership (often used as a proxy variable for income), education and qualifications, and social class.

The picture produced was on the whole one of high levels of unemployment, high proportions of lone parents, little access to transport, large families, and large numbers of children aged under five. In short, mothers in these family centres were living in neighbourhoods of high unemployment, low income and family stress.

It was clear from this study that large numbers of children, in all kinds of families, were growing up in disadvantaged circumstances in these neighbourhoods – even if they were not 'referred' by social workers. It is often assumed that referred families are more disadvantaged than non-referred families, and services may be restricted to those who can satisfy this criterion. Indeed the level of disadvantage is often taken as a threshold criterion for referral to the social services department and thus access to services.

The family centre study raised serious questions about this assumption. In terms of disadvantage, there was not much difference between 'referred' and 'open access' families. Indeed, it was the disadvantage of lone parents, and their children, that stood out.

Mapping Need

'Mapping need' in the family centre study was done by analysing data from the most recent census (in this case, the 1991 census) for the wards approximating best to each centre's catchment area. This method allowed us to estimate the differences between the six areas on variables including numbers of children aged 0-4, lone parent families, unemployment, or social class composition. It also effectively demonstrated that 'disadvantage' or 'need' cannot be tapped by a single measure but is multidimensional. Some centres' catchment areas, for example, had lower levels of unemployment, but higher levels of households headed by young lone parents and by lone parents not in the labour market. But the measure remained a relatively crude estimate of need at a neighbourhood level. Census data rapidly becomes out of date. Wards contain smaller neighbourhoods with very different levels of need, which is masked by ward level data; and catchment areas may vary in size and density according to the type of service. Thus, it was clear that we had to develop techniques which could map *actual* catchment areas of services, and to acquire more 'dynamic' data sets, which would provide information at more frequent intervals and for smaller areas.

Two subsequent studies provide further examples of later work in progress. The first (Noble and Smith, 1994) was a pilot project exploring the use of Geographical Information Systems (GIS) and Housing Benefit/Council Tax (formerly Community Charge) Benefit data sets in the strategic planning of social services provision. The first stage was to extract information on variables such as family composition, the degree of dependency on state benefits, age and number of dependent children, and disability within the family from the HB/CTC data sets and map it to enumeration district (ED) level. This identified potential pockets of need in relation to services for children and families. The second stage was to map actual client data drawing on the postcoded social services client information system on current clients, reasons for referral, and resources allocated. We also mapped the actual location of provision such as day nurseries, family centres and registered childminders. We could then compare indicators of need with distribution of resources. These techniques allowed us to compare 'need' (for example, children under four living in families dependent on benefit) with 'supply' (for example, full time equivalent places in a range of day care services). We thus identified areas where 'need' was largely met, and, conversely, areas where there was considerable need not met by existing provision for further investigation by the local authority.

The second study (Platt and Smith, 1998) explored further the possibility of comparing need with resource allocation at neighbourhood level. We developed and mapped a number of different indicators of need at enumeration district (ED) level using Housing Benefit/ Council Tax Benefit data – for example, families in low waged employment drawing Family Credit, families dependent largely on state benefits drawing Housing Benefit and Council Tax Benefit, unemployed families drawing Income Support, family structure, family size, families with children under four, disability, working parents using childcare, and referrals to childcare by social workers and health visitors. We then superimposed location maps of different types of service. Finally we mapped actual catchment areas as identified by users of different services from the (postcoded) registers kept by the services in question. This study drew once again on Housing Benefit/Council Tax Benefit data sets. But this time we could make a more sophisticated comparison of user demand and catchment areas between 'referred clients' and 'working parents' using day care services through the use of postcoded data. The next stage will be to add in data from education, health and voluntary sector services.

These two studies provide us with a different outcome measure – a measure of 'service provision' (of different kinds) in relation to need (of different kinds) at the very local level.

The link between the two types of study reported is this. Mapping can give us trend data on concentrations of need, service provision and take-up and the match or mismatch between these three. But it cannot explain the variations in take-up: why potential users make use or fail to make use of services provided – the problem of 'accessibility'. This is what user studies can tell us.

Family Centres, Need and Users' Views

There is no doubt that family centres offering a range of services in disadvantaged neighbourhoods provide much needed resources to families with young children. A study of the effectiveness of providing such services would have to start by defining the type of centre and services offered. Phelan's comment (1983) is still valid:

> There is no quick definition of a family centre ... A centre is not just a building – it is a whole philosophy.(Phelan, 1983, p. ix)

Today we are clearer about the 'philosophy'. And we have clearer evidence as to need, take-up of services, and outcomes.

References

Bruner, J. (1980), *Under five in Britain*, London, Grant McIntyre.

Calam, R. and Franchi, C. (1987), *Child abuse and its consequences*, Cambridge, Cambridge University Press.

Cannan, C. (1992), *Changing families, changing welfare: family centres and the welfare state*, London, Harvester Wheatsheaf.

Cigno, K. (1988), 'Consumer views of a family centre drop-in', *British Journal of Social Work*, 18, pp. 361–75.

Daines, R., Lyon, K. and Parsloe, P. (1990), *Aiming for partnership*, Barkingside, Barnardo's.

De'Ath, E. (1988), *Focus on families: the family centre approach*, The Children's Society Briefing Paper, London, The Children's Society.

Ferri, E., Birchall, D., Gingell, V. and Gipps, C. (1981), *Combined nursery centres: a new approach to education and child care*, London, Macmillan/National Children's Bureau.

Ferri, E. and Saunders, A. (1991), *Parents, professionals and pre-school centres*, London, National Children's Bureau/Barnardo's.

Fogell, C. (1986), 'Dilemmas for staff working in informal settings', *British Journal of Social Work*, 16, Supplement.

Gibbons, J. with Thorpe, S and Wilkinson, P. (1990), *Family support and prevention: studies in local areas: purposes and organisation of preventive work with families*, London, HMSO.

Hallam, A. and Knapp, M. (1997), 'Costing services in family centres' in Netten, A. and Dennett, J. (eds), *Unit costs of health and social care*, Canterbury, PSSRU/University of Kent.

Higginson, J. (1990), 'Partners not problems: developing new roles for staff and consumers' in Darvill, G. and Smale, G. (eds), *Partners in empowerment: networks of innovation in social work*, London, National Children's Bureau.

Holman, B. (1986), 'Research from the underside', *British Journal of Social Work*, 16, Supplement.

Holman, B. (1988), *Putting families first: prevention and child care*, Basingstoke, Macmillan.

Holman, B. (1992), *Family centres*, Highlight No. 111, London, National Children's Bureau.

Holtermann, S. (1997), *The benefits and costs of preventive work with families*, paper presented at a Joseph Rowntree Foundation seminar on 25 November 1997.

Leeming, A. (1985), *Radford Family Centre – evaluation*, Department of Child Health, University of Nottingham, mimeo.

Lloyd, E. (1997), 'The role of the centre in family support' in Cannan, C. and Warren, C. (eds), *Social action with children and families: a community development approach to child and family welfare*, London, Routledge.

Macdonald, G. and Roberts, H. (1995), *What works in the early years? Effective interventions for children and their families in health, social welfare, education and child protection*, Barkingside, Barnardo's.

MacFarlane, W. (1989), 'Langlees Family Centre: a community social work approach to services for families' in Smale, G. and Bennett, W. (eds), *Pictures of practice: volume I: community social work in Scotland*, London, National Institute for Social Work.

Makins, V. (1997), *Not just a nursery ... multi-agency early years centres in action*, London, National Children's Bureau.

Noble, M. and Smith, T (1994), '"Children in need": using Geographical Information Systems to inform strategic planning for social service provision', *Children and Society*, 8 (4), pp. 360–76.

Phelan, J. (1983), *Family centres: a study*, London, Children's Society.

Platt, L. and Smith, T. (1998), *Mapping needs and services for under fours in Birmingham*, Social Disadvantage Research Group, Department of Applied Social Studies and Social Research, University of Oxford, mimeo.

Schweinhart, L. Barnes, H. and Weikart, D. (1993), *Significant benefits: the High/Scope Perry Pre-school study through age 27*, Michigan, High/Scope Press.

Shinman, S. (1986), *Soho Family Centre September 1985 – August 1986*, Brunel University, mimeo.

Shinman, S. (1988), *Two years on; Soho Family Centre September 1986–January 1988*, Brunel University, mimeo.

Sinclair, R. Hearn, B. and Pugh, G. (1997), *Preventive work with families: the role of mainstream services*, London, National Children's Bureau.

Smith, T. (1996), *Family centres and bringing up young children*, London, HMSO.

Statham, J. (1994), *Childcare in the community: a study of community based, open access services for young children in Save the Children Fund (UK) family centres*, London, Save the Children Fund.

Whalley, M. (1994), *Learning to be strong: setting up a neighbourhood service for under fives and their families*, Sevenoaks, Hodder and Stoughton.

PART IV
DISSEMINATION AND IMPLEMENTATION

8 Adopting and Implementing Empirically Supported Interventions: A Recipe for Success

CAROLYN WEBSTER-STRATTON AND TED K. TAYLOR

Summary

- *Over the past 30 years, hundreds of carefully controlled studies have demonstrated that there exist today a number of effective therapies and services for children and families which can reduce behaviour problems and delinquency, improve mental health, assist abusive parents to improve their child-rearing, and increase family functioning (Weisz and Weiss, 1993).*
- *Yet in spite of this evidence, few empirically supported interventions have been widely adopted in applied settings (Kazdin, Bass, Ayers, and Rodgers, 1991).*
- *In this paper, we describe an empirically supported parenting intervention developed and evaluated by the first author, including the strategies used to make it easy for clinicians in the field to implement with integrity.*
- *Next, we describe the process by which four applied settings adopted and implemented this intervention.*
- *We believe that the lessons learned from these four examples can guide clinicians, administrators, and researchers on how to facilitate the process of adopting empirically supported interventions.*

Introduction

Over the past 30 years, hundreds of carefully controlled studies have demonstrated that there exist today a number of effective therapies and services for children and families which can reduce behaviour problems and delinquency, improve mental health, and increase family functioning (Weisz and Weiss, 1993). Among empirically supported interventions, parenting interventions based on cognitive/social learning theories have perhaps the greatest evidence of their effectiveness (Serketich and Dumas, 1996; Taylor and Biglan, 1998). Cognitive behavioural parenting interventions are one of the most effective strategies for treating disruptive behaviour problems in children, including aggressive behaviour, Oppositional Defiant Disorder and Conduct Disorder (Dumas, 1989); (Kazdin, 1995) and Attention Deficit Hyperactivity Disorder (Barkley, 1996; Pisterman, McGrath, Firestone and Goodman, 1989) Together these problems represent the majority of referrals for children's mental health services (McMahon and Wells, 1989). Behavioural family interventions have also been identified as one of the best strategies for the treatment (Becker et al., 1995), and prevention of child abuse (Wolfe, Reppucci and Hart, 1995). They also appear promising for preventing future drug abuse among at-risk youth (Dishion and Andrews, 1995), and for treating chronic delinquents (Bank, Marlow, Reid and Patterson, 1991). Cost-benefit analyses suggested that parent training was one of the most cost-effective strategies for preventing future juvenile delinquency and adult criminal behaviour (Greenwood, Model, Rydell and Chiesa, 1996).

Yet despite this evidence, few empirically supported interventions such as behavioural parent training have been widely adopted in applied settings (Kazdin, Bass, Ayers and Rodgers, 1991; Weisz, Donenberg, Han and Weiss, 1995). Instead, these settings have overwhelmingly adopted a wide assortment of therapeutic fads, which change every few years, and which have no empirical evidence to support their effectiveness. This state of affairs has led some reviews to suggest that, if this trend holds up, we may be faced with the following dilemma: 'The good news is child psychotherapy works; the bad news is, not in real life' (Weisz and Weiss, 1993, p. 96).

> *'Eat these lima beans: they are good for you!'*

Why have clinicians failed to adopt empirically supported treatments, such as parent training interventions? It reminds us of a common fact of life that even though most people know that vegetables are good for them, most still leave their lima beans on their plate and eat their fatty dessert!

But is this a problem of the research interventions not being tasty enough for clinicians to want to try them out or is it that researchers have not provided readily available descriptions of their interventions and clear recipes for clinicians to be able to offer successful interventions? Certainly it is far from easy for clinicians to find and identify empirically validated interventions. It requires the clinician to review dozens of journals, none of which are typically available in a clinical agency let alone town. Moreover to identify a best-practice for a single problem, the clinician must wade through a sea of opinion papers and poorly designed studies which claim their intervention is the best. In order to evaluate the interventions, the clinician must be versed in statistical procedures, from t-tests to structural equation modelling. Even then the research papers provide scant descriptions about the actual treatment processes and methods requiring the clinician to continue his or her pursuit to determine if a treatment manual exists. All this time (usually conducted in the clinician's spare time) is necessary to identify a single intervention for a single problem in a single population. It is perhaps no wonder that so few clinicians use research articles to help them implement treatment and are more likely to implement whatever brand of intervention is heavily marketed that year.

Researchers by and large have done a good job of developing and refining a number of creative interventions for a variety of problems experienced by children and families. However, they have done a poor job of ensuring that this information is systematically shared with people who can most use it, such as clinicians and administrators in the field or with politicians and policy makers who have the power to fund such programmes. This too is understandable. In the 'publish or perish' environment of academia, original research and publications in peer reviewed journals helps to advance the researcher's career but efforts to disseminate earn relatively little prestige and is often considered a task unworthy of a significant amount of a scientist's time. Moreover, those who develop and research new interventions often have no funding to provide technical assistance to potential adopters of their programmes and may perceive it as an onerous burden when they are struggling to keep their own research programmes afloat! Nonetheless, given that we now have a number of empirically supported interventions widespread use of which could result in high social benefits (Biglan, 1995), it is time for scientists to adopt a public health perspective on these problems. We must recognise that to significantly reduce their prevalence we must focus on strategies for disseminating empirically supported interventions to clinicians and service providers (Biglan and Metzler, in press). This should be considered a priority not a luxury.

In this paper, we describe an empirically supported cognitive-behavioural parenting intervention developed and evaluated by the first author, including the strategies used to make it easy for clinicians in the field to implement with integrity. Next, we describe four case examples of applied settings adopting and implementing this intervention. The first, beginning 1992, involved a series of Head Start preschool centres in Puget Sound, Seattle which occurred as a result of the initiation of the first author, the developer of the programme.

The second, beginning in 1993, involved a children's mental health centre in Thunder Bay, Canada where the second author was working as a clinician at the time of adoption of the programme. The third, beginning in 1994, involved a children's mental health centre in Timmins, Canada, to which the second author consulted. The fourth, beginning in 1995, involved a state-wide intervention/prevention programme in Delaware which occurred as a result of the joint-initiation and collaborative efforts of the Department of Services for Children, Youth and their Families, through its Division of Family Services and the Department of Education with strong administrative and financial support from Governor Carper. All four of these sites continue to offer this programme as a part of their regular service today. For each of these examples, we describe how the decision to change first began, how administrators and clinicians were involved in supporting the new intervention, and the strategies used to ensure that the clinical integrity of the programme was maintained. We believe that the lessons learned from these four examples can guide clinicians, administrators, policy-makers, and researchers in how to facilitate the process of adopting empirically supported interventions.

The Development of the Parents and Children Series Programmes

Content and Methods of the Programmes

The original 12-week parent programme, entitled BASIC, was heavily guided by the modelling literature and focused on teaching parents interactive play skills and reinforcement skills based on the early theoretical work and research of Hanf (1970) and Eyberg and Matarazzo (1980), as well as a specific set of nonviolent discipline techniques including Time Out and Ignore as described by Patterson (1982) and Forehand and McMahon (1981), logical and natural consequences, and problem-solving strategies (D'Zurilla and Goldfried, 1971; D'Zurilla and Nezu, 1982). In 1987 the programme was broadened to address other family risk factors (e.g., depression, marital distress, poor coping skills, lack of support) (ADVANCE). In 1992 it was further revised in order to make the programme more culturally sensitive, more prevention-oriented, and more usable outside of the Pacific Northwest; for instance, the programme included a higher percentage of people of colour (40 per cent) as models in the video-tape examples. Next, an older age version of the programme was developed so that it could be used with parents of children up to age nine or 10 (grade 3). This included the development of a new programme entitled *Supporting Your*

Child's Education aimed at teaching parents how to strengthen their children's reading and general academic readiness as well as promoting strong home/ school connections. Finally, we developed a comprehensive child training intervention (Dinosaur Curriculum) which could be used by teachers and school counsellors as a prevention programme for an entire classroom of students or by child therapists for directly training children with behaviour problems in feeling language, social skills, anger management and effective problem-solving.

All the interventions described above were designed to be offered as group discussions (with 12 to 14 parents per group) facilitated by trained group leaders. In the parenting programme each parent is encouraged to have a partner or close friend participate in the programme. The group format was chosen because it fosters a sense of community support, reduces isolation and normalises parents' experiences and situations. Moreover the group approach allows for diverse experiences with problem-solving regarding a variety of family situations as well as a cost-effective way of reaching more families.

All the family interventions have relied heavily on video-tape modelling as a therapeutic method. Because the extent of conduct problems has created a need for service that far exceeds available personnel and resources, the author was convinced of the need to develop an intervention that would be cost-effective, widely applicable, and sustaining. Video-tape modelling promised to be both effective and cost-efficient. Bandura's (1977) modelling theory of learning suggested that parents could improve their parenting skills by watching video-taped examples of parents interacting with their children in ways that promoted pro-social behaviours and decreased inappropriate behaviours. Moreover, it was felt that this method of training would be more accessible, especially to less verbally oriented parents, than other methods (e.g., didactic instruction, written handouts) and would promote better generalisation (and therefore long-term maintenance) by portraying a wide variety of models in a wide variety of situations. Furthermore, video-tape modelling has a low individual training cost when used in groups, and lends itself to mass dissemination. For a more detailed description of the programme, see Webster-Stratton and Hancock (1998).

Evaluation of the Programmes

The first author has spent the last 20 years in an academic setting engaged in the process of developing and evaluating the parent, teacher and child training interventions described above as a means to help families of young children with early onset conduct problems. More recently she has begun to evaluate these programmes as prevention programmes for high risk populations (Webster-Stratton, in press). In the late 1970s she theorised that early intervention with parents of young children (ages three to seven years) would prevent young highly aggressive children from continuing on the trajectory to school drop out, drug abuse and delinquency. She proceeded to evaluate her family interventions following standard scientific procedures. These studies, published in peer reviewed journals, involved randomised controlled trials in which effects were measured according to changes in parent behaviour as well as child behaviour, using parent and teacher reports as well as actual observations of behaviour at home and in the laboratory. After much research and six randomised control group studies with various populations, she concluded that her parent interventions had sustaining effects for up to five years for at least two thirds of families (Webster-Stratton, 1996b). Results of these studies consistently showed that parenting skills and confidence were enhanced (i.e., producing more positive, nurturing and less physically aggressive and critical parenting behaviours) and children's conduct problems were significantly decreased while their social competence was increased (Webster-Stratton, 1997; Webster-Stratton, in press). Furthermore, research suggested that adding the broader-based family focus (ADVANCE) to the parent training as well as direct training for children in social skills and problem-solving (Dinosaur Curriculum) significantly enhanced treatment outcomes in terms of marital improvements and children's peer relationships (Webster-Stratton, 1994). A believer in science and logic, this researcher naively thought she had proven her point – but little did she know she was only initiating the process of being a change agent.

Preparing the Programme for Others to Use

A number of strategies are used to implement the parents' and children's interventions with high levels of clinical integrity. First, the programmes are packaged in an uncomplicated format enabling the clinician to readily learn the skills required. The reliance upon a series of video-tapes to illustrate concepts and skills not only adds to the clinical effectiveness and efficiency of the intervention (Webster-Stratton, Kolpacoff and Hollinsworth, 1988) but it allows the clinician to focus more on the process of facilitating groups, without having to memorise and present all of the content. The video-tapes are supplemented with materials for parents, including a book (Webster-

Stratton, 1992) as well as weekly home activities, refrigerator magnets, and refrigerator notes summarising the key principles taught. Clinician/group leaders receive not only a session-by-session guide, but also a book which outlines the theory and collaborative process of leading groups (Webster-Stratton and Herbert, 1994) as well as a Leaders' Guide with practical guidance on topics ranging from setting up the location and room for the first session, to suggestions for engaging low income families (Webster-Stratton, 1998) and ways to promote parent support both within and outside the parent group (Webster-Stratton and Hancock, 1998).

To supplement the programme materials, training workshops are offered to introduce clinicians not only to the intervention materials and content, but also to the collaborative process involved in leading the groups. A collaborative approach to facilitating groups was chosen because it is more empowering to clients than a more hierarchical approach which is prescriptive and tends to 'lecture' to parents. A collaborative approach which permits parents to determine their own goals and priorities is more likely to increase parents' self-efficacy, to promote engagement in the intervention, to reduce dropout and resistance, and to give parents and group leaders a joint stake in the outcome of the intervention (Dweck, 1975; Meichenbaum and Turk, 1987; Seligman, 1975). Additionally, the collaborative approach is more flexible and adaptable and more likely to fit the needs of different populations.

Recognising that receiving the materials and attending a workshop is not a guarantee that the intervention will be implemented with integrity, a group leader certification process was developed. The requirements for certification include: parent weekly and final evaluations for two complete parent group interventions (each lasting 12 weeks), two peer evaluations for each programme offered, and completion of authorised training workshops. Satisfactory peer review, parent evaluations and group attendance indicate leaders have satisfactory mastery of the content and therapeutic process to become certified as group leaders. Not only does this certification process allow clinicians to continue the learning process after the initial introduction to the programme, but it offers formal recognition to those who make the extra effort to demonstrate that they are competent to implement the intervention. Clinicians who become certified can reasonably anticipate to achieve effects similar to those achieved in the published outcome studies evaluating the programme. Clinicians who become certified group leaders are also eligible to work towards eventual certification as a trainer of other group leaders. With these materials and procedures in place, all that was needed was some applied settings with a desire to change and try something new.

The Decision to Adopt the Intervention

Introducing empirically supported interventions and innovative services into existing organisations is not an easy task. The fact that so few agencies have adopted such services is proof of this. Fortunately, researchers in a variety of fields have studied the process by which innovations diffuse, and have identified a number of critical issues (Rogers, 1995). In this section we will draw from four successful experiences the authors have had in assisting applied settings to adopt and implement the Parents and Children Series programmes with a high level of clinical integrity. Two of these were evaluated in randomised controlled trials (Taylor, Schmidt, Pepler and Hodgins, in press; Webster-Stratton, in press). The positive results in these studies gives us confidence that we have identified a process which can lead to adoption and implementation in applied settings while maintaining the clinical integrity of the intervention.

Based upon our experience, we suggest that there are four critical tasks to achieve in assisting applied settings to adopt and implement a new intervention with a high level of clinical integrity. The first, and in some ways most important step is developing a desire or taste for change within someone in the system. Our experience suggests that this desire for change can occur at almost any level of the system, including front-line clinician, administrators of an agency, or the governor's office. The second step in the process involves obtaining key administrative support and recognition of the need for the new intervention. The support of administrators is essential, because they have the ability to manipulate the organisational structure, job descriptions and contingencies so that new programmes can be carried out successfully. The third step involves obtaining the support of the clinicians. These will be the front-line individuals who will be responsible for the quality of the implementation of the intervention. The final step involves implementing the programme in a manner that ensures that the clinical integrity of the programme is maintained. If these four steps are taken, there is a high likelihood not only that a self-sustaining process can be achieved to maintain the programme's implementation, but the system may initiate on its own the adoption of other empirically-validated interventions as well. Examples of how this process unfolded in four applied settings is described below. It is hoped that this description may tempt others to try some of the ingredients in this recipe for success.

Developing a Taste for Change

Researchers who study the diffusion of innovations have identified that the process begins by one or more individuals in a system learning about an innovation, forming a favourable opinion about it, and deciding to adopt it (Rogers, 1995). Below we describe how this process occurred in each of the four adopting sites.

The Puget Sound Head Start experience One of the first agencies to adopt the Parents and Children Series programmes as a prevention programme in an applied setting occurred in the Head Start centres housed within the Puget Sound Educational Service District in Seattle, Washington.[1] The potential use of the parents, teacher and child training programmes in Head Start was of particular importance because this agency serves a population of families who are at higher risk for having children with conduct problems because of the increased number of stresses associated with living in poverty. As a result, in 1992 the first author and her colleagues from the Parenting Clinic at the University of Washington established an 'information exchange relationship' (Rogers, 1995) with the administrators of the Puget Sound Head Start organisation, including the education, mental health and family service coordinators. They discussed the Head Start agency goals in that district in regard to involving parents and teachers in training for managing children's behaviour problems and strengthening children's social competence. The first author presented the research showing the connection between early onset aggression in young children and later delinquency and then proceeded to present her own research evidence indicating that early aggression could be reduced considerably with the Parents and Children Series training programmes (Webster-Stratton, 1996a; Webster-Stratton, 1996b).

Head Start, as a national organisation, has historically had a long standing commitment to parent involvement and parent education but in this particular district there was a clear administrative desire to offer more comprehensive parent programmes which were less fragmented and offered more continuity of leadership throughout the year. On the other hand, the administrators in this district had less interest in training teachers to offer a social skills and problem-solving training curriculum for the children in their classrooms. Thus we established some compatible goals and a clear desire for change on the part of the administrators to strengthen their parent education programmes. This extensive consultation process resulted in the agency's senior management identifying a desire for change.

The Thunder Bay experience In contrast to the above example, the desire for change in the Thunder Bay began in 1993 with a front-line clinician, the second author of this paper, who had just begun working as a psychologist in a Children's Mental Health Centre. He had done an exhaustive review of the literature of parent training programmes during his PhD (Taylor and Biglan, 1998) and was familiar with the outcomes of the Parents and Children Series programme, and was eager to implement the programme personally. Realising that other more established clinicians would need to be on board for this new programme to be accepted, he shared information about the programme with another psychologist in a number of meetings soon after arriving. That psychologist also had a strong commitment to the importance of empirically supported interventions, and became a critical ally in the further promotion of the programme. The decision of this individual, an established and well-respected front-line clinician, to support the desire for change was critical before efforts were made with any other clinical or administrative levels to achieve support for the new programme.

The Timmins experience In Timmins, the desire to change was first established by the executive director of a small children's mental health centre who had heard about the programme being initiated in Thunder Bay. The second author established an 'information exchange relationship' with this director, keeping him updated on the progress of the parenting groups in Thunder Bay. He, in turn, passed this information on to a group of front-line staff who became quite interested in learning more about the programme. In 1994, one year after Thunder Bay had started the programme, the executive director invited the second author to come and train some of his staff in the implementation of the programme.

The Delaware experience In Delaware, the desire for change first was begun at a different level from the previous examples. In this state the Director of Child Mental Health (Julian Tapplin) from the Department of Services for Children, Youth and Families had spent two years researching the results of studies evaluating parenting programmes and had chosen two interventions (one targeted at young children and one at adolescents) which he wanted to implement in his state. Simultaneously, Governor Carper committed to the notion of funding mental health services for children in kindergarten through third grades who were experiencing behaviour problems. It was felt that by offering these services to targeted children early in their lives that their academic success would be enhanced, school failure reduced and ultimately crime prevented. Most importantly, administrators and policy makers in this state had decided that they would only fund interventions which had strong empirical support. Ultimately, representative Maroney and Senator McDowell were responsible for getting the funding for this project.

Even though Delaware adopted this programme later than the previous three sites, this combination of an influential administrative champion and new funding which could only be used for programmes with scientific evidence of their effectiveness, resulted in the largest adoption and implementation of the programme to date. First, a K-3 Programme was established as a collaborative partnership between the Department of Education and the Department of Services for Children, Youth and Families under the Division of Family Services in order to design a team approach to address behaviour problems in elementary schools. The efforts of this group resulted in the decision to contact the developer of the programme in 1995, and request training for family crises workers and clinicians to conduct both parent and child training groups in schools as part of the initiation of their K-3 Early Intervention Programme.. Thus the desire for change in this setting began at a very high level, and resulted in enthusiastic administrative support.

Obtain Key Administrative Support and Recognition of the Need for the New Intervention

As the above examples illustrate, we believe the desire for change can be stimulated either by people inside the system or outside, and that it can first take root at almost any level of the system. Once, the desire for change has taken root somewhere, the next critical task involves getting the appropriate administrative support and recognition of the need for the new intervention. This typically involves sharing information about the potential advantages of the intervention as well as its research evaluation with the key administrators of the organisation where it is hoped the intervention will be disseminated. For interventions to be offered in schools this will mean involving superintendents, principals, and teachers in informational discussions. For use in clinical agencies and health maintenance organisations it will mean involving agency directors and senior staff members. These key administrators need to be provided with written summaries of the research evaluating the intervention as well as clear descriptions of the programme's short and long-term goals. In order for an organisation to consider adoption of a new intervention, the key administrators must first see that the new programme's goals are compatible with the general goals and needs of their organisation.

Moreover, they must perceive the relative advantages of the innovation over their existing services, particularly in terms of providing maximum gain for the largest number of clients in their organisation.

The Puget Sound Head Start experience After initial acceptance of the concept of offering parenting intervention at the Head Start administrative level, it was then necessary to generate the interest and cooperation of the superintendents, principals and other key administrative staff associated with each individual school district. This acceptance was important because Head Start centres are based within school districts and family services workers are actually hired by them, although supervised by Head Start coordinators. During meetings with these key administrators we helped translate the research for non researchers so that they understood the importance of randomised designs, control groups and observational data in obtaining an unbiased evaluation of programme outcomes. In essence we helped them understand how to critically evaluate research regarding the effectiveness of different interventions. We provided summaries of the literature in general regarding the effectiveness of parenting and child programmes along with information about how our specific programme had been evaluated and was being used in different settings with different populations.

The Thunder Bay experience In a similar manner to that described above, in Thunder Bay the second author engaged in writing summaries of the research on the programme, and highlighting the advantages of using it within a Children's Mental Health Centre. Issues of cost-effectiveness were highlighted. Additionally, the value of evaluating the programme in an applied setting was highlighted, along with the practical issues of randomisation and wait-list control groups. Ultimately middle and senior management of the agency authorised the purchase of the materials of the programme, and authorised the groups to be offered and to be evaluated.

The Timmins experience In contrast to Thunder Bay where the second author worked and had regular personal contact with management staff, in Timmins, the communication efforts consisted of mail and occasional phone calls with the Executive Director sharing similar information to that shared in Thunder Bay. The second author sent several written summaries concerning the programme, and kept him updated concerning the experience of implementing the groups in Thunder Bay. This information was, in turn passed on to a middle manager and a small group of front-line staff. After a year of hearing about the groups being successfully offered in Thunder Bay, sufficient interest was developed among management in Timmins to support trying the programme as well.

The Delaware experience Although there existed top level administrative support for the programmes, the programmes were completely unfamiliar to middle management staff such as principals of schools or supervisors of family crises workers or to the teachers. Since the plan was to place family crises workers in designated schools to implement the child and parent programmes, we felt it was essential that school personnel be informed. Thus when both authors were invited to Delaware to conduct their first week-long workshop we asked our administrative supporters to invite principals (of targeted schools), teachers, and school counsellors to a presentation where we reviewed the research efficacy for the programmes as well as an overview of the content, philosophy and therapeutic skills embedded in the interventions. Also attending this meeting were the family crises workers who would be trained in delivering the programme. This exchange permitted clinicians and school personnel to discuss ways they could support each other's efforts.

Mother:	*What shall we bake today?*
Child:	*How about chocolate chip cookies?*
Mother:	*Well oatmeal-raisin cookies are probably better for you.*

Obtain the Support of the Clinicians

Of course, like the administrators the clinicians need to be made aware of the empirical validity of the new intervention as well as its potential advantages over existing services. However, since clinicians will be primarily responsible for the actual delivery of the intervention, it is essential that they understand more precisely the therapeutic model underpinning the intervention. Their attitudes, prior education and concerns about the therapy model must be taken into account. If this does not happen early on in the decision making process, interventions may be impeded or actively resisted because of faulty understandings of the therapeutic model or because clinicians perceive a lack of control of programmatic decisions.

The Puget Sound Head Start experience We began this process in this district by inviting teachers, family service workers and parents from the different schools to focus groups. At these meetings we elicited their input about their priorities for what kind of content they would like covered in parenting programmes, how long they felt the parent sessions should last and what factors would motivate parents to attend. We approached the Head Start parent board to get their support and input into the programme content. At the same time we began to share with these groups some of the specifics about the philosophy and objectives of our parenting programme. For example we showed them samples of the training video-tapes and training manuals. We discussed how the programme could meet their stated priorities, and what was involved in order for their staff (i.e. family service workers) to become trained as leaders of parent groups. For although the administration of Head Start was in agreement to offer more intensive parent training, the next important decision to be made was whether this particular brand of parent education was consistent with their administrative, clinician and parent values.

We found in Seattle that there was a general mistrust of behavioural approaches by the family service workers and Head Start teachers. There was concern about specific parenting approaches described in our programme such as the use of rewards and Time Out. These approaches were perceived by some of the more psychodynamic clinicians as inhuman, mechanistic and not appropriate for preschoolers. Other clinicians were threatened because they had no prior training in learning principles. Still others saw their role as case workers but did not see their professional role as including comprehensive parent education and this initially created some role identity issues. As we discussed these issues we frequently found that the behavioural jargon was foreign to them and created psychological barriers. For example, the word reward seemed to conjure up for them Skinnerian notions of giving pellets to pigeons, but on the other hand, the use of terms such as celebrations, surprises, and descriptive encouragement for children were acceptable. While the teachers professed not to believe in Time Out they were very comfortable with using a Calm Down technique which upon further examination was very similar to our Time Out approach. Thus once we got past the semantic differences and began to focus on the underlying principles (e.g., fostering parent empowerment, collaboration, nurturing and nonviolent discipline) we found many compatible philosophies and values. Being 'child directed' is a key element to Head Start philosophy and once they viewed our play training tapes which are based entirely on this principle they began to see the congruence in philosophies.

However, despite the family service workers' growing enthusiasm for the programme there was considerable concern about their daily work pressures, stresses and their ability to take on any more work in an already heavy case load. In addition, we found they had prior experiences with offering brief parent education evenings on a monthly basis resulting in poor parent turnouts. Consequently, they were somewhat pessimistic about the possibility of success with a more comprehensive group-based parent programme. Their overall motivation for change in the beginning was guarded. We listened to their concerns, acknowledged the barriers, and discussed with them their ideas for how they felt family turn out could be increased.

Finally, after a year of meetings and focus groups, the administrators and clinicians made the decision to try out the parenting intervention but to postpone offering the teacher intervention. Teachers could be involved in so far as they would be trained in the parent programme but would not be expected to offer the Dinosaur social skills curriculum in classroom. We agreed upon a three year commitment to evaluate the parent programme in eight Head Start centres. This concept of trialability was attractive to them because it allowed them to see how the programme worked with parents before they adopted it on a larger scale.

The Thunder Bay experience The process of obtaining clinician support for implementing the programme was carried out by the second author and his colleague. Copies of some of the video-tapes were ordered to preview before purchasing, and these were shown to interested clinicians and middle management personnel. Brief handouts from the programme were copied and distributed, and a number of copies of the book for parents (Webster-Stratton, 1992), were shared and read by clinicians. The second author and his colleague committed to leading groups, and other volunteers were solicited from among the clinicians to co-lead groups. After four months of advocating, the first parenting groups began.

The Timmins experience The first contact that the second author had with clinicians in the Timmins Children's Mental Health Centre was a 90-minute phone call with the Executive Director, a middle manager, and six interested clinicians. In this meeting the second author listened to staff's descriptions of their interests and goals, and described the programme to them, highlighting how it was compatible with their goals. Approximately two months later the second author visited the agency and offered a training workshop for the six interested individuals. At this agency this subgroup of six front-line staff were quite eager to try the programme, believing that the current strategies they were using were not effective, and recognising that their large caseloads required some form of group treatment. Shortly after the workshop, these staff immediately started leading groups.

The Delaware experience In Delaware as we have said, we started with administrative support for our programmes. In fact our first contact with the front-line clinicians was when we arrived in Delaware to conduct a four-day group leader-training workshop for family crises workers. We encountered considerable clinician resistance to the intervention at first.

Some of the resistance occurred because the clinicians felt mandated to offer this service and had not been consulted by their administrators. Family crises workers told us that when they were hired by the department they had not been told that conducting parent or child groups in schools was part of their job description. Some of them told us they felt unprepared to work directly with children in groups and others were concerned about their skills offering parent groups. In general there was anxiety and some anger about having to learn two different treatment approaches at the same time.

In addition, some of the resistance had to do with the notion of offering a behavioural 'packaged' group programme. Those with more psychodynamic backgrounds were convinced that one-on-one individual therapy approaches with exploration of parents' family of origin was far more effective than the less private and more standardised group approach. There were also misconceptions about the use of a video-based programme, assuming that a video-tape programme would be rigid, inflexible, non-therapeutic and culturally insensitive. We explained the collaborative nature of the intervention, how the video-tapes were used to stimulate debate, discussions and group process, how past family history informed group discussions at times, and how the intervention focused on individual family goals and priorities. In essence, we needed to dispel the notion that because the intervention was packaged and somewhat structured, it did not mean that it was inflexible, nor did it assume a 'one size shoe fits all' philosophy. Moreover, it required not less therapy skill on the part of clinicians but rather a high level of group process skill and leadership.

In both the Delaware and Seattle experience it was key for the developer and trainer of the intervention programmes to have personal contact with the clinicians. Listening to the concerns and anxieties from the clinicians about the interventions helped us to clarify misperceptions about the intervention philosophy and to explain its success with a variety of populations. It also helped us to understand how stressful role change was for them and the necessity of clinicians being empowered as part of the change process within their organisations. In fact, there is a considerable body of research attesting to the importance of clinicians being involved in the planning for any new intervention (Backer, Liberman and Kuehnel, 1986). Without considering the emotional reactions of the clinicians to the change, resistance to change may occur which will sabotage almost any innovation. In fact, personal contact as an implementation strategy has been cited as the single most important variable in promoting adoption among mental health professionals, regardless of the nature of the intervention (Backer et al., 1986).

Implementation of the Intervention with Integrity

> Mother: *I think you can make these cookies by yourself now, but be sure to follow the recipe carefully for cookie dough. Put in exactly what the recipe says.*
> Child: *Oh I am!* (mutters to self) *I think I'll put less flour and more sugar, that will taste even better!*

An essential aspect to successful implementation of an intervention is hinged upon whether the intervention was actually carried out as intended. The absence of intervention integrity is not an uncommon flaw in programme dissemination. An intervention may not show effects when delivered in community settings, not because the programme was flawed but because the programme was inadequately implemented with inexperienced or untrained people or clinicians who did not adhere to the intervention protocols.

Once the decision has been made to adopt a new intervention in a setting then there are at least nine key elements to successful implementation. These are: 1) training in the intervention; 2) helping clinicians understand their role as change agents; 3) implementing the entire intervention, without eliminating major components or shortening the intervention substantially; 4) providing ongoing supervision and peer support to clinicians; 5) providing organisational support and internal advocates; 6) involving an external agent; 7) assuring maximal participation; 8) providing support to participants; and 9) pairing of new leaders with experienced staff.

Training in the Intervention

As we have noted earlier, training workshops lasting two to four days were offered in all four sites to prepare group leaders in the parent training programme. This interactive training familiarised group leaders with the content, methods and processes of the intervention and permitted clinicians to ask questions and to role play group processes. These workshops have been found to be invaluable in assuring that the collaborative process is understood by clinicians (for more information, see Webster-Stratton and Herbert (1994)).

Helping Clinicians Understand Their Role as Change Agent

Successful implementation requires clinicians to recognise their role as change agents. Our experience suggests that it is best if the first clinicians to implement a new intervention are eager to do so. For the clinician who decides s/he wants to implement a new programme s/he becomes an 'innovator' in the system they work in. These people are often called 'early adopters', because they are willing to take risks and try new ideas before they have become well-established interventions in the organisation (Rogers, 1995). However, sometimes early adopters are unaware of what it means to be a change agent and don't realise that they must engage in the process of 'social marketing' – of being a champion for their new services to families and their professional colleagues. They also need to be prepared to deal with organisational resistance to their efforts. Part of our initial training workshops focuses on preparing these clinicians for the processes involved in becoming an innovator within their organisational system.

The most successful clinicians will be flexible, confident, enthusiastic, and committed to the programme. In addition, they must also be non-authoritarian, collaborative, well-respected, well-educated, organised, well-prepared, pro-active and have a high morale. In short, they are leaders. Organisation administrators would be well advised to start with training clinicians with these characteristics who indicate a willingness to try out new programmes rather than to mandate all clinicians to follow suit. Those who are not risk takers are called 'late adopters' and they will reluctantly venture into new programmes only after their well respected colleagues have been shown to be successful with the programme (Rogers, 1995).

Child:	*Okay, the recipe is for three dozen?*
Mother:	*No that's too many! It will take too long.*
Child:	*Maybe we can cook them faster if we put the temperature higher.*
Mother:	*You might think so. But if you put it higher for less time, they end up burned on the outside, but raw inside.*

Implementing the Entire Intervention

Another common aspect of the implementation in all four sites was that the programme was offered in full with all core components of the programme offered over a 12 to 14 week time frame. We are well aware that administrators and clinicians may believe that they can eliminate parts of a mental health intervention or shorten it to be more cost effective. Experience with other empirically supported interventions shows this usually weakens or eliminates the positive effects of the programme altogether (Corrigan, MacKain and Liberman, 1994). For example, we know from the research regarding conduct disordered children that interventions of at least 20 hours in length are more effective than other shorter programmes. We also have learned that such children and their families need ongoing and continual support. Thus intervention programmes, offered early in a family's child rearing life (for example, prior to starting school) should not be thought of as an inoculation for life. Rather, successful prevention/intervention will necessitate ongoing programmes offered at critical stages in family development (e.g., preschool, transition to kindergarten, middle school and high school).

Moreover, if an intervention has been researched based on 12 sessions, two hours a week then the clinician must assume the same standard in order to get the same results. Fewer sessions than this will dilute the effectiveness of the programme. Moreover, most intervention programmes are offered in some kind of logical order with each session building on a prior session. If the clinician suddenly decides to omit a session or start in the middle of the programme, the efficacy of the programme may be compromised considerably or may even result in harmful effects for the family.

An important distinction must be made between implementing the core elements of the programme and stifling clinical skills or flexibility. It is easy for the former to be misconstrued as the latter. For our intervention at least, group leaders are encouraged to bring their skills, experience and ideas when implementing the programme. Group leaders often bring newspaper articles, comic strips about parenting, or other similar materials to groups, as well as their own experiences and metaphors to help parents understand certain concepts. They also bring their own clinical judgement about when to take time in the group to explore an issue in greater depth, or to address a problem not related to the immediate content of the day. Thus, rather than treating the programme as a precise script to be recited at parents in a didactic manner, clinicians come to understand the fundamental principles that guide the programme include flexibility, parents collaboration in setting the agenda, and having fun. When clinicians understand this, they realise that rather than limiting the use of their clinical skills and judgement, the programme fosters and encourages it. Our experience suggests that the willingness of clinicians to continue to implement this intervention hinges on their willingness to retain the core elements of the intervention, while still bringing their clinical skills, judgement and creativity to bear in the implementation.

Providing Ongoing Supervision and Peer Support to Clinicians Throughout the Programme

The formal training and workshop only starts the training process. In all four sites, group leaders met in regular (typically weekly) peer review sessions to review clinicians' progress and group difficulties and to provide support to each other. We are convinced that this peer support is key to the success of interventions, regardless of the degree of expertise of the group leaders involved. Often times group leaders can become discouraged or demoralised by particular families or children and their lack of apparent success with the programme. The peer group support and objectivity helps the group leader maintain optimism for the families and to find new ways of approaching resistant parents or children. In all four sites, a peer group was established which met on a weekly or bi-weekly basis. Additionally, in Thunder Bay and Delaware, groups were video-taped in order to assess the quality of the intervention delivered. The group leaders then picked segments of these video-tapes to show in their weekly peer group meetings. They could chose to share a successful strategy with their peer group or a situation in which they wanted feedback and help in finding alternative therapeutic strategies. Additionally, leaders from Thunder Bay and Delaware both sent selected tapes to the trainer for review in Seattle. This feedback to the developer and trainer of the programme was extremely helpful in designing follow-up workshops and knowing the areas of the intervention which were particularly difficult for the clinicians to implement. For example, when we reviewed tapes of the family crises workers' first groups we found that few of them were using role plays or reviewing homework activities to bring families' personal problems to life. Most were preoccupied with the video-tapes and curriculum rather than the therapeutic group process. Teaching and agendas tended to be non-collaborative and prescriptive. While this is to be expected when first learning to do groups, the information was helpful to the follow-up workshops where the trainer focused on role plays and group process with the clinicians and discussed with them ways to deal with parental resistance.

Providing Organisational Support and Internal Advocates

Successful implementation also involves organisational support for the intervention. Implementation of new services requires the allegiance and active support of administrative parties. For example, job descriptions might have to be rewritten to recognise the time commitment involved for clinicians starting up and carrying out parenting groups. Even though group approaches are more cost effective than individual approaches there is still considerable clinician time spent outside the group calling parents weekly, assuring transportation and food are provided for each session, and preparing handouts and materials for the sessions. This time must be budgeted for in the clinician's day. In the beginning the administrators must provide adequate release time for the clinician to be trained in the new intervention. This will involve more than the initial training workshop. Sometimes administrators are surprised to find that the initial training does not adequately prepare their clinicians to start groups the following week! It is imperative that administrators understand that learning a new intervention will also involve considerable time studying the video-tapes and training manuals and practising with their colleagues.

Additionally it is important for administrators to understand that once parent groups are started it is still necessary to provide ongoing peer support. Group leaders will need to meet for regular supervision and review of their group dynamics. These peer review sessions between group sessions are essential to maintaining the quality of the interventions.

It will be the administrators' role to push for high quality implementation. Without these efforts, the requirement for maintaining quality falls upon those implementing it to do so on their own time, without any recognition or support for the work involved in doing it well. One of the most important ways the organisation can do this is to ensure that there are one or more internal administrative champions of the programme. These people will assure ongoing support for the programme and will see that the clinicians who are adopting the programme are well recognised for their extra work and rewarded within the system. Internal advocates should be familiar with local agencies, persons with power, and know how decisions are made in the system. In other words, they are familiar with local politics. This is important because these internal advocates will need to help clinicians deal with some of the organisational resistance and unintended side effects of the new programme. Research shows that if clinicians are left to champion a programme without an active administrative champion, the clinicians who first adopt the intervention quickly burn out from the extra work, get resentful about the lack of support, and often leave the agency (Liberman and Corrigan, 1994). Research has indicated that the interpersonal contact provided by the internal advocate is a critical ingredient in promoting adoption of new programmes, regardless of the nature of the programme (Backer et al., 1986). In many ways, the administrative champions are more important to the long-term success of the intervention than the clinicians themselves.

In our Head Start project, the administrators altered some of the family service worker job descriptions so that the material covered in the parenting programme could substitute for some of the other required training areas. In addition, they funded the release of the family service workers on a monthly basis for support and supervision meetings. The time spent in supervision could be substituted for some of their other required in-service training time. They assigned part of one administrator position to oversee this new service and to communicate with the clinicians and developer/trainer about areas of concern.

In Thunder Bay and Timmins, staff were allowed to participate in a regular peer group meeting of group leaders, and the groups were promoted as one of the services offered regularly at the centre. Additionally, staff were allowed to take time off during the day time because of the increased work in the evenings for the groups.

In Delaware the job descriptions were completely rewritten to describe the family crises worker's role in schools as parent and child group leader. Each worker would be assigned to two schools where they would offer on going groups. In addition, workers provided these targeted families with weekly home visits, 24-hour crises services, individual and family counselling, and linkages to needed resources as necessary. When new family crises workers were hired their roles as child and parent group leaders in the schools were clearly described. Consequently when we conducted a second workshop a year later with new family crises workers, there was virtually no clinician resistance. By that time, job descriptions were clear and there was a support system in place. Each summer during the first two years of implementation, family crises workers spent a day a week reviewing tapes and manuals and practising leading groups. In the second year, new workers paired up with more experienced group leaders to conduct their first groups.

Successful Implementation Involves an External Agent

The external agent is usually the person who developed the intervention or a person who has been certified in the intervention as a trainer and has had extensive experience using it. This person serves as trainer of workshops, helps the clinicians with how to use manuals, video-tapes, and handouts and provides ongoing feedback and review of group process and if possible, review of video-tapes of groups. The external agent provides ongoing consultation to the programme and collaborates with the 'internal advocate' to plan further training and implementation. This person also provides consultation to both the clinicians and administrators regarding the process of change itself and helps them with understanding some of the psychological resistance and unintended side effects of the intervention. The external agent/developer is also in an excellent position to advise the administrators in ways to support and reinforce the clinician's change efforts. Finally this person helps the clinician understand how to bring about innovation in the system.

Assuring Maximal Participation in the Intervention Programmes

Another threat to the success of an intervention particularly with prevention programmes is concerned with low attendance and attrition. An intervention may not be successful because very few people perceive the need for the intervention. For example, in our Head Start project we offered parent training to all parents enrolled. However, initially parents did not perceive the need for such a programme. In fact, the consensus in that community was that only parents who were court ordered or mentally ill would attend parenting programmes. Some parents may not want to participate because they resent the intrusion into their private life, personal values and priorities. If they are experiencing difficulties with their children they may feel somehow blamed or stigmatised by an approach which emphasises parent training. Moreover, they may not have the time or flexibility in their schedules to attend parent groups. Even highly motivated parents may not be able to continue participation because of work commitments, illness or other life events. The clinicians are critical in the marketing of the new interventions and organising their delivery so that as many barriers be they psychological or physical are removed for families as possible.

Provide Support Services to Participants

The most carefully implemented intervention will not achieve very much if families don't come out. Expecting highly stressed families to rush home from work, feed their children, arrange childcare, and travel to a group held far from home is simply not realistic. Our experience is that this stress and difficulty getting to evening groups is true for middle class, two-parent working families and even more so, for low-income, disadvantaged families. For example, in the Head Start project, we provided childcare and dinner was arranged for all families, and offered groups in sites close to family's homes (sometimes in housing units). In Thunder Bay, parents were encouraged to arrange their own child care, but a single baby sitter was hired to be at groups regularly for those who could not, or whose alternative plans fell through at the last minute. Additionally, rides were arranged for those families who could not get to the group another way. After these strategies were implemented, the attendance of single parents went up dramatically. In Delaware, funding was provided for buses to transport parents to their groups from their homes as well as for child care and food for parent groups. They also made funding available for helping families with particular resources, such as clothing for children and special education needs.

Pairing New Leaders with Experienced Leaders

In our Seattle project we were fortunate to be able to pair up our trained and experienced parent group leaders from our Parenting Clinic with each of the new family service workers from Head Start. This arrangement provided ideal training because the new clinicians were mentored by a certified group leader.

In Thunder Bay, there were no experienced group leaders available for the first group. Additionally, at the time that the groups began, only the one clinician (the second author), had attended training with the programme developer. In an effort to ensure treatment fidelity, the second author spent considerable time reviewing all materials in the programme, and co-led the first three parenting groups simultaneously with three different leaders. When these groups were finished, five new groups began, each with at least one experienced group leader. Later several group leaders attended a training session with the developer, and ever since, all new group leaders have conducted their first group with an experienced leader.

In Timmins, four therapists attended a training workshop on the programme, and then spent additional time reviewing the materials together, and began the first two groups simultaneously so that they could offer each other mutual support. After this, they also followed the process of pairing new leaders with experienced leaders.

In Delaware, following a training workshop in the spring, the family crises workers spent one day a week during the summer months practising in groups with each other to be ready for their groups to start in the fall. After the initial year of implementation, all new groups always had at least one experienced leader.

Other Recommendations

Some of the following strategies were used in a few of the sites to help ensure maximal participation in their intervention programme. We theorise that using some of these strategies will lead to stronger community buy-in to the programme which will ultimately lead to interventions that continue to be used in the long-run.

Induce the Community to Feel Ownership of the Programme

Engage key community leaders as collaborators or partners in an advisory capacity with the intervention evaluation team. The Delaware and Seattle programmes had advisory boards consisting of community leaders including superintendents of education; director and programme administrators of the Division of Family Services, Department of Services for Youth, Children and Families in Delaware (DSCYF) and Puget Sound Educational Service District in Seattle; principals of the school districts involved in offering the programmes; parent, family service worker and teacher representatives; and University of Delaware and University of Washington representatives. These advisory groups met periodically to give input into the training, delivery and evaluation of the interventions.

Make the Programmes Flexible in Times and Places they are Offered

Among the four sites, the intervention has been offered in mental health centres, housing units, churches and schools near where the parents were living. Night time groups were the most successful in attracting two partners and working parents, although daytime groups were easier for some families because their children were in school.

Moreover, if the programme is being offered as prevention programme in the community make sure its advertising does not give a blaming message regarding the cause of mental health problems. For example, we advertised our Head Start programme to families as a programme designed to help children succeed in school, not a programme to reduce behaviour problems. This less stigmatising way of recruiting parents resulted in a high turnout of parents to the programme.

Provide Opportunities for Interested Community Members to Participate in Development, Organisation, Implementation, and Evaluation of the Programmes

In the Seattle project we asked for parent volunteers to help with family recruitment, day care , transportation and programme evaluation. In the second year of the project, 75 per cent of the parents who had been trained the year before offered to participate in some way either by helping run day care for new parents or by attending parent orientation nights at the schools to help explain the programme and motivate new parents to participate. In the third year of the project we trained parents who had shown themselves as 'natural leaders' to be co-leaders of parent groups with the family service workers. This involvement helped parents develop a sense of ownership and investment in the programme's success and began to change the meaning of the programme in the community.

Make Sure the Intervention Programme is Culturally Sensitive and Adaptable to the Changing Needs of the Community

It is important that the programme reflect the needs and characteristics of the community it serves. In Seattle, we translated the programme into Spanish and Vietnamese to try to meet some of the language needs. We hired leaders representing different minority groups to do the evaluation interviews and to be trained to lead the groups.

Part of the collaborative process involved in this programme is to ask parents in the first session to identify their goals for the programme and to list the behaviours they want to promote in their children. Each family has their own unique goals for their children based on their values and culture. The programme then focuses on management principles which they can apply to their personal goals. In this way the programme can be culturally sensitive to individual needs and values.

In addition to trying to set up programmes that are responsive to the cultural context and the needs, demands and priorities of communities so that maximal participation is ensured, it also helpful, if possible, to collect data concerning the people who refuse to participate or drop out from the programme and why they do not want to participate. Such data helps to provide understanding of who the programme is best suited for and which groups do not find it helpful.

It is not clear whether people who do not participate are those most in need of the programme or those who least need it! This information could help further the development and focus of the intervention programme (Price, Cowen, Lorion and Ramos, 1989).

Provide Incentives

Particularly in the case of prevention programmes for high risk populations (where parents are not seeking help), we found it important to provide some incentives (other than food) to motivate parents to attend the parenting programme. We offered course credits to those who needed the credits for school. Occasionally lotteries were held. For example everyone who attended a group had their name put in a jar and one name was pulled out for a prize at the end of each session. All the children and parents received certificates at the end of the training programme and a special celebration party of their success. In the Head Start project we also offered a $25 bonus to parents who attended more than two-thirds of the sessions (Webster-Stratton, 1998). Many parents told us that the incentives initially attracted them to the programme but after attending the session felt they would have attended anyway regardless of whether there were lotteries or bonuses.

Mother:	*Well, how do the cookies look?*
Child:	*They're gooier than yours are – but that's how I like them.*
Mother:	*Let's see how they taste ...*

Evaluation of the Intervention Programme

Even though a programme has been evaluated in a research setting its effectiveness within particular organisations or communities must be determined. Simple self-report measures of parenting skills and children's behaviour can be administered pre and post intervention. Consumer satisfaction measures can be completed at the end of each session as well as the end of the intervention to get feedback on the particular content of the programme covered as well as the leader skills and methods used (i.e. use of video-tapes, group discussion, use of book and audio-tape, homework activities, buddy calls, etc.). It is important to try to assess who the programme works for and who it doesn't work for.

In the Head Start project we had research money to evaluate our programme so we completed a detailed analyses of the programmes' effects. Results revealed significant improvements in parenting nurturance and discipline competence, increases in parent involvement with teachers and reductions in child behaviour problems that were sustained one year later in kindergarten. Consumer satisfaction at the end of the programme was very high with 85 per cent of families attending two thirds of the programme (Webster-Stratton and Hammond, in press). Five years later our interventions are still being offered in these centres and Puget Sound Head Start have moved on to train other family service workers in our programmes in many of their centres. Because of their success new Head Start districts are consulting with them about starting these services. Some of the centres have written grants themselves and obtained money from charities to cover their food costs, books and other necessary supplies.

In Thunder Bay, funding was obtained from the Ontario Mental Health Foundation to evaluate the programme. Results indicated that the programme was effective at reducing behaviour problems in children, and that the programme was at least as effective and more satisfying to parents than usual services at the centre (Taylor et al., in press).

In Delaware, each year they phase in five–six new schools and train new family crises workers. They provided a budget for their own evaluation staff in conjunction with the University of Delaware who are generating reports regarding their focus groups, and baseline inventory data. They plan to present post intervention data on the families at the end of grade three. They are currently offering programmes in 24 schools and 10 school districts. Focus groups with teachers, nurses, principals, and guidance counsellors are held at the end of each school year. These indicate that principals cannot imagine their school without a family crises worker who is conducting the parent and child groups. Teachers acknowledge the value of family crises workers in helping resolve student's behaviour problems and feel they are spending more time teaching and less time disciplining students. They report better communication with parents, increased student attendance, and reduced aggressiveness. However, this year focus groups also indicated that teachers felt left out of the loop and wanted more intensive training in classroom management skills and how to engage in social skills and problem-solving training for all their students and not just for the targeted students. Consequently the administrators are planning phasing in this third aspect of their services for the next school year.

Maintenance of the Intervention Programme

In all four of the sites, the parenting programme continues to be used today, three and six years after the initial adoption of the programme. Where there has been strong administrative support for the programme, the continued maintenance is easier, and the number of groups offered has continued to grow each year. In some sites, administration placed a strong value on the use of empirically supported interventions. They asked regularly about how the groups were doing, and made it known to all staff that leading these groups was important. As a result, clinicians felt that their work was valued. Additionally, when administrators placed an expectation that clinicians would lead these groups, they also gave them the time to prepare and organise them as well. In contrast, in other sites where implementation of the intervention was voluntary, clinicians had to decide to work evenings to lead the groups while their colleagues chose to see their clients individually during the day. They often had to do the extra planning and coordinating involved in leading the groups on their own time. Yet in spite of these obstacles the clinicians have continued to offer the groups. This has occurred largely as a result of the dedication of individual clinicians who became champions of the programme in their centre. These individuals advocated for the programme when others resisted it. They gave of their time to ensure it was offered. This dedication and commitment ultimately resulted in new individuals joining them to offer the programme.

Expanding to Adopt Other Empirically Supported Interventions

An additional, unanticipated pattern we observed in each site was that, following the initial successful implementation of the first interventions, other empirically supported interventions were adopted by the same sites. In Puget Sound Head Start, success with the parent intervention programme led them to think that there might be further benefits from the teacher training component. Currently teachers from selected centres are engaged in workshops one day a month and working with us to evaluate and further refine a teacher training curriculum that meets their needs. In Timmins, they have adopted the Dinosaur Social Skills and Problem-solving Curriculum (Webster-Stratton, 1997), and in Thunder Bay they have adopted the Dinosaur Curriculum as well as another empirically validated parenting programme for adolescents, the Adolescent Transition Programme (Dishion and Andrews, 1995). And as we mentioned earlier, in Delaware they are starting to offer our teacher training intervention in classroom management skills and how to teach all their students social skills and problem-solving skills.

These four case examples lead us to believe that a positive experience with one empirically supported intervention gives clinicians and clinical agencies a taste for other empirically supported interventions. If this is the case, this has significant implications for disseminating other empirically supported interventions. The recent failure of the large-scale Fort Bragg 'System of Care' demonstration project (Weisz, Han and Valeri, 1996) has been attributed to the failure to use empirically supported interventions as basic components of the system of care. If positive experiences with one empirically supported intervention make service providers more receptive to other empirically supported interventions, then this suggests that the first intervention to be introduced should be selected carefully to be one which has a high likelihood of success. Once an agency or system has adopted one such intervention, it might be approached to integrate other interventions gradually until such an empirically supported system of care is in place.

Mother:	*Hey they taste good!*
Mother:	*How did you get them like that? Did you use less flour?*
Child:	*No I followed the recipe but ... I added extra chocolate chips!*
Mother:	*Yummy, let's see if Gram likes them too.*

Rarely have prevention/intervention programmes shared in detail the core ingredients of their intervention recipes and therapy processes. Such information is essential in order for interventions to be successfully implemented by clinicians. For example, if the child making cookies had cut out a core ingredient such as the flour or baking soda the cookies would have been unsuccessful. On the other hand, by including all the core ingredients and adding chocolate this child improved upon the taste – particularly for those in his family who like chocolate. Similarly, the clinician is encouraged to keep the core ingredients (not cut things they don't like such as Time Out) and then supplement the programme with their own stories, analogies, and other materials which reflect the uniqueness of the population they are working with.

Conclusion

In summary, these four experiences give us confidence that applied centres can be persuaded to adopt and implement empirically supported intervention with a high level of clinical integrity, and that they will often continue to offer these interventions after the change agent has ceased to be involved. The process began in all four sites by developing the desire for change within someone in the system. Next, support was obtained from administrators and clinicians. With this support, the implementation began, beginning with training in the intervention. In all four sites the entire intervention was implemented, with administration supporting the use of ongoing supervision and peer support. As new staff were brought into the process they received training and co-led their initial groups with an experienced leader who mentored them through the initial process. All four sites maintained contact with the programme trainer after the initial training, with clinical feedback ranging from consultation to detailed feedback on video-tapes of sessions. The evaluation data available on these implementations suggests that they were effective. This recipe, like the programme itself, was sufficiently flexible to respond to the unique needs of each of the four sites, while offering sufficient guidance to ensure that the ultimate product was what the sites initially expected.

Acknowledgements

This research was supported by funding from the Prevention Research Branch of the National Institute of Mental Health (NIMH), National Institute of Health (NIH) and a Research Scientist Development Award MH00988-05 from NIMH and the NIH National Centre for Nursing Research Grant #5 RO1 NR01075-11 and Grant N. DA 09678 from the National Institute on Drug Abuse. The author is grateful to a number of people who were 'internal advocates' and instrumental in the dissemination of our programmes – John Bancroft, Mary Fickes, Ronnie Gilboa, Nancy Pearsall, Fred Schmidt, Julien Taplin, Katherine Way, Valerie Woodruff and all the family service administrators and workers, family crises workers and therapists at the participating sites. Correspondence concerning this article should be sent to Carolyn Webster-Stratton, Parenting Clinic, Box 354801, School of Nursing, University of Washington, Seattle, WA 98195.

Note

1 Other agencies purchased the programme prior to this, but since the developer had little or no contact with them, she has no knowledge of whether this was done with clinical integrity, or whether they maintained the programme.

References

Backer, T.E., Liberman, R.P. and Kuehnel, T.G. (1986), 'Dissemination and adoption of innovative psychosocial interventions', *Journal of Consulting and Clinical Psychology*, 54, pp. 111–8.

Bandura, A. (1977), *Social learning theory*, Englewood Cliffs, Prentice-Hall, Inc.

Bank, L., Marlow, J.H., Reid, J.B. and Patterson, G.R. (1991), 'A comparative evaluation of parent-training interventions for families of chronic delinquents', *Journal of Abnormal Child Psychology*, 19 (1), pp. 15–33.

Barkley, R.A. (1996), 'Attention Deficit/Hyperactivity Disorder' in Mash, E.J. and Barkley, R.A. (eds), *Child Psychopathology*, New York, Guilford Press.

Becker, J.V., Alpert, J.L., BigFoot, D.S., Bonner, B.L., Geddie, L.F., Henggeler, S., Kaufman, K.L. and Walker, C.E. (1995), 'Empirical research on child abuse treatment: Report by the child abuse and neglect treatment working group, American Psychological Association', *Journal of Clinical Child Psychology*, 24, pp. 23–4.

Biglan, A. (1995), *Changing cultural practices: A contextualist framework for intervention research*, Ren, Nv.,Context Press.

Biglan, A. and Metzler, C.W. (in press), 'A public health perspective for research on family-focused interventions' in Ashery, R.S. (ed.), *Research Meeting on Drug Abuse Prevention through Family Interventions*, NIDA Research Monograph.

Corrigan, P.W., MacKain, S.J. and Liberman, R.P. (1994), 'Skill training modules – A strategy for dissemination and utilization of rehabilitation innovation' in Rothman, J. and Thomas, E.J. (eds), *Intervention research: Design and development of human service*, New York, Hawthorne Press.

D'Zurilla, T.J. and Goldfried, M.R. (1971), 'Problem solving and behavior modification', *Journal of Abnormal Psychology*, 78, pp. 107–26.

D'Zurilla, T.J. and Nezu, A. (1982), 'Social problem-solving in adults' in Kendall, P.C. (ed.), *Advances in cognitive behavioral research and therapy*, Vol. 1, New York, Academic Press.

Dishion, T.J. and Andrews, D.W. (1995), 'Preventing escalation in problem behaviours with high-risk young adolescents: Immediate and 1-year outcomes', *Journal of Consulting and Clinical Psychology*, 63 (4), pp. 538–48.

Dumas, J.E. (1989), 'Treating antisocial behavior in children: Child and family approaches', *Clinical Psychology Review*, 9, pp. 197–222.

Dweck, C. S. (1975), 'The role of expectations and attributions in the alleviation of learned helplessness', *Journal of Personality and Social Psychology*, 31, pp. 674–85.

Eyberg, S.M. and Matarazzo, R.G. (1980), 'Training parents as therapists: A comparison between individual parent-child interaction training and parent group didactic training', *Journal of Clinical Child Psychology*, 36 (2), pp. 492–9.

Forehand, R.L. and McMahon, R.J. (1981), *Helping the noncompliant child: A clinician's guide to parent training*, New York, Guilford Press.

Greenwood, P.W., Model, K.E., Rydell, C.P. and Chiesa, J. (1996), *Diverting children from a life of crime. Measuring costs and benefits*, Santa Monica, Ca., Rand.

Hanf, C. (1970), 'Shaping mothers to shape their children's behavior', unpublished manuscript, Portland, University of Oregon Medical School.

Kazdin, A.E. (1995), *Conduct disorders in childhood and adolescence*, Thousand Oaks, Ca., Sage Publications.

Kazdin, A.E., Bass, D., Ayers, W.A. and Rodgers, A. (1991), 'Empirical and clinical focus of child and adolescent psychotherapy research', *Journal of Consulting and Clinical Psychology*, 58 (6), pp. 729–40.

McMahon, R.J. and Wells, K.C. (1989), 'Conduct disorders' in Mash, E.J. and Barkely, R.A. (eds), *Treatment of childhood disorders*, New York, Guilford Press.

Meichenbaum, D. and Turk, D. (1987), *Facilitating treatment adherence: A practitioner's guidebook*, New York, Plenum Press.

Patterson, G.R. (1982), *Coercive family process*, Eugene, Or., Castalia.

Pisterman, S., McGrath, P.J., Firestone, P. and Goodman, J.T. (1989), 'Outcome of parent-mediated treatment of preschoolers with attention deficit disorder with hyperactivity', *Journal of Consulting and Clinical Psychology*, 57 (5), pp. 628–35.

Price, R.H., Cowen, E.L., Lorion, R.P. and Ramos, M.J. (1989), 'The search for effective prevention programmes: what we learned along the way', *American Journal of Orthopsychiatry*, 59 (1), pp. 49–58.

Rogers, E.M. (1995), *Diffusion of innovations*, New York, The Free Press.

Seligman, M.E.P. (1975), *Helplessness*, San Francisco, Ca., Freeman.

Serketich, W.J. and Dumas, J.E. (1996), 'The effectiveness of behavioral parent training to modify antisocial behavior in children: A meta-analysis', *Behavior Therapy*, 27 (2), pp. 171–86.

Taylor, T.K. and Biglan, A. (1998), 'Behavioral family interventions for improving child-rearing: A review for clinicians and policy makers', *Clinical Child and Family Psychology Review*, 1 (1), pp. 41–60.

Taylor, T.K., Schmidt, F., Pepler, D. and Hodgins, H. (in press), 'A comparison of eclectic treatment with Webster-Stratton's Parents and Children Series in a Children's Mental Health Centre: A randomized controlled trial', *Behavior Therapy*.

Webster Stratton, C. (1994), 'Advancing videotape parent training: A comparison study', *Journal of Consulting and Clinical Psychology*, 62 (3), pp. 583–93.

Webster-Stratton, C. (1992), *The incredible years: A trouble-shooting guide for parents of children ages 3–8 years*, Toronto, Umbrella Press.

Webster-Stratton, C. (1996a), 'Early intervention for families of preschool children with conduct problems' in Guarlnick, M. (ed.), *The effectiveness of early intervention: Second generation research*, Paul H. Brookes Company.

Webster-Stratton, C. (1996b), 'Videotape modeling intervention programs for families of young children with oppositional defiant disorder or conduct disorder' in Jensen, P.S. and Hibbs, E.D. (eds), *Psychosocial treatments for child and adolescent disorders: Empirically based approaches*, Washington, DC, APA.

Webster-Stratton, C. (1997), 'Treating children with early-onset conduct problems: A comparison of child and parent training interventions', *Journal of Consulting and Clinical Psychology*, 65 (1), pp. 93–109.

Webster-Stratton, C. (1998), 'Parent training with low-income clients: Promoting parental engagement through a collaborative approach' in Lutzker, J.R. (ed.), *Handbook of Child Abuse Research and Treatment*, New York, Plenum Press.

Webster-Stratton, C. (in press), 'Preventing conduct problems in Head Start children: Strengthening parent competencies', *Journal of Consulting and Clinical Psychology*.

Webster-Stratton, C. and Hammond, M. (in press), 'Conduct problems and level of social competence in Head Start children: Prevalence, pervasiveness and associated risk factors', *Clinical Child Psychology and Family Psychology Review*.

Webster-Stratton, C. and Hancock, L. (1998), 'Parent training: Content, Methods and Processes' in Schaefer, E. (ed.), *Parent training*, New York, Wiley and Sons.

Webster-Stratton, C. and Herbert, M. (1994), *Troubled families – Problem children: Working with parents: A collaborative process*, Chichester, Wiley and Sons.

Webster-Stratton, C., Kolpacoff, M. and Hollinsworth, T. (1988), 'Self-administered videotape therapy for families with conduct-problem children: Comparison with two cost-effective treatments and a control group', *Journal of Consulting and Clinical Psychology*, 56 (4), pp. 558–66.

Weisz, J.R., Donenberg, G.R., Han, S.S. and Weiss, B. (1995), 'Bridging the gap between laboratory and clinic in child and adolescent psychotherapy. Special Section: Efficacy an effectiveness in studies of child and adolescent psychotherapy', *Journal of Consulting and Clinical Psychology*, 63 (5), pp. 688–701.

Weisz, J.R., Han, S.S. and Valeri, S.M. (1996), 'What can we learn from Fort Bragg?', *Journal of Child and Family Studies*, 5 (2), pp. 185–90.

Weisz, J.R. and Weiss, B. (1993), *Effects of psychotherapy with children and adolescents*, London, Sage Publications.

Wolfe, D.A., Reppucci, N.D. and Hart, S. (1995), 'Child abuse prevention: Knowledge and priorities', *Journal of Clinical Child Psychology*, 24, pp. 5–22.

9 Introducing Evidence-based Social Welfare Practice in a National Child Care Agency

EVA LLOYD

Summary

- *This chapter describes the contribution of the Barnardo's research and development team to the introduction of evidence-based social welfare practice in the UK's largest voluntary child care agency.*
- *Barnardo's has made an explicit commitment to evidence-based services, and is the first child welfare organisation to do so.*
- *Current approaches to evidence-based social welfare practice are illustrated and their relationship to the model provided by evidence-based medicine is discussed.*
- *To clarify the links between research and practice, analogies are drawn with the processes by which research is thought to influence policy.*
- *Examples are provided of promising strategies for supporting developments in services for children and families on the basis of the best possible evidence for their effectiveness.*

Introduction: The Role of Research and Development (R&D)

Barnardo's works with some of the most disadvantaged children and their families and with young people, in all four countries that make up the UK. Forty per cent of its work involves children under eight and their families and in 1997 this work attracted some £30 million of Barnardo's total expenditure Day care and family support, community development and educational initiatives, structured therapeutic interventions for children who have suffered or are at risk of abuse, adoption and fostering services, as well as community-based parenting education groups, they all form a part of the range of services provided by Barnardo's for children and their parents. Additionally, Barnardo's provides a raft of services and advocacy for young people, including those leaving care or in contact with the youth justice system.

The Research and Development function in Barnardo's Children's Services

Department is located in the Policy, Planning and Research Unit based at its head office in Barkingside, Essex. This resides with the R&D team, comprising a coordinator, four principal officers research and development (three of these outposted) and a senior research officer.

While each team member holds a specialist national brief for particular subject areas of Barnardo's work, they also have specific support responsibilities for two geographical areas.

The R&D team is matched with a team of principal officers Policy and Practice; these two teams are further complemented by a development officer HIV/Aids and health education, an education advisor, an information officer, parliamentary and policy officer, an administrator and a sizeable library team; all supported by a range of administrative staff. Together, they make up one of the largest policy, planning and research units in the voluntary child care sector.

Members of the R&D team fulfil a number of different roles within the Unit, mainly working with senior and Children's Services field managers, as well as with a range of colleagues in the Marketing and Communications Department.

In order to further their own professional development and keep their skills up-to-date, each team member has an honorary attachment to a university in each of their designated geographical areas. The author of this chapter for example, in addition to holding the research and development brief for Barnardo's family support work in the widest sense, including child protection activities, has honorary research fellow attachments to Cambridge University's Centre for Family Research and the Queen's University's Centre for Child Care Research in Belfast.

The broad remit of the Barnardo's R&D team can be summarised in four points:

- to train practitioners in monitoring, research and self-evaluation methodologies and to enable them to engage in reflective practice;

- to commission evaluative research intended to assess service effectiveness; (e.g. Buist and Fuller, 1997; Sachdev et al., 1996);

- to support practitioners with the development of practice based on the best available evidence of effectiveness; and

- to commission and contribute to publications on *What Works* in each area of Barnardo's work (e.g. Stein, 1997; Beresford et al., 1995) and to write or commission reports used for Barnardo's lobbying, campaigning and advocacy work in relation to children's welfare policy (e.g. Roberts and Sachdev, 1996; Policy Development Unit, 1996: Lloyd et al., 1997).

In addition, the team work closely with colleagues to develop the voice of children and young people as users of Barnardo's service, or recipients of public and social policies as they affect children.

How the team attempts to realise the four objectives listed above in the work with practitioners will be described below, once the question of why it is important to do so has been addressed. To this end links between research and practice need exploring in some depth.

The Links Between Research and Practice: The 'Why' of Evidence-based Social Welfare Practice

In common with many other social welfare practitioners, Barnardo's believes that the use of the best possible evidence of effectiveness is as important for the work of a child care agency as it is for medical practice. Evidence-based medicine has been defined as an approach which attempts the integration of individual clinical expertise and the best external evidence (Sackett et al., 1996; Barnes-McGuire et al., 1997).

Research units such as the NHS Centre for Review and Dissemination at York University, as well as the Centre for Clinical Outcomes, Research and Effectiveness established by the British Psychological Society at University College, London, bear witness to the importance being attached to the development of clinical audit and related activities within the medical profession and that of clinical psychology respectively.

Experience with evidence-based medicine, in particular that achieved via the Cochrane Collaboration, has demonstrated that the common assumption both among lay people and professionals that current medical practice is routinely based on the best possible evidence of effectiveness, may be misplaced (Chalmers, 1996).

If this is true for a discipline like medicine which aims to be scientifically based, then how much more likely is this to be true of social work practice, which employs methodologies from a variety of disciplines, not all with a foundation in scientific methods (Macdonald and Sheldon, 1992).

The definition of evidence-based medicine used above, can equally well be applied to social welfare practice, provided that the term clinical is replaced with a term like 'practitioner'.

Evidence-based social work focuses on the use of methodologically sound research both in selecting and in evaluating social welfare interventions. Its adherents demand more rigorous evidence of social work effectiveness than that preferred by narrative reviews of current research, even when those are described as meta-analyses (Gorey, 1996).

Within the developing debate around evidence-based social work practice, two trends can be distinguished. One could be described as being towards a more strict or hard-line approach, the other veers towards eclecticism, or pragmatism.

As far as the more hard-line approach is concerned, the case for the use of methodologically sound research, in particular randomised controlled trials, in striving to create evidence-based social work practice, has been strongly made by Macdonald and Roberts (1995), Macdonald (1996), McNeish and Newman (1996) and Newman and Roberts (1997).

Fuller (1996) is more pragmatic in his approach. A relatively pragmatic approach to evaluation research is represented by Cheetham's (1997) work. Similar to the approach adopted by Barnes-McGuire (1997) towards children's mental health, these papers suggest minimum standards for any research that makes use of less robust research methods than the randomised controlled trial. For a discussion of the place of evidence-based social work research among other types of social work research see Trinder (1996) and Little (1998).

It is worth noting at this point a different line of argument which has been proposed by some researchers, to bring about a reconciliation between the demands for accountability and a realistic appraisal of the complexity of evaluating the impact of human services.

Simeonsson and Bailey's (1991) work represents this perspective, building on a model proposed by Smith (1981). These authors employ the framework of law as a model for evaluating the levels of certainty of evidence for the impact of early intervention programmes with young children and their parents, an area bedevilled by long-term impact uncertainties. In this model, three levels of evidence are considered: suggestive, preponderant and conclusive evidence.

With suggestive evidence, several explanations remain possible for the observed impact; in the case of preponderant evidence competing explanations for change are reduced, while conclusive evidence rules out competing explanations for change and defines the final level of certainty.

In the context of measuring the impact of early intervention programmes, three important implications of viewing evidence within a levels of certainty framework present themselves, according to Simeonsson and Bailey.

First of all, such a perspective enables programme evaluations to be expanded beyond experimental designs; secondly events and outcomes may vary in precision and certainty and finally the qualifications of findings can be formalised.

This approach may have some use in evaluating the evidence of effectiveness of different types of interventions, especially if resources to fund rigorous and independent outcome evaluations are limited. We will return to it in the final section of this chapter.

The fact remains that, while all the studies discussed here indicate that progress is beginning to be made with the rigorous evaluation of outcomes for children and families who use social welfare services, a considerable gap remains between research and practice.

The Links Between Research and Practice: The Role of Dissemination

The familiar contribution academics have traditionally made to the adoption of evidence-based or other approaches by social work practitioners has been via the production of research findings. More recently, a greater awareness has emerged among the research community and the large research funding agencies of the need to find more accessible formats for the dissemination of such findings.

The publication of research in academic and practitioner orientated journals is now often complemented by the production of brief 'findings' of individual research initiatives, and brief overviews of a raft of current research in particular areas.

The Rowntree Foundation's series of 'findings' and 'social policy summaries' are a shining example of the former, as is a recent ALBSU publication (Bynner and Steedman, 1995). The HighLight series produced by the National Children's Bureau in association with Barnardo's represents the latter.

A study of the use of research in local authorities commissioned by the Department of Health (Sinclair and Jacobs, 1994) indicated not only a heavy reliance on findings or summaries, but also that three quarters of those interviewed had used findings from any piece of research they had read. Respondents considered research central to effective policy making; this issue will be explored further in a separate section below.

Researchers may be increasingly aware of their responsibility for giving practitioners information in a form that can be translated into effective intervention strategies. But by which process are such findings assimilated into practice? Is merely publishing them in accessible formats sufficient?

This would appear not to be the case. The dissemination of research findings to practitioners by the research community is a different process from the processes required for the incorporation of the lessons from research into service development by practitioners themselves.

Dissemination of research findings in accessible formats, then, is a necessary but not a sufficient condition for the introduction of evidence-based social work practice. Dissemination by itself will not ensure that the gap between research and practice is closed, as the next section illustrates.

Closing the Gap between Research and Practice: The Case of Family Support

Concern that the results of research are not used to inform decision making regarding social welfare services is still widespread (Department of Health, 1994). A case in point is formed by the lessons that can be learned about the effectiveness of family support services in relation to the protection of children from abuse. What we know about the long-term effect of day care in particular (Gibbons, 1991) is not yet reflected in changes in family support practice.

Admittedly, there is the general problem that the effectiveness of general preventative services is hard to prove, since there is no easily identified target population to measure, nor any obvious measurable outcome (Jeffrey, 1996).

The important 1991 study by Gibbons aimed at filling this void. She followed families for four months after they had been referred to social services. She found that of a range of different family support services provided, day care alone had a significant positive effect on these children and their parents.

There is real evidence, too, that in terms of longer-term outcomes for children and families, open access family centres, which provide day care as part of their programmes, may be at least as effective, if not more so, than the client centred ones, which provide more 'therapeutic' interventions (Smith, 1996; Statham, 1994).

Gibbons (1990) reviewed the literature on the effectiveness of family support services predating the Children Act's implementation. What she found particularly striking was the absence of controlled evaluations of measures aimed at preventing serious child-rearing problems and the removal of children from home, i.e. child protection interventions. However, Macdonald and Roberts (1995) identified good evidence for the effectiveness of some forms of systemic family therapy, which is practised in some of Barnardo's family centres.

Little and Gibbons (1993) also found that the results of traditional approaches to child protection in England and Wales meant that only a small proportion of abused children were registered as at risk, as a result of different registration criteria and different styles of investigation by different levels of staff.

Add this fact about the investigation process to the finding about the absence of sound intervention studies and surely the conclusion is warranted that in principle open access family support provision offering day care among its services is no less likely to reach children in need of protection than the client-focused centres are.

In fact, of all the different components of the family support packages offered by family centres, the evidence for the effectiveness of day care for children in need is actually the strongest.

This state of affairs highlights some of the problems surrounding the adoption of evidence-based social work in the area of so-called preventive services, as described by, for instance, Sinclair, Hearn and Pugh (1997).

Analogies with the Process Linking Research and Policy

While there should there be clear links between research and practice, the same is true for research and policy. The routes by which social research may influence policy would appear to have been explored more thoroughly than those between social research and practice. What lessons can be applied from that particular relationship to achieve the successful incorporation of research findings into social welfare practice? What has been learned about any barriers to such a process?

In the course of a discussion of the influence that qualitative research may have on the policy process, Rist (1994, p. 456) observed that:

> Policy making is multi-dimensional and multi-faceted. Research is but one (and often minor at that) among the number of frequently contradictory and competing sources that seek to influence what is an ongoing and constantly evolving process.

This observation echoes a similar one by Tizard (1990, p. 438), who said:

> ... it can plausibly be argued that research findings on their own have never played a crucial role in any major policy decision.

It has even been suggested that mental health policy for instance has been influenced more by political values than by evidence (Ham et al., 1995), and it certainly is not unique in this respect.

It would seem appropriate then to view practice as similarly subject to competing influences, one of which is research. Indeed, even in a historical case of the documented influence of research on practice – the closure of Barnardo's residential homes in favour of work with families and of fostering and adoption – doubt was cast by the principal researcher on the degree of impact the research itself had on this decision.

Tizard (1990), the principal researcher in question, postulated not only that the agency in question was 'ready' for this decision, but also that the research in the agency's own residential homes provided them with a justification for it (1996, p. 13).

Are there further parallels that can be drawn between the process by which research is likely to influence policy and the process by which it may influence practice? Rist (1994, p. 547) analysed the different phases of the policy cycle and identified three points where research ought to inform decisions. This was: 1) at the point of policy formulation; 2) at the point of policy implementation; and 3) in respect of policy accountability, i.e. concerning its intended and unintended consequences.

In respect of the influence of research on practice, a similar analysis can be applied to the three phases of service development where research and development input is required to inform Barnardo's practice and strengthen its evidence base. At the point of service formulation, of service implementation and of service accountability, an evidence-based approach has much to offer.

Encouraging Evidence-based Practice at the Point of Service Formulation

How can new service developments be supported with the best available research evidence for effectiveness? At the point of service formulation?

The R&D team's input at the point of service formulation consists of a number of different strands. One of these is training in monitoring and self-evaluation methodologies and impact assessment, delivered by team members to managers in the different geographical regions where Barnardo's operations are located. A training pack is available which was produced in support of this training (Ware, McNeish and Parish, 1994).

Another one of these strands is the provision of detailed comments on different stage of individual service proposals by team members with expertise in a particular subject. Particular attention is paid to the formulation of aims and objectives which lend themselves to impact assessment and to ensuring that practitioners are in a position to use internal and external evidence critically. This work may be done in partnership with the relevant principal officers policy and practice in the Policy, Planning and Research Unit.

Part of the research and development team's remit is to encourage greater correspondence between service planning and the findings of research and evaluation, so that models of intervention are selected which are known for their effectiveness. At the early stages practitioners may refer to Barnardo's own *What Works* series of research reviews to inform the choice of the appropriate intervention methodologies.

The *What Works* series of publications from Barnardo's aim to be compendia of methodologically sound research pertinent to the different areas of Barnardo's work. While they do not constitute a systematic review in the strict sense of the term, they nevertheless could be said to be a 'hybrid' form of such reviews, amply illustrated with practice examples informed by sound research.

Written in an accessible style, they are aimed at an audience of practitioners and policy makers. They are being used by managers in designing new services, and in negotiations with local authority partners.

The authors of the first title in the series (Macdonald and Roberts, 1995, p. 5) acknowledge that good work on the effectiveness of interventions can only be achieved with the enthusiastic participation of those at the sharp end, the practitioners themselves. They set out the series' main objective as follows:

> Until we are able to assemble good evidence on the effectiveness or otherwise of our current interventions with children, it is all too likely that they will be as informed by the same mixture of passionate conviction, ideology and good and poor research, as has been the case in the past.

Other titles so far have dealt with children with disabilities (Beresford et al., 1995), family placement (Sellick and Thoburn, 1996), leaving care (Stein, 1997), and inclusive education (Sebba with Sachdev, 1997). In the pipeline are publications dealing with parents with learning difficulties (McGraw, forthcoming); child protection (Macdonald, forthcoming); and parenting education (Lloyd et al., forthcoming).

Two volumes in this series are intended to spread the message about evidence-based social work practice as widely as possible. Both are collections of seminar papers, edited by the coordinator of the Barnardo's research and development team, in partnership with the director of the University of London's Social Science Research Unit (Oakley and Roberts, 1996; Roberts and Oakley, 1996). They address an audience of both academics and practitioners. The ESRC funded Barnardo's and the Social Science Research Unit to organise these seminars to explore the use of reliable methodologies, including randomised controlled trials.

The establishment of a new service may be preceded by a development period in which mapping, survey or other research and development activities are undertaken in the area where the new service is to be located. Reports based on such activities, together with literature reviews and the use of the *What Works* evidence, aim to ensure the optimal application of the available evidence in service design.

Finally, needs assessments are an essential requirement for evidence-based practice. It is no good initiating apparently effective interventions which users do not want.

Encouraging Evidence-based Practice at the Point of Service Implementation

How can the findings from methodologically sound research best be used to inform ongoing developments in practice? At the point of service implementation and beyond?

A current initiative concerning family support is directly relevant to the question of how to make *What Works* work. Members of the team are working on a collaborative proposal, with colleagues in a social services department in central England and with The Centre for Research into Parenting and Children at Oxford. It is concerned with developing an evidence-based programme of family support services in this county.

By evidence-based is meant implementing policies, procedures and interventions that the best available evidence suggests will be most successful in achieving the intended objectives. Two studies should result from this initiative, one concerning what works in promoting evidence-based practice in child welfare services, another reviewing what works in family support.

On a modest scale, the Policy, Planning and Research Unit newsletter is used by the R&D team to update colleagues in the field on developments in research. Recently a series of short items on Cunningham and Bremner's (1995) work in Ontario, Canada, attracted a lot of attention from colleagues. These researchers employed a randomised controlled trial to measure the effectiveness of community-based parenting education group training versus clinic based interventions with children and their parents. Experiments with a research bulletin board using the Barnardo's wide-area computer network are in progress. The research team have also provided updates for the different areas of work as part of several organisational strategic reviews.

Another potential resource for evidence-based practice in Barnardo's is the introduction of a computerised client records monitoring system. This is gradually being implemented to facilitate a range of relevant monitoring activities to enable evaluation to take place at different stages of service development and to facilitate the production of annual and other management reports.

Encouraging Evidence-based Practice in Service Accountability

How can the outcomes of Barnardo's work with children and families best be evaluated by means of methodologically sound evaluative research? At the point of service accountability?

It is to be expected that the conditions for methodologically sound research apply to evaluation studies carried out on Barnardo's own interventions. Their success or otherwise ought to be measured against the findings from other sound evaluation research into similar interventions.

Barnardo's research and development practice in this area can be compared to Jacobs's (1988) five-tiered approach to a service or system evaluation, which is employed at various stages of service development. Jacobs recommends a formative evaluation at the pre-implementation stage and moves to an outcome or summative evaluation to measure the service or system impact, via accountability, clarification and progress to objectives stages which each require detailed and different kinds of monitoring activities.

Examples of evaluation at some or all of these service levels can be identified for most of Barnardo's services. The use of formative evaluations at the pre-implementation stage has already been mentioned in the context of service formulation. However, outcome evaluations are relatively infrequently encountered, yet these are potentially the most important contribution that a learning organisation can make to evidence-based practice.

Two Scottish examples of outcome evaluations of Barnardo's services are an externally commissioned study of a service for young people who sexually abused others (Buist and Fuller, 1997) and an internal evaluation, largely indebted to the high quality monitoring data collected by the head teacher, of a residential school for children with emotional and behavioural difficulties (Sachdev et al., 1996).

There is also a need to build on initial developments in cross-organisational evaluation of programmes, so that findings can be fed into service development on an ongoing basis. Ensuring that a focus is kept on realistically achievable service outcomes which are, moreover, comparable across the organisation, is a major challenge.

Currently it remains problematic for practitioners to take on board the lessons from existing research and evaluation findings from their own services in developing evidence-based services.

Evidence-based Social Welfare Practice and the Barnardo's Research and Development Agenda

The points raised so far concern the practical utility of research in child welfare services. Despite any inherent contradictions between problem-oriented research, basic research and applied research, all three types of research must contribute to the knowledge base that is required for social welfare and allied professionals if they are to provide the most effective services.

The integration of research findings into social welfare practice, according to Cheetham (1997), is a subtle, often lengthy process subject to both organisational influences and professional judgements.

Changes in training are also needed as a way forward. Cheetham (1997, p. 305) argues that social work education at all levels needs to encourage research-minded practice. In her view evaluative research has a specific role to play in relation to practice:

> ... most evaluative research does not – and should not, given its focus and methods – present unequivocal prescriptions for action. More often it presents a basis for critical review and reflection, perhaps including a comparison of different ways of providing similar services, an analysis of factors that influence quality and a pointer to unintended or unexpected outcomes.

Combining multidisciplinary education and research is another strategy

Cheetham promotes. Different types of action research are identified as a promising way of fostering evidence-based social welfare practice. An example of this is an experiment carried out at the National Institute of Social Work in the early 1990s.

NISW, sponsored by the Department of Health and the Rowntree Foundation, experimented with a programme in which researchers helped policy makers and practitioners to translate research findings into action plans first and then to evaluate their implementation (Neill and Williams, 1992).

The adoption of evidence-based social welfare practice is bound to benefit from the recent establishment of the Centre for Evidence-based Social Services at the University of Exeter, with Professor Brian Sheldon as director.

This partnership project has been jointly funded by the Department of Health and 15 social services departments in the south and south west of England. Apart from initiating studies of the evidence base for a range of social welfare services, the centre also hopes to develop optimal formats for the training of social workers in critical appraisal skills – the kind of skills Cheetham has identified as indispensable to the profession.

Another useful development is the impending registration, within the Cochrane Collaboration, of a review group dedicated to children's developmental, psychosocial and learning problems which will complement other groups where issues are represented across the age groups.

Research and development activities in Barnardo's will profit from these developments. For the time being, and in the absence of sufficient resources, an incremental approach will continue to be employed towards the evaluation of programme impact, along the lines suggested by Smith (1981).

On their own, R&D teams like the Barnardo's one, cannot hope to provide sufficient support to secure evidence-based practice across the board throughout a social welfare organization as large as Barnardo's. However, they are not entirely alone. They are supported by a strong training structure across the children's services department, as well as a corporate one.

They are also fortunate to be supported by contributions from a number of Barnardo's managers and senior practitioners with established reputations in action research and with publications to their name (Stones, 1994; Gill, 1994; Fratter, 1996).

Conclusion

Another important trend in research is also recognised by those responsible for research and development in Barnardo's. This is that at the same time as evidence-based social welfare practice is gaining ground, a trend can be detected in other disciplines, like social and developmental psychology (Richardson, 1996; Phoenix et al., 1992), towards the incorporation of more qualitative and mixed research methodologies, including grounded theory (Pidgeon and Henwood, 1996). Although this is a departure from the rigorous experimental methods previously employed, such developments should be viewed as complementary research strategies.

While the arguments for the adoption of the most robust methodologies for defining effectiveness which are put forward by proponents (Macdonald and Macdonald, 1995) of evidence-based social welfare practice are accepted in principle, the Barnardo's team acknowledges that there is, again, a need for an incremental approach to the adoption of such practice. Greater levels of certainty are particularly needed when interventions may have major implications for the future lives of children and their families.

For the purposes of research and development in Barnardo's, effectiveness continues to be defined in terms of robust evidence that the services provided by Barnardo's are achieving their stated aims in supporting children, young people, and their families.

Finally, evidence-based social welfare services are not an academic exercise. Children and their parents, the subject of this book, have a right to know about the likely impact of child welfare services and about the evidence for their effectiveness.

It is crucial to the quality of all such evidence that it reflects the views of those who are at the receiving end of Barnardo's interventions – and that includes children – on the impact achieved. Users of services are an expert source of knowledge on effectiveness who are too often ignored in research.

In listening to user views, Barnardo's strives to incorporate those of visible and invisible minorities. There can be neither effective research nor practice without doing so. For instance, Black perspectives on Barnardo's services for children in need were explored by a research team from the National Children's Bureau (Caesar, Parchment and Berridge, 1994).

The views of students in colleges of further education on the inclusion of students with disabilities were explored by a research team including three further education students who themselves had a disability (Ash, Bellew, Davies, Newman and Richardson, 1995).

Barnardo's also actively promotes the involvement of children in service design, implementation and evaluation, as well as high standards in research with children (Alderson, 1995). To do justice to a discussion of these issues is however beyond the scope of this chapter.

References

Ash, A., Bellew, J., Davies, M., Newman, T. and Richardson, L. (1995), *Everybody in? The Experience of Disabled Students in Colleges of Further Education*, Barkingside, Barnardo's.

Alderson, P. (1995), *Listening to Children: Children, Ethics and Social Research*, Barkingside, Barnardo's.

Barnes-McGuire, J., Stein, A. and Rosenberg, W. (1997), 'Evidence-Based Medicine and Child Mental Health Services', *Children and Society*, Vol. 11, pp. 89–96.

Beresford, B., Sloper, P., Baldwin, S. and Newman, T. (1995), *What Works in Services for Families with a Disabled Child*, Barkingside, Barnardo's.

Buist, M. and Fuller, R. (1997) *A Chance to Change: an Intervention with Young People who Have Sexually Abused Others*, The Scottish Office Home Department Central Research Unit, Edinburgh

Bynner, J. and Steedman, J. (1995), *Difficulties with Basic Skills: Findings from the 1970 British Cohort Study*, London, The Basic Skills Agency.

Caesar, G., Parchment, M. and Berridge, D. (1994), *Black Perspectives on Services for Children in Need*, Barkingside, Barnardo's in association with the National Children's Bureau.

Chalmers, I. (1996), 'Assessing the Evidence: the Cochrane Collaboration' in Roberts, H. and Oakley, A. (eds), *What Works? Effective Social Interventions in Child Welfare*, Barkingside, Barnardo's and the Social Science Research Unit, University of London.

Cheetham, J. (1997), 'Evaluating Social Work: Progress and Prospects', *Research on Social Work Practice*, Vol. 7, 3, pp. 291–310.

Cunningham, C., Bremner, R. and Boyle, M. (1995), 'Large Group Community-Based Parenting Programmes for Families of Pre-Schoolers at Risk for Disruptive Behaviour Disorders: Utilization, Cost Effectiveness and Outcome,' *Journal of Child Psychology and Psychiatry*, Vol. 36, 7, pp. 1141–60.

Department of Health (1994), *A wider strategy for research and development relating to personal social services*, London, HMSO.

Fratter, J. (1996), *Adoption with Contact: Implications for Policy and Practice*, London, British Agencies for Adoption and Fostering.

Fuller, R. (1996), 'Evaluating Social Work Effectiveness: a Pragmatic Approach' in Roberts, H. and Oakley, A. (eds), *What Works? Effective Social Interventions in Child Welfare*, Barkingside, Barnardo's and the Social Science Research Unit, University of London.

Gibbons, J. (1990), *Family Support and Prevention: Studies in Local Areas*, London, HMSO.

Gibbons, J. (1991), 'Children in Need and Their Families: Outcomes of Referrals to Social Services', *British Journal of Social Work*, Vol. 21, pp. 217–27.

Gill, O. (1994) *Parenting Under Pressure*, Barkingside, Barnardo's.

Gorey, K. M. (1996), 'Social Work Intervention Effectiveness Research: Comparison of the Findings from Internal Versus External Evaluations', *Social Work Research*, Vol. 20, pp. 119–28.

Ham, C., Hunter, D.J. and Robinson, R. (1995), 'Evidence Based Policy Making', *BMJ*, Vol. 3, 10, pp. 205–10.

Jacobs, F.H. (1998), 'The Five-Tiered Approach to Evaluation: Context and Implementation' in Weiss, H.B. and Jacobs, F.H. (eds), *Evaluating Family Programs*, Hawthorne, NY, Aldine de Gruyter.

Jeffrey, J. (1996), 'Targeting: from Principles to Practice' in Allen, I. (ed.), *Targeting Those Most in Need: Winners and Losers*, London, Policy Studies Institute.

Little, M. (1998), 'Whispers in the Library: a Response to Liz Trinder's Article on the State of Social Work Research', *Child and Family Social Work*, Vol. 3, 1, pp. 49–56.

Little, M. and Gibbons, J. (1993), 'Predicting the Rate of Children on the Child Protection Register', *Research, Policy and Planning*, Vol. 10, 2, pp. 15–8.

Lloyd, E., Hemingway, M., Newman, T., Roberts, H. and Webster, A. (1997), *Today and Tomorrow: Investing in Our Children*, Barkingside, Barnardo's.

Lloyd, E. with Barlow, J. and Webster-Stratton, C. (forthcoming), *What Works in Parenting Education*, Barkingside, Barnardo's.

Macdonald, G. (1996), 'Ice Therapy: Why We Need Randomised Controlled Trials' in Roberts, H. and Oakley, A. (eds), *What Works? Effective Social Interventions in Child Welfare*, Barkingside, Barnardo's and the Social Science Research Unit, University of London.

Macdonald, G. (forthcoming), *What Works in Child Protection*, Barkingside, Barnardo's.

Macdonald, G. and Macdonald, K.I. (1995), 'Ethical Issues in Social Work Research' in Hugman, R. and Smith, D. (eds), *Ethical Issues in Social Work*, London, Routledge.

Macdonald, G. and Roberts, H. (1995), *What Works in the Early Years: Effective Interventions for Children and Their Families in Health, Social Welfare, Education and Child Protection*, Barkingside, Barnardo's.

Macdonald, G. and Sheldon, B. (1992), 'Contemporary Studies of the Effectiveness of Social Work', *British Journal of Social Work*, Vol. 22, 6, pp. 614–43.

McGraw, S. (forthcoming), *What Works for Parents with Learning Disabilities*, Barkingside, Barnardo's.

McNeish, D. and Newman, T. (1996), 'Evaluating Child Welfare Interventions', *Research, Policy and Planning*, Vol. 14, 1, pp. 53–8.

Neill, J. and Williams, J. (1992), *Leaving Hospital: Elderly People and Their Discharge to Community Care*, London, HMSO.

Newman, T. and Roberts, R. (1997,) 'Assessing Social Work Effectiveness in Child Care Practice: the Contribution of Randomised Controlled Trials', *Child-Care, Health and Development*, Vol. 23, 4, pp. 287–95.

Oakley, A. and Roberts, H. (eds) (1996,) *Evaluating Social Interventions*, Barkingside, Barnardo's.

Phoenix, A., Woollett, A. and Lloyd, E. (eds) (1992), *Motherhood: Meanings, Practices and Ideologies*, London, Sage.

Pidgeon, N. and Henwood, K. (1996), 'Grounded Theory: practical implementation' in Richardson, J.T. (ed.), *Handbook of Qualitative Research Methods for Psychology and the Social Sciences*, Leicester, British Psychological Society Books.

Policy and Development Unit (1996), *Transition to Adulthood*, Barkingside, Barnardo's.

Richardson, J.T. (ed.) (1996), *Handbook of Qualitative Research Methods for Psychology and the Social Sciences*, Leicester, British Psychological Society Books.

Rist, R.C. (1994), 'Influencing the Policy Process with Qualitative Research' in Densin, N. and Guba, S. (eds), *Handbook of Qualitative Research*, London, Sage.

Roberts, H. and Oakley, A. (eds) (1996), *What Works: Effective Social Interventions in Child Welfare*, Barkingside, Barnardo's and the Social Science Research Unit, University of London.

Roberts, H. and Sachdev, D. (eds) (1996), *Young People's Social Attitudes*, Barkingside, Barnardo's with Social and Community Planning Research.

Sachdev, D. with Potter, S. and Hughes, M. (1996), *An Evaluation Blackford Brae Project: 6 Years on*, Barkingside, Barnardo's Policy, Planning and Development Unit.

Sackett, D.L., Rosenberg, W.M.C., Muir Gray, J.A., Haynes, R.B. and Richardson, W.S. (1996), 'Evidence-Based Medicine: What It Is and What It Isn't', *British Medical Journal*, Vol. 312, pp. 71–2.

Sebba, J. with Sachdev, D. (1997), *What Works in Inclusive Education*, Barkingside, Barnardo's.

Sellick, C. and Thoburn, J. (1996), *What Works in Family Placement*, Barkingside, Barnardo's.

Simeonsson, R.J. and Bailey, D.B. Jr (1991), 'Evaluating Programme Impact: Levels of Certainty' in Mitchell, D. and Brown, R.I. (eds), *Early Intervention Studies for Young Children with Special Needs*, London, Chapman and Hall.

Sinclair, R. and Jacobs, C. (1994), *Research in Personal Social Services: the Experience of Three Local Authorities*, London, National Children's Bureau.

Sinclair, R., Hearn, B. and Pugh, G. (1997), *Preventive Work with Families: the Role of Mainstream Services*, London, National Children's Bureau.

Smith, N. L. (1981), 'The Certainty of Judgements in Health Evaluations', *Evaluation and Programme Planning*, Vol. 4, pp. 273–8.

Smith, T. (1996), *Family Centres and Bringing up Young Children*, London, HMSO.

Statham, J. (1994), *Child Care in the Community: the Provision of Open Access Services for Young Children in Family Centres*, London, Save the Children.

Stein, M. (1996), *What Works in Leaving Care*, Barkingside, Barnardo's.

Stones, C. (1994), *Family Centres in Action*, London, Macmillan.

Tizard, B. (1990), 'Research and Policy: Is There a Link?', *The Psychologist*, Vol. 3, 10, pp. 435–40.

Tizard, B. (1996), 'An Interview with Barbara Tizard' in Bernstein, B. and Brannen, J. (eds), *Children, Research and Policy*, London, Taylor and Francis Ltd.

Trinder, L. (1996), 'Social Work Research: the State of the Art', *Child and Family Social Work*, Vol. 1, 1, pp. 233–42.

Ware, C., McNeish, D. and Parish, A. (1994), *Successful Evaluation: a Barnardo's Resource Pack*, Barkingside, Barnardo's.

10 A Consensus

ANN BUCHANAN

Summary

- A consensus emerges from the interdisciplinary group contributing to this book, about what needs to be done to prevent or at least to limit the disabling effects of emotional and behavioural disorders in children.
- In this final chapter findings from the previous chapters are summarised and linked to related research findings.

Parenting cuts to the very core of our emotions. Be we medical practitioners, researchers, teachers, social workers, or clinical psychologists, we have one thing in common: some of our strongest emotions and our strongest-held views are elicited by our own experience of being parented and if we have children, of being a parent. Add to this different professional training, role expectations and objectives, as well as different theoretical backgrounds, and research experience, there was considerable anxiety when we came together as a group that controversy rather than consensus would rule the day. Loseke and Gelles (1993, p. xv.), writing about 'experts' from the field of family violence, commented:

> Too much controversy in the family of family violence experts has, at times, led to professional family dysfunction, with enemies rather than colleagues, opposition rather than co-operation, sabotage rather than assistance, silence rather than communication.

Against expectations, however, there emerges from this book some consensus, and I believe a coherent agenda on what needs to be done to prevent, or at least limit, the disabling effects of emotional and behavioural disorders in children. The credit for this rests not only with the authors who have contributed to this book, but to a growing consensus amongst the research community at large that the weight of evidence from other studies around the world as well as from those outlined in this book, is pointing in a similar direction.

- *The number of children with emotional and behavioural problems is rising.*

• *Depending on the age of the child, sex, disorder, diagnostic criteria, area in which they live and period in which they have been brought up, the prevalence of children with emotional and behavioural disorders can be as high as one in four (boys) and one in five (girls). These children are a major concern, to themselves, to their parents and to society in general. Such disorders are a major cause of educational failure and social exclusion. Lack of emotional well-being in childhood is linked to mental ill health and major illness and disease in adult life, as well as to unemployment.*

There is considerable evidence that despite improving health and educational standards, the number of children with emotional and behavioural disorders appears to be rising (Rutter and Smith, 1995; Kovacs and Devlin, 1998). Prevalence rates vary according to the age of the child, sex, disorder, diagnostic criteria, area in which the child lives and period in which they have been brought up. Anderson, Williams and McGee (1987) in a study of 792 children age 11 years from the general population in New Zealand found an overall prevalence of disorders at 18 per cent with a sex ratio (boys:girls) of 1.7:1. Newman et al. (1996) have shown that internalising disorders for girls rose to 19 per cent at ages 21. Rutter et al. (1975) using the Rutter 'A' Health and Behaviour Checklist in an inner London area, found an overall prevalence rate of disorders for boys of 25 per cent and for girls of 13 per cent.

This means that up to one in four (boys at age 11) or one in five (girls at age 21) in any given area are being disabled by emotional and behavioural problems. This is a tragedy for both the children and their families and a huge economic waste of potential for society as a whole.

In chapter 2, Sarah Stewart-Brown, taking a Public Health or 'population' perspective, talks of an 'epidemic'. Given the strong associations between problems in childhood and adult mental and physical health, children with emotional and behaviour disorders are indeed an NHS Public Health concern. She also argues convincingly that such children do not have a separate disorder or disease, but are at an extreme end of a continuum of emotional and behavioural expression seen in all children. Anything that can be done to improve the emotional well-being of all children is likely also to benefit children with emotional disorders.

We need, however, to ask whether population approaches such as public health and educational measures will be sufficient to tackle this epidemic or whether there is also a need for specific interventions for children at high risk of emotional and behavioural disorders. The concern is, how will these children be identified? Although there are now well validated and easy-to-use assessment schedules (for example, Goodman, 1997), Dr Stewart-Brown believes that a national screening programme will not be helpful. There are very real concerns that children picked up by such a screening programme will be further handicapped by 'labelling'. Despite these concerns, it is important that such tools are made more widely available to assess the efficacy of interventions, and especially to assess certain high-risk groups such as children in care.

Kathy Sylva and Paul Colman taking an educational perspective, see the challenge as preventing children with emotional and behavioural disorders being excluded from school and becoming educational failures. The critical period is often before children have ever entered school. The number of school exclusions is a simple indicator of the number of children with emotional and behavioural difficulties. These have risen dramatically in the last four years. The message from the High/ Scope study in the US (Schweinhart and Weikart, 1993) is that over 27 years, there is a $7 return for every $1 spent on structured preschool education. Sylva and Colman conclude:

> If early education can encourage inclusion, then it's likely that these social gains will outweigh the direct cognitive benefits related to school-like skills (Sylva and Colman, this volume).

- *Children with 'emotional' and 'behavioural' problems are part of a continuum of emotional and behavioural expression seen in all children. The prognosis for those with 'emotional' disorders or who 'internalise' their distress is rather different from those with 'behavioural' disorders or who 'externalise' their difficulties. There is a strong risk in both groups of children that they will have continuing problems in adulthood. There is some overlap between the two groups.*

Children with emotional disorders are part of the continuum of behaviours expressed by all children. Mild anxiety, depression and mood swings are part of the normal pattern of ups and downs in all children. Anxiety is very common in young children (Kovacs and Devlin, 1998) and depression or mood swings are quite common amongst adolescents, particularly girls. There is considerable evidence that 'internalising' disorders, however, are more 'within the child'. Their temperament or biology may make them more anxious or liable to mood swings and as a result more sensitive to family adversities. For example, in chapter 3 we saw that family conflict was a risk factor for 'unhappy' type behaviour. Kovacs and Devlin (1998) found that many of these children develop anxiety or depression in later life. Some of these children, however, may develop 'externalising' problems in adolescence, perhaps as a way of masking their internal distress. Plomin (1994, p. 817) noted:

> We should not lose sight of the fact that the same genetic data provide the best available evidence for the importance of non-genetic factors. Rarely does genetic influence account for more than half of the variance of behavioural dimensions and disorders.

Using Bronfenbrenner's (1979) 'ecological' model, there is therefore much that can be done by parents and others to manipulate the environment so that the child can find the 'niche' in which he/she operates best. For more serious cases, cognitive behavioural therapy and medication may be used to treat symptoms (Goodman, 1997).

Children with 'externalising' disorders are also part of a continuum of normal behaviour. At the extreme end, those with severe problems are more likely to be boys and in some cases may have a biological tendency to over-activity; but the expression of their maladaptive behaviour is strongly linked to parenting 'style' and family adversities. This group of children is at risk of developing a 'conduct disorder' and antisocial behaviour in adolescence and in adult life. In adult life, however, some children who had 'externalising' disorders can become depressed, perhaps because they face the reality of lost life opportunities, for example children who have been in care (Buchanan and Ten Brinke, 1997). As many authors in this book report, structured home based and school programmes based on behavioural principles are extremely helpful for these children with externalising disorders and can be effective in up to two thirds of cases (Webster-Stratton, this volume). In extreme cases of Attention Deficit Hyperactivity Disorder (ADHD), some children may be helped by medication.

- *Parenting 'style' is a key factor in the aetiology of 'behavioural' disorders, and a factor in some 'emotional' disorders, but blaming parents is not helpful.*

Again there is considerable agreement that how children are parented, or parenting 'style', is a key factor in the aetiology of behavioural disorders in children. The challenge for parents is to match their 'style' to the child. Parents whose parenting style lacks 'warmth', and parents who are punitive and critical, are particularly damaging to children with both emotional and behavioural disorders. The good news is that more positive parenting styles can be learnt, as we see from Frances Gardner's and Carolyn Webster-Stratton's work.

All contributors to this book agree that a culture of 'blaming' the parents is unhelpful. Indeed the heightened sense of guilt associated with feelings of failure may, in the extreme cases, be associated with child maltreatment (Buchanan, 1996). Parents whose relationships break down are particularly vulnerable to these feelings of guilt. Recent research supports Ann Buchanan and JoAnn Ten Brinke's (1997) finding that in these situations, the long term psychological damage to children comes from conflict, extreme disadvantage and parenting breakdown (an experience of being in 'care') rather than family breakdown. There are costs to children's emotional well-being from family breakdown, but these can be limited if conflict is kept to the minimum.

*   *It can no longer be assumed that parenting 'just comes naturally'. Parenting was always a complex, highly skilled task. Skills learnt from our own parents may not be appropriate in a fast changing world.*

In chapter 1 we noted the great changes that are occurring in families and family life. Most of us learn our parenting skills from our own parents. These skills evolved over generations and most skills that were passed on were those likely to safeguard and promote the well-being of children. Some men and women, however, have a legacy of punitive and abusive parenting and up to a third of this group will have difficulties when bringing up their own children (Buchanan, 1996).

In recent times, families have also become more mobile and grandparents may not be around to help with the grandchildren (Buchanan and Ten Brinke, 1997; Morrow and Richards, 1996). Young parents, removed from the vicinity of their families of origin, have had to find other forms of support. In addition, with much larger numbers of women entering the workforce, the old skills need to be updated – how do you bring up three children on your own while working at the same time?

In this changing world, we can no longer assume that new parents have the necessary knowledge and skills. In the past, parent training has been associated with parents who are failing parents. Sarah Stewart-Brown suggests that parent training should be available to all parents rather like immunisation. Jane Barlow's current research, as described in chapter 6, takes the evaluation of parent-training programmes one stage further. The home-school linked parent-training programme, based on the work of Bavolek (1996), provides parent-training and emotional literacy skills not only for parents, but for teachers and children as well. This represents an important advance on the more traditional parent-training programmes which have been used in this country to date.

Recent research on developing parenthood education in schools (for example, Hope and Sharland, 1997) approaches the problem from another angle. Their key finding was that when parenthood education was delivered well in schools, there was a measurable and positive impact on students' knowledge, skills and understanding of parenthood. Their key recommendation was that:

> The School Curriculum and Assessment Authority (SCAA) should establish a pilot scheme to develop a comprehensive parenthood syllabus and programmes for 11 to 13 year-olds and 14 to 16 year-olds. The syllabus should be based upon the values of caring for children and the importance of relationships, avoid promoting a single model of family structures or cultures, and be structured around five main themes: what it means to be a parent; what parents need; parent child relationships; rights and responsibilities; health and development. (Hope and Sharland, 1997, p. 8).

- *Parenting occurs within the interacting 'ecology' of the world in which the child grows up: child/parent(s); child/parent(s)/family; child/parent(s)/ family/school/community/wider social environment. Interventions at person, family, school, community, population levels are complementary.*

All contributors agree that parenting takes place within an interacting 'ecological framework': factors in the child, such as the child's temperament, interact with factors in the parent(s), the wider family, school/community and the macro social environment.

Different researchers, however, place different emphases on the role of parenting and/or the context of the parenting. These different emphases complement rather than contradict each other. They reflect professional training and roles, research experiences, expectations and opportunities within their specific professions.

Teresa Smith coming from a community work background demonstrates the value of identifying disadvantaged areas and placing open-access resources such as Family Centres in these areas. Severely disadvantaged communities are likely to be high-risk areas for children with emotional and behavioural disorders.

As a social worker, Ann Buchanan is interested in identifying risk and protective factors in the 'ecological' framework so that compensatory experiences or 'buffers' can be set in place. This, rather than any concept of therapy, is the main intervention used by social workers in voluntary and statutory agencies, although they may not have identified the theory as such. An important 'buffer', for example for children from multiply disadvantaged backgrounds, is a preschool experience such as that advocated by Kathy Sylva.

Frances Gardner, as a clinical psychologist, suggests that individual work that teaches parents to play with their children and find enjoyment in their activities as well as to manage conflict has long-term benefits. Carolyn Webster-Stratton started her long professional career as a Nurse Practitioner also working with individual parents. In her carefully controlled trials, she found that group interventions 'normalise parents' experiences and situations' and are also more cost-effective.

- *There is considerable evidence that some interventions are more effective than others, but there may be other interventions that are also effective but they have not been evaluated.*

Kathy Sylva demonstrates convincingly that particular preschool structured programmes lead to positive gains for the children. There is also longitudinal evidence of the efficacy of this approach from the High/Scope (Schweinhart and Weikart, 1993). Jane Barlow's literature review of parent-training programmes and Carolyn Webster-Stratton's and Frances Gardner's contributions also give evidence that we now know 'what works'. From her literature review, Jane Barlow demonstrates that group-based parent-training programmes are remarkably effective in helping children with behaviour disorders, and the group-based behaviour modification programmes appeared to be the most successful.

In the UK, however, although there are a large number of different parenting programmes in existence, there is a paucity of methodologically rigorous research. In simple language this means that some programmes currently provided may not work, or at worst may even be damaging.

Carolyn Webster-Stratton, however, working in the US, can be more confident. Over the past 30 years, numerous rigorously controlled studies have demonstrated that there exist today a number of effective therapies and services for children and families that can reduce behaviour problems and delinquency, improve mental health, assist abusive parents to improve their child-rearing, and improve family functioning (Webster-Stratton and Hooven, 1998). Among the most successful and most clearly demonstrated as effective are her series of programmes with young children (age 3–8 years). Carolyn

Webster-Stratton can confidently predict that utilising her parent programmes, around two-thirds of children with behaviour problems will make sustained improvements. This leaves a 'hard core' who may need to be further treated by other methods. For example, Webster-Stratton's research further suggests that combining child-training and teacher-training in conjunction with parent-training, will lead to greater improvements for the third that do not show sustained effects with parent-training alone.

Although we may know what works, there may be other interventions that are effective but to date have not been evaluated. In the UK, parent-support programmes are often set up by voluntary organisations who have to work hard to raise their core funding. As there is rarely any spare cash for evaluation, only a handful of these programmes have been properly assessed.

It may also be that some parents and children do not need the 'full' Webster-Stratton or High/ Scope preschool treatment, or there may be ways of meeting their needs more cost-effectively. We need ways of assessing this. Knapp (1997) and Goodman (1997) argue that along with evaluations of treatment efficacy we also need economic evaluations so that judgements can be made about the comparative costs/benefits of interventions for different types and severity of emotional and behavioural disorders.

- *Different types of evaluations give different levels of confidence that an intervention is effective. If we going to compare the effectiveness of different programmes, common measures need to be used.*

As Eva Lloyd notes in her chapter, greater levels of certainty are needed when interventions may have major implications for the future lives of children and their families. Different research methodologies provide different levels of certainty. When a range of studies using different samples and different methods all point to the same conclusion, this increases confidence that an intervention is effective. Research studies are therefore incremental, building upon each other. Frances Gardner (this volume) also includes a helpful discussion about the value of different methodologies.

Every research methodology has its strengths and limitations. Users' views give us a clue about what types of services and interventions they prefer, for example, Teresa Smith's study on Family Centres. They can be extremely informative and give a totally new perspective. Issues that may seem important to outside researchers may be considerably less important to the user. Rutter (1995, p. 45) notes:

[i]n a previous era there was often an implicit assumption that psychosocial stresses or adversities could be considered as absolutes without reference to either their personal meaning or their cognitive processing by the individual. It is now obvious that this makes little sense.

Research based on longitudinal cohort studies, such as in Ann Buchanan and JoAnn Ten Brinke's studies, have the advantage that they follow up groups of children from a large national cohort over time. The major limitations of such studies is attrition, that is, some members fail to take part at different times and so vital information is missing. The other concern is that over thirty years or so, the data collected reflects different social conditions.

It is generally felt that evaluations that are based on Randomised Controlled Trials (RCTs) are the gold standard in research. Following the medical or scientific experimental model, groups of children or parents are randomly allocated to a particular intervention programme or to a comparison group. Assessments, using well-validated schedules, for example emotional and behavioural checklists and direct observations, are taken both before and after in order to measure change. If we are going to be able to compare results between different trials, it is essential that common measurements be used so that results can be compared. Carolyn Webster-Stratton's work has been extensively evaluated in such trials and so there is reasonable confidence that her programmes are effective. To be sure that her programmes are effective in the UK, we need the results of similar trials here. In these and in other trials, common measures need to be used so that results can be compared. Unless some agreement is reached about such measures, we will never be able to compare the effectiveness of different programmes.

One of the difficulties is that setting up Randomised Controlled trials for children with emotional and behavioural disorders is rather different from medical trials. By the very nature of their problems, the group is hard to access. In medicine it is relatively easy, ethical considerations permitting, to set up an RCT where the intervention involves medication. Most people want to 'get better' so they are highly motivated to take part. Parents may be less sure about taking part in a parenting programme. Many of the people who were involved in the child protection studies needed additional monetary incentives (Department of Health, 1995). This may mean that those who took part were biased, or nonrepresentative, because of the incentives. Many researchers would feel this was quite an acceptable bias, if it exists. Research is always a balance between methodologies that will lead to a high level of confidence with results that can be relied upon and methodologies that lead to lesser levels of confidence but with findings of more general relevance. Those who have a role in deciding where money should be spent need to be alert to how the evidence for the programme was collected.

When measuring change in populations, both education and health have always used indicators. In health, each Health Authority will be able to plot from areas to communities, the number of deaths relating to a specific condition and the number of cases of a specific disease. Standard Achievement Tests in schools serve a similar purpose in monitoring educational improvements. Teresa Smith's work on plotting disadvantage using geographical information mapping is another variant of this.

More generally, national indicators of emotional and behavioural well-being in children need to be developed. It could be that some of these may come from education. Standard Achievements tests, and reading scores, especially in disadvantaged areas, will measure not only educational gains but gains in children's emotional and behavioural well-being.

- *To date, not enough effort has been put into dissemination of research findings. Senior people in agencies need to take the lead in initiating change and implementing programmes.*

Chapters 8 and 9 in this book look at these issues in detail. Carolyn Webster-Stratton and Ted Taylor comment in their chapter:

> Researchers have by and large done a good job of developing and refining a number of creative interventions for a variety of problems experienced by children and families. However, they have done a poor job of ensuring that this information is systematically shared with people who can use most use it, such as clinicians and administrators in the field or with politicians and policy makers who have the power to fund such programmes.

Carolyn Webster-Stratton and Ted Taylor describe in detail, step-by-step, how they implement the Webster-Stratton programmes in four areas. The process in all four sites started by developing *the desire for change* from a lead person within the system. Secondly *support from the administrators and clinicians* was obtained. The programme was sufficiently flexible to respond to *the unique needs of each site*. After this, an implementation phase began, firstly, with *training*. In all four centres the entire programme – not a shortened version – was *implemented with integrity*. The temptation for administrators is always to cut back and save money but half a programme is a different intervention. Staff implementing the programme received *ongoing supervision and peer support. New staff received training* and initially co-led groups with an experienced leader. Contact was maintained with the trainer after the initial training for *consultation and feedback. Evaluation* in all four sites showed that the programme had been successful.

The second chapter on introducing evidence-based child welfare practice is by Eva Lloyd of the UK charity, Barnardo's. Here the agency has made a specific commitment to providing evidence-based services and is the first UK child welfare organisation to do so. Examples are provided of promising strategies for supporting developments in services for children and families on the basis of the best possible evidence for their effectiveness. Barnardo's works with some of the most disadvantaged children in the UK. Most of the children they deal with are either at high risk of emotional or behavioural disorders or already have considerable problems.

Eva Lloyd notes some of the difficulties in implementing evidence-based practice. The first problem, with a few notable exceptions such as Joseph Rowntree, is that the research funding councils have not disseminated their research findings in accessible formats. She highlights another important issue. Often research focuses on the effectiveness of one intervention. This does not answer the dilemma of the agency who has to make choices between the costs/benefits of different types of services/interventions.

In overcoming this dilemma in Barnardo's, the Research and Development team input at a number of levels. Barnardo's are developing their own series of *What Works*: accessible summaries of key research findings covering the main child welfare topics. Managers are also trained in monitoring and evaluation and given detailed feedback on proposals. In addition, Barnardo's actively promotes the involvement of children in service designs.

In this communication-dominated age, it may be that academic researchers have been slow to make the necessary links with the media, or those with the necessary skills to communicate a message through the media. Although a number of funding councils such as the ESRC and the Joseph Rowntree Foundation are now sending their researchers on Talking to the Media training courses.

Quite apart from disseminating a message at a policy or a practice level, the media can be very effective in communicating basic parenting information to the general public. Adrienne Katz (1997), who is also a journalist, working with the Department of Applied Social Studies and Research, received huge media coverage for her *'Can-Do Girls'*. One of the key messages from her survey of young women, was that although most parents are loving, more confident and self-motivated girls had parents who also listened to them, guided them, and respected their opinions. On the other hand the less confident and motivated young women *'Low Can-Do Girls'*, had more controlling and highly critical parents. The message on how to be a more effective parent was not dissimilar to that outlined by the contributors in this volume, but the method of communication meant the message reached a very wide audience.

- *There is a need for more interdisciplinary co-operation at every level. From central government down, the interests of children and families are split between a number of different ministries and agencies. How resources are allocated works against interagency/interdisciplinary work in universities, and research/dissemination/practice work.*

The new Social Exclusion Unit that is part of the Cabinet Office is a notable exception in central government. Here representatives from a number of different ministries sit together to develop a common policy agenda on specific topics including school exclusion and school truancy. At local authority level, Children's Services Plans are now mandatory. Some areas have been more successful in bridging the health/education/social divide than others. The Cabinet Unit and Children's Services Plans do, however, provide a vehicle for people to talk to each other.

Similarly in the UK universities the 'publish or perish' ethos mentioned by Carolyn Webster-Stratton is equally strong. Attached to publications, which should be in 'refereed' journals, are Research Assessment Exercises (RAEs) from which, depending on how well they do, each Department receives resources. Research assessment exercises place departments in competition with other departments. In the social sciences, particularly in matters relating to parenting, 'refereed' journals have limited circulation. Considerable uncertainty exists from one RAE to another as to how the marks will be allocated. Some assurance that extra credit will be awarded for interdisciplinary work and also extra credit for being involved in dissemination into practice will help break down the barriers.

Conclusion

While bringing this book to a conclusion, I was invited to have lunch with Anne Watts, the Equal Opportunities Director of the Midland Bank. For more than 20 years she has been developing 'family friendly' initiatives for the benefit of the Midland's employees. Almost all employees taking maternity leave now return to the bank either full-time or part-time. Among their 'family friendly' policies are working parents network meetings in lunch hours; emergency family leave of up to five days a year; paternity leave; career break schemes; flexible working hours; and a range of childcare initiatives including nurseries and holiday play-schemes.

With larger numbers of women entering the workforce, or being encouraged to do so in the *Welfare to Work* programmes, 'family friendly' policies in the workplace are playing an increasingly important role. At the beginning of this book, I reflected on the momentous education, health and social achievements of the last hundred years that have done so much to improve the well-being of children and I asked the reader to consider from where the next great leap forward will come. This book is full of well-validated ideas on how to help parents and limit the costs and consequences of children with emotional and behavioural disorders so that they can be re-included in society. In the next hundred years, health, education and social services will continue to play an important role but an increasingly valuable partner, as long as employment rates hold up, will be the employer.

Before I had lunch with Anne Watts, I felt some satisfaction at the scope covered in this book.

Francis Bacon warned in his erudite 1605 edition of the *Advancement of Learning*: 'They are ill discoverers that think there is no land, when they can see nothing but sea'. As a mother who spent much of her early working life in 'family unfriendly' workplaces, the land that I had somehow omitted to see was the possibility of some help from my employer.

Hopefully, the next series of Seminars at the Oxford Centre for Research into Parenting and Children, and its next publication, will focus more on the role of 'family friendly' workplaces.

References

Anderson, J.C., Williams, S., McGee, R., and Silva, O.P.A. (1987), 'DSM-III disorders in preadolescent children', *Archives of General Psychiatry*, 44, pp. 69–76.

Bacon, F. (1605), *Advancement of Learning*, Book II. vii. 5.

Bavolek, S.S. (1996), *Research and Validation Report of the Nurturing Programs. Effective Family-based Approaches to: treating and preventing child abuse and neglect*, Family Resources Inc., USA.

Bronfenbrenner, U. (1979), *The Ecology of Human Development: Experiments by Nature and Design*, Cambridge, Mass, Harvard University Press.

Buchanan, A. (1996), *Cycles of Child Maltreatment. Facts, Fallacies and Interventions*, Chichester, John Wiley and Sons Ltd.

Buchanan, A. and Ten Brinke, J-A. (1997), *What happened whey they were grown up? Outcomes from Parenting experiences*, York, Joseph Rowntree Foundation.

Department of Health (1995), *Child Protection, Messages from Research*, London, HMSO.

Goodman, R. (1997), 'The Strengths and Difficulties Questionnaire: a research note', *Journal of Child Psychology and Psychiatry*, 38, 5, pp. 581–7.

Hope, P. and Sharland, P. (1997), *Tomorrow's Parents. Developing parenthood education in Schools*, London, Calouste Gulbenkian Foundation.

Katz, A. in association with Buchanan, A. and Ten Brinke, J-A (1997), *Can-do Girls. Women of the Millennium Study*, Department of Applied Social Studies and Research, University of Oxford and The Body Shop.

Knapp, M. (1997), 'Economic Evaluations and interventions for children and adolescents with mental health problems', *Journal of Child Psychology and Psychiatry*, 38, 1, pp. 3–26.

Kovacs, M. and Devlin, B. (1998), 'Internalizing Disorders in Childhood', *Journal of Child Psychology and Psychiatry*, 39, 1 pp. 47–63.

Loseke, D.R. and Gelles, R.J. (1993), 'Examining and evaluating controversies on family violence' in Gelles, R.J. and Loseke, D.R. (eds), *Current Controversies on Family Violence*, Newbury Park, Ca., Sage.

Morrow, V. and Richards, M. (1996), *Transitions to Adulthood: a family matter?*, York, Joseph Rowntree Foundation.

Newman, D.L., Moffitt, T.E., Caspi, A., Magdol, L., Silva, P.A. and Stanton, W.R. (1996), .Psychiatric disorder in a birth cohort of young adults: Prevalence, co-morbidity, clinical significance and new case incidence from ages 11 to 21', *Journal of Consulting and Clinical Psychology*, 64, pp. 552–62.

Plomin, R. (1994), 'The Emmanuel Miller Memorial Lecture 1993: Genetic research and identification of environmental influences', *Journal of Child Psychology and Psychiatry*, 35, 5, pp. 817–35.

Rutter, M, (1995), 'Individual development and social change' in Rutter, M. and Smith, D. (eds), *Psychosocial disorders in young people*, Chichester, John Wiley and Sons Ltd.

Rutter, M. and Smith, D. (eds) (1995), *Psychosocial Disorders in Young people*, Chichester, John Wiley and Sons Ltd.

Rutter, M., Cox, A., Tupling, C., Berger, M. and Yule, W. (1995), 'Attainment and adjustment in two geographical areas I the prevalence of psychiatric disorder', *British Journal of Psychiatry*, 126, pp. 493–509.

Schweinhart, L.J. and Weikart, D. (1993), *A summary of significant benefits: The High/Scope through age 27*, Ypsilanti, Michigan, High/Scope Press.

Webster-Stratton, C. and Hooven, T.H. (1998), 'Parent Training for Child Conduct Problems' in Ollendick, T. (ed.), *Comprehensive Clinical Psychology, Vol. 5: Children and Adolescents*, Oxford, Elsevier.

Author Index

Subject Index